INC.
YOURSELF

How to Profit by Setting Up Your Own Corporation

EIGHTH EDITION

Judith H. McQuown

HarperBusiness
A Division of HarperCollins Publishers

FIRST EDITION

Designed by Irv Perkins Associates

ISBN 0-88730-748-5

95 96 97 98 99 CC/HC 10 9 8 7 6 5 4 3 2 1

In loving memory of four remarkable women
Bessie Rosenberg, my grandmother
Pearl Hershkowitz, my mother
Isabel Rosenberg, my aunt
Rhoda Haas, my godmother

CONTENTS

ACKNOWLEDGMENTS · xi

PREFACE TO THE EIGHTH EDITION · xiii

INTRODUCTION · xvii

1 SO YOU WANT TO BE A CORPORATION · 3

2 GETTING READY · 22

3 AND NOW THE PAPERWORK · 47

4 YOUR OFFICE: *Home or Away?* · 53

5 YOUR BUSINESS PLAN: *Preparing for Success* · 61

6 LIMITED LIABILITY COMPANIES (LLCs): *The Newest Business Entity* · 72

7 HOW TO PROFIT FROM YOUR S CORPORATION · 75

8 ESPECIALLY FOR WOMEN AND MINORITIES: *Taking Advantage of Minority-Supplier Contracts and Business Incubators, and Avoiding a Different "Mommy Trap"* · 113

9 YOUR EMPLOYEES · 124

10 "FREE" INSURANCE · 129

11 MEDICAL BENEFITS · 135

12 ALL ABOUT ERISA: *Tax-Sheltered Pension and Profit-Sharing Plans* · 142

13 BUT I ALREADY HAVE A KEOGH PLAN! · 156

14 INVESTING YOUR CORPORATE SURPLUS · 161

15 PUTTING IT ALL TOGETHER   172

16 RETIRE WITH THE BIGGEST TAX BREAK POSSIBLE   202

17 LONG-TERM PLANNING FOR YOURSELF AND YOUR
   HEIRS   209

18 IF YOU SHOULD DIE FIRST   214

19 BACK TO THE FUTURE—AND THE PRESENT   215

APPENDIX A STATE REQUIREMENTS FOR GENERAL
   BUSINESS AND PROFESSIONAL CORPORATIONS   217

APPENDIX B SAMPLE MINUTES AND BYLAWS FOR A
   SMALL CORPORATION   243

APPENDIX C ADOPTION AGREEMENT   265

INDEX   273

"The critical ingredient is getting off your rear end and starting something."

—NOLAN BUSHNELL, founder of Atari

"An essential aspect of creativity is not being afraid to fail."

—DR. EDWIN LAND, inventor of the
Polaroid camera

"The future belongs to those who believe in the beauty of their dreams."

—ELEANOR ROOSEVELT

ACKNOWLEDGMENTS

This book could not have been written without the help of many experts, for whose time, knowledge, patience, and enthusiasm I am most grateful.

In particular, I wish to thank Martin Askowitz, Senior Vice President, Investments, Smith Barney Inc.; "Sales Doctor" Brian Azar; Melody Borchers, Manager, Women's Business Resource Program, Ohio Department of Development; Howard J. Golden, Partner, Kwasha Lipton; and Leonard B. Stern, President, Leonard B. Stern & Co., Inc.

Special thanks go to the wonderful people at Coopers & Lybrand L.L.P. In New York: Murray Alter, Tax Partner; Peter R. Collins, Director, National Entrepreneurial Advisory Services; Neil J. Rosenberg, Esq., Tax Partner; Andrew H. Solomon, Senior Associate, Multi-State Tax Division, and Maggie O'Donovan, Manager, National Public Relations, and her hardworking staff, who helped arrange these interviews. In Columbus, Ohio: Carrie L. Clay, Partner and Coordinator of Women's Business Activities. And in Washington, D.C.: Richard S. Wagman, Esq., Senior Tax Specialist.

As always, I am grateful for the help and advice of Dominick Abel, my agent.

PREFACE TO THE EIGHTH EDITION

Adjacent headlines: "Raytheon Offers 2,300 Workers Buyout Package to Retire Early" (Boston); "Corestates [Financial] to Slash 2,800 Jobs, Close 37 Branches to Trim Costs" (Philadelphia). Those 5,100 jobs lost, reported by *Investor's Business Daily* on March 30, 1995, were just the latest in the decade-long corporate restructuring and downsizing that has cost Americans over 3 million jobs. And, for the first time in U.S. history, more executives, managers, and professionals have lost their jobs than have blue-collar workers.

Welcome to the Age of the Accidental Entrepreneur! People just a few years older than the baby boomers, who started working for major corporations or organizations in the 1960s or 1970s, were led to believe that as long as they did pretty good work they had guaranteed jobs and periodic promotions. The last ten years have proved the falsity of that corporate fairy tale. Now no one is safe—not executive vice presidents, not tenured professors. While hundreds of thousands of twenty- to thirty-year-olds have lost their jobs, people in their forties and fifties have been especially hard hit. Many search for new jobs for more than a year. Where only a generation ago corporate employment was safe and entrepreneurism was hazardous, now it is clear that the risks are reversed. The rewards were always greater in entrepreneuring!

All this may explain the dramatic rise in the number of corporations formed during the past ten years:

xiii

1986	702,738	
1987	685,572	
1988	685,095	
1989	677,397	
1990	647,366	
1991	628,604	
1992	666,800	
1993	706,537	
1994	753,000	(estimate—based on figures through 9/30/94)
1995	730,000	(estimate)
	6,883,109	

And the trend is accelerating—1995 should mark the third year in a row of new corporations numbering over 700,000, a total of more than 2 million in three years!

So, welcome to the eighth edition of *Inc. Yourself: How to Profit by Setting Up Your Own Corporation.* When I first wrote *Inc. Yourself,* 19 years and 350,000 copies ago, the decision to incorporate was a fairly simple one to make.

It isn't anymore.

Since 1981, nearly every year has produced major tax legislation that has impacted the small corporation:

1981	Economic Recovery Tax Act
1982	Tax Equity and Fiscal Responsibility Act (TEFRA)
1982	Subchapter S Revision Act of 1982
1984	Deficit Reduction Act of 1984
1986	Tax Reform Act of 1986
1987	Omnibus Budget Reconciliation Act of 1987 (usually referred to as the Revenue Act of 1987)
1988	Technical and Miscellaneous Act of 1988 (TAMRA)
1989	Omnibus Budget Reconciliation Act of 1989 (OBRA)
1990	Revenue Reconciliation Act of 1990
1993	Omnibus Budget Reconciliation Act of 1993

1995   Tax Fairness and Deficit Reduction Act of 1995*
         S Corporation Reform Act*

Many of the changes have benefited small corporations. Tax rates for most small corporations have been lowered, as shown below:

	1981	1995
Under $25,000	17%	15%
$25,001–$50,000	20	15
$50,001–$75,000	30	25

A corporation whose net income was $50,000 would have paid $9,250 in federal income taxes in 1981 but only $7,500 in 1995, a decrease of 19 percent.

Only for personal service corporations in the following professions was the corporate rate boosted to a flat 34 percent by the Revenue Act of 1987:

> . . . health, law, engineering, architecture, accounting, actuarial science, performing arts or consulting. . . .
> (Internal Revenue Code §448)

For individuals in these fields, it still may pay to *Inc. Yourself.* By using an S corporation, they can enjoy the legal and business status of a corporation while being taxed at what may be a slightly lower individual rate.

Another option is one that did not exist when I wrote the seventh edition of this book: the limited liability company (LLC), which is the subject of an entire new chapter in this edition of *Inc. Yourself.*

Clearly, there are many compelling business and tax reasons to *Inc. Yourself.* This book will help you make the right decision.

*Legislation pending—passage expected late 1995.

INTRODUCTION

This book is not designed to substitute for your lawyer or accountant, but rather to serve as a guide and enable you to make the most of their professional help. While you *can* incorporate and set up tax shelters yourself without legal advice, it is far more desirable not to go it alone. Tax laws are complicated and often change from year to year; it takes a skilled professional to stay on top of them.

You don't have to be a professional to incorporate—if you're a self-employed salesman, plumber, real estate agent, antique dealer, or hairdresser, this book can save you money. If you can show a net profit, this book can save you money. All you have to do is form a corporation, and this book will show you how it can be done, step by step.

While we'll discuss corporations completely in Chapter 1, "So You Want to Be a Corporation," for now let's define a *corporation* simply as a body of persons granted a charter that legally recognizes them as a separate entity with its own rights, privileges, and liabilities. But don't let the "body of persons" wording scare you; every state permits one person to incorporate (see chart, Appendix A).

Depending on the state you live in, your business or profession may require you to incorporate as a *professional corporation* (see Appendix A), but this means only that your professional practice is now able to enjoy all the benefits and privileges of corporations that had earlier been prohibited. There is no difference in the *tax* treatment of professional versus business corporations; the only difference is a legal and supervisory one: if you form a professional corporation, all the shareholders and officers of the corporation must be licensed as professional practitioners in the state of incorporation. Your husband or wife and children

xvii

cannot own stock in the corporation—even as minority stock-holders—unless they, too, are licensed as professionals.

Thus, in terms of the law, a professional corporation is more restrictive in structure than a general business corporation; if your state permits you to choose, it is better to incorporate as a general business corporation. But whatever you do, if you are earning enough money and want to shelter substantial portions of it from taxes, you should consider incorporation.

Now sit back, read carefully, and you, too, can *Inc. Yourself* and *Profit by Setting Up Your Own Corporation.*

INC.
YOURSELF

1

SO YOU WANT TO BE A CORPORATION

Now that your appetite has been sufficiently whetted by visions of tax-free sugarplums, let's get down to basics.

DO YOU HAVE WHAT IT TAKES TO BE AN ENTREPRENEUR?

Consultant Brian Azar, "The Sales Doctor," has worked with several thousand people in the past ten years. He has created the following quiz to predict entrepreneurial success:

On a scale of 1 (lowest) to 5 (highest)

1. Can you work on your own, independent of others, for long periods of time?_____

2. Can you sell yourself, your ideas, products, concepts, services? In other words, can you persuasively and effectively communicate to others and be able to draw them into your point of view or project as collaborators, supporters, customers?_____

3. Do you have good people skills:

bonding and rapport?_____

coaching and managing skills?_____

sales skills?_____

4. Do you have good organizational skills:

time management?_____

communications—oral and written?_____

3

5. Are you organized, structured, disciplined?_____

6. Can you make decisions quickly while maintaining your flexibility?_____

7. Can you learn from your mistakes?_____

8. Can you take calculated risks, as opposed to procrastinating?_____

9. How well do you handle money?_____

10. Do you know your bank manager's first name?_____

11. Do you have persistence, tenacity, stamina—especially when the going gets tough?_____

12. Do you have a "mastermind"? (A mastermind is a group of people—mentors, role models, peers, or other entrepreneurs or small business owners—who support and may assist your vision and goals in various ways.)_____

Finally, and most important:

13. Do you have an idea, service, or product that you love?_____

believe in?_____

A perfect score is 85; a very good score is 60 or higher. Use this quiz to identify the areas in which you need to improve your entrepreneurial skills.

Don't slough this self-examination. According to Azar, four out of five small business owners go out of business within five years, and it's not for financial reasons. The top four reasons are:

1. Lack of organizational skills
2. Poor attitude
3. Poor sales and marketing skills
4. Poor people skills

Don't be a casualty—be a success!

ADVANTAGES OF INC.—ING YOURSELF

Until now, most self-employed people have been operating as sole (or individual) proprietorships, a form of business organization in which the individual provides the capital, starts and runs the business, and keeps all the net profits and is taxed on them. As a sole proprietorship, the individual assumes total liability.

One step up in complexity from the sole proprietorship is the partnership, in which two or more people act as joint proprietors: they provide joint funding, joint management, and joint financial responsibility. Unfortunately, like the sole proprietorship, the partners are *personally* liable to an *unlimited degree* for all the other partners' errors.

A corporation is the most sophisticated—and protective—form of business organization. It is a "legal person," completely separate from the individuals who own and control it. A corporation has the power to do anything any person may do: carry on business, own property, lend and borrow money, sue and be sued. Most important, it offers its shareholders limited liability: its stockholders can lose no more than their original investment; they are not liable for the debts of the corporation.

In terms of limited exposure to liability alone, it pays to incorporate to protect your assets; if you incorporate, no one can attach your house, car, or Ming vases if your business fails or if you lose a lawsuit. While this point is particularly important in such obvious professions as medicine, dentistry, law, architecture, and the construction industry, there are lesser-known areas in which limited liability plays an important role.

One of my friends incorporated himself to produce illustrated science fiction and children's books. For him, too, the primary benefit of incorporation has been limited liability: "I publish authors whose work some people might find offensive, and they might sue me, as the publisher. Rather than reject authors whose work I respected, but who might be dangerous, it seemed safer to incorporate. If I were sued, I wouldn't be personally liable."

Although limited liability may be the most attractive feature of incorporating, there are many others. For many people, there is greater ease in doing business. Some stores favor corporate accounts and offer discounts. Yes, even Tiffany's.

Incorporating can make job possibilities more attractive to new or future employees. There's a feeling of working for a profitable enterprise associated with incorporation; you can offer employees greater benefits out of pretax dollars; and, of course, you can always offer them a promotion in title instead of a raise.

Then, too, there are medical, life, and disability insurance benefits. Although the Tax Equity and Fiscal Responsibility Act finally let Keogh Plan contributions achieve parity with corporate pension contributions, your benefits will be still greater if you incorporate. Incorporation offers you free life and disability insurance. There is even one kind of insurance you can't get as a self-employed person but can get as the employee of your corporation, even if you are the *only* employee—workers' compensation.

Medical benefits alone can make it worth your while to incorporate. If you pay your medical bills as a sole proprietor, the amount you can deduct from taxable income is reduced by 7.5 percent of your adjusted gross income. For most people, these deductions can wipe out over $5,000 in medical bills every year.* But your corporation can write off *all* your family's medical bills—they're considered a business expense.

Is your business so profitable that you've been investing in stocks? Good. Whereas before, as a sole proprietor, you had to pay income tax on all your dividends, now, if your corporation invests in those stocks, 70 percent of those dividends are completely excluded from income tax, and the remaining 30 percent are taxed at only 15 percent if your corporate net taxable income was $50,000 or less and at only 25 percent if your corporate net taxable income was between $50,000 and $75,000. The maximum rate is 39 percent on corporate net income between $100,000 and $335,000. Then it drops back to 34 percent on net income between $335,000 and $10 million.

*Pursuant to legislation enacted in mid-April 1995, sole proprietors may deduct 30 percent of their health-insurance premiums for 1995 and subsequent years in calculating their Adjusted Gross Income. Unfortunately, this works out to less than $100 in actual tax dollars for most taxpayers, as shown on page 140.

That's the good news. There are a few drawbacks, but they're mostly minor ones. There will be more paperwork, and you will have to set yourself a salary and live within it. There will be a greater number of taxes to pay, but your total tax bill will be much lower than it was as a sole proprietorship—especially if you live in states or cities which impose taxes on unincorporated businesses.

It's pretty clear that the advantages far outweigh the disadvantages, and that's why more and more people are following their lawyers' and accountants' advice and incorporating!

THE MYTH OF DOUBLE TAXATION

A little knowledge is a dangerous thing. Here's proof: if you tell friends and colleagues that you're thinking of incorporating, sooner or later one of them will say to you, "But you don't want to do that—you'll be subject to double taxation."

This statement is fallacious at best and disingenuous at worst. It confuses two separate issues. You *will* have to pay two taxes— corporate and personal—but *you won't be taxed twice on the same money*. What's more important, *your total taxes will be less*—often by 30 to 50 percent, as compared with an individual proprietorship.

> **The issue of double taxation—which means that your corporation's profits are first taxed at the corporate level and then at your own personal level, when your corporation pays you dividends—is a red herring. There is never a need for your corporation to pay you a dividend when it simply can raise your salary or pay you a bonus, neither of which is taxed at the corporate level.**

Let's look at some examples. In the first set of figures, our entrepreneur hasn't incorporated. Using 1994 tax rates, he would have to pay $9,300 if he was single and $5,917 if he was married, assuming that he had no children and was filing a joint return with no other income:

	Single	Married
Net income	$ 50,000	$ 50,000
Less exemption(s)	−2,450	−4,900
	$ 47,550	$ 45,100
Less standard deduction	−3,800	−6,350
Net taxable income	$ 43,750	$ 38,750
Income tax	$ 9,300	$ 5,917

However, if our entrepreneur incorporates, pays himself $25,000 a year, and retains $25,000 in the corporation, the numbers change dramatically:

	Single	Married
Retained corporate earnings	$ 25,000	$ 25,000
Taxed at corporate rate	× 15 %	× 15 %
Corporate tax	$ 3,750	$ 3,750
Salary	$ 25,000	$ 25,000
Less exemption(s)	−2,450	−4,900
	$ 22,550	$ 20,100
Less standard deduction	−3,800	−6,350
Net taxable income	$ 18,750	$ 13,750
Income tax	$ 2,816	$ 2,066
Corporate tax	3,750	3,750
Total taxes	$ 6,566	$ 5,816
Income tax on $50,000	$ 9,300	$ 5,917
Amount saved	$ 2,734*	$ 101*
Percentage saved	29%*	2%*

*The amounts and percentages saved are really much higher than those shown because the $16,250 after-tax corporate income could be invested to produce $1,300 in dividends, of which $910 would be tax-free and $390 would be taxed at only 15 percent. Thus, the total tax on $1,300 of dividends would be only $58.50. In comparison, taxpayers whose net income was $50,000 and who received $1,300 in dividends would be taxed $364 on the dividends if they were single or if they were married.

The more money you earn, the more you can save by incorporating. Splitting a net income of $75,000 into $25,000 salary and $50,000 retained corporate earnings results in much greater savings, especially for married entrepreneurs, where the percentage of taxes saved zooms from 2 percent to 26 percent:

1994 Corporate Tax Rates		1994 Personal Income-Tax Rates*			
		Single		Married	
$0–$50,000	15%	$0–$22,750	15%	$0–$38,000	15%
$50,000–$75,000	25	$22,750–$55,100	38	$38,000–$91,850	28
$75,000–$100,000	34	$55,1000–$115,000	31	$91,850–140,000	31

*Net income, after deductions and exemptions.

The following table shows how favorable corporate tax rates are compared to personal income-tax rates:

	Single	Married
Personal income tax on $25,000	$ 2,816	$ 2,066
Corporate income tax on $50,000	7,500	7,500
	$10,316	$ 9,566
Personal income tax on $75,000	$16,715	$12,917
Amount saved	$ 6,394	$ 3,351
Percent saved	38%	26%

Thus, on the first $75,000 in income each year, incorporating can save you $3,400–$6,400 a year on your federal income taxes. At that point the gap narrows, but for most one-person corporations, corporate tax rates are still always lower than or equal to personal tax rates.

But the most important point, of course, is that by incorporating, you can divide your income into *two portions,* as shown earlier, *each of which is taxed at a lower rate.*

ARE YOU EVER TOO YOUNG
TO INCORPORATE?

Although the voting age has been lowered to eighteen, in some states you still must be twenty-one to incorporate. From a practical point of view, most experts recommend incorporating as soon as possible. Incorporation has many intangible benefits for young people. The young publisher I mentioned earlier says, "I find it easier to deal as a corporation. I have less trouble in getting good people to work for me; they feel that a corporation is more responsible financially. It seems to increase my financial stature, even in my personal life. I had fewer credit-investigation problems when I wanted to rent an expensive apartment."

ARE YOU EVER TOO OLD?

Of course, the older you are, the fewer years you have in which to accumulate tax-sheltered retirement funds. Still, according to Boston banker Dean Ridlon, "people in their fifties can still incorporate profitably; it all depends on how much money they're earning every year. A successful professional can certainly make use of incorporation in order to provide substantial retirement funds even if retirement is ten, five, or even only three years away."

HOPE FOR CORPORATE CASUALTIES

I hope that these comments will give much-needed hope to the corporate casualties, the 1.1 million people who were laid off in 1993 and 1994 alone: 615,186 in 1993 and 516,069 in 1994. Layoffs for 1995 are estimated at 500,000.

Here are the Top Ten corporate layoffs in 1993 and 1994:

	1993		*1994*	
IBM	63,500	Digital Equipment	26,000
Sears, Roebuck	50,000	GTE	17,000
Boeing	31,000	NYNEX	16,800
Philip Morris	14,000	AT&T	15,000
NCR	13,100	Delta Airlines	15,000
Procter & Gamble	13,000	Scott Paper	10,500
Woolworth	13,000	Boeing	10,100
Eastman Kodak	12,000	Ameritech	10,000
McDonnell Douglas	10,700	Pacific Bell	10,000
United Technologies	10,600	Sara Lee	9,900
Total Top Ten	230,900	Total Top Ten	140,300
Total 1993	615,186	Total 1994	516,069

Many of these people who have been laid off have years of experience which they can put to good use when they go into business for themselves.

ARE YOU EVER TOO RICH TO INCORPORATE?

Yes, Virginia, there is such a thing as making too much money to incorporate. Your corporation can accumulate $150,000/$250,000*—no questions asked. Above that figure, you must prove that your corporation needs the money for business purposes. Otherwise, the IRS will take the position that your company has liquid assets that are "greatly in excess of its reasonable business needs" (IRS regulations quoted) and will impose additional punitive taxes on the corporation.

The corporation then comes to the crossroads, where it must either declare a dividend, on which the stockholders would be

*The IRS limits corporations whose principal function is "services in the field of law, health, engineering, architecture, accounting, actuarial science, performing arts, or consulting" to $150,000. The limit for all other corporations was raised to $250,000 in 1981.

taxed, or justify the accumulation by showing "specific, definite, and feasible plans" (IRS regulations quoted) for the use of that accumulation. (Office or inventory expansion would be considered such a reasonable use.) If the accumulation cannot be justified, the IRS sets a penalty tax on the "accumulated taxable income": the retained earnings in excess of $150,000. The tax is 27.5 percent of the first $100,000 of this accumulated taxable income and 38.5 percent of everything in excess of $100,000. This corporate tax is an *additional* tax on top of the normal corporate income tax, so the *total* tax can go as high as 75 percent.

Thus, if your corporation's retained earnings are approaching the $150,000/$250,000 limit, it should avoid this tax by raising your salary, paying you a bonus, investing in new office or other equipment, or preparing plans that would justify the accumulated capital to the IRS.

Only a corporation that has been grossing about $200,000 or $250,000 a year, however, or a corporation that has been in existence a number of years (long enough to have accumulated a substantial surplus) and is considered "mature" is faced with these problems. For most people who are thinking of incorporating, consideration of the accumulated earnings tax on surplus is premature and it should not be a factor in their decisions.

There's another point, too. Until 1976, the amount a corporation could set aside as surplus without penalty was only $100,000; the Tax Reduction Act of 1975 increased that allowance to $150,000, and the Economic Recovery Tax Act raised that limit for many corporations to $250,000. With inflationary pressures influencing legislation, it is likely that in another five or ten years that allowance will be increased again, just because money today isn't worth what it used to be. If your corporation's net after taxes is $15,000, it would take ten years to reach the IRS limit, and many tax changes are likely between now and then.

ARE YOU EVER TOO POOR?

Yes, again. It doesn't pay for someone who is earning $10,000 or $12,000 a year to incorporate. The real benefits start at around $30,000 a year. At $30,000 net taxable income, single entrepreneurs are in the 28 percent bracket. However, if they draw a salary of $20,000 instead and retain $10,000 in the corporation, they are taxed at approximately 15 percent on the $20,000, and the corporation is taxed at 15 percent on the $10,000. For married people, real tax advantages start at around $40,000 net taxable income.

BUT YOU CAN BE TOO UNDISCIPLINED

For some people, the joys of corporate tax savings just don't outweigh the extra paperwork and planning that are involved. In contrast to the "good old days" of sole proprietorship, when you could write yourself a check or raid petty cash whenever you ran short, now you must clearly differentiate between the corporation and yourself and act in accordance with the fact that you are now an employee of the corporation—even if at the same time you are its president and only employee. The corporation is a *separate legal entity,* and as such, there are certain formalities and restrictions. One of the tests the IRS uses to disqualify a corporation is "the corporate pocketbook"—the mixing together of personal and corporate funds: are you recognizing that you and the corporation are two separate, distinct legal entities, and does your bookkeeping reflect that fact, or are you still commingling corporate and personal income and expenditures? Of course, I know one man who does this and even pays the milkman with a corporate check—he leaves the mess to his accountant, who straightens it out every year. But this procedure is—to say the least—highly inadvisable.

In order to avoid having your corporation disqualified on these grounds, it is necessary that you set yourself a liberal salary—and to live within it, since you can no longer tap the bank account whenever you run short.

MORE TALK ABOUT SALARIES

But deciding on a salary is not as simple as it seems at first glance. If you operate a business as a sole proprietor, you pick up all the income of your business. But if you incorporate and pay yourself a high salary, the IRS may attack your salary as unreasonably high and disallow it. Or the IRS may hold that your salary is reasonable, but that if you don't have a history of paying dividends and your income has been accumulating, part of your salary may be deemed by the IRS to be a dividend and will be taxed to you accordingly.

Part of the question of reasonable versus unreasonable salary depends on what other people in the same business or profession or a comparable one are earning. However, even this point can be gotten around. For example, if you are in a creative profession, the IRS really cannot find an equivalent: there's just no way of comparing two artists or two writers—or their income.

But what about too low a salary? If you pay yourself a very low salary, your personal income taxes will be minimal, and your retained corporate earnings, which will be proportionately greater, will also be taxed at minimal corporate rates—15 percent up to $50,000.

This sounds like a wonderful solution, but there are some drawbacks. First, you may not be able to live on a very low salary—and remember, you must avoid the corporate pocketbook at all costs. Second, the more rapidly money accumulates as corporate surplus, the more quickly you may reach the limit of $150,000/$250,000 and be forced to declare a dividend or be liable for the punitive tax on accumulated taxable income over $150,000/$250,000, as explained earlier.

There may also be other considerations involved in how much or how little you pay yourself. If your corporation earns $40,000 a year, the IRS may look askance at your paying yourself $5,000—even if you can live on it—and retaining $35,000 in the corporation at the minimum tax rate of 15 percent. If you drew $15,000 in salary and retained $25,000 in the corporation, there would be less question of the IRS's involvement in the issue of your salary.

Third—and possibly most important—both your Social Security and pension contributions (and eventually payments) are based on your salary; the lower your salary is, the lower these contributions and payments to you will be.

Let's look at that $40,000 to see how this might work with respective salaries of $15,000 and $25,000, based on 1994 rates:

	$15,000 Salary	*$25,000 Salary*
Net pretax earnings before salary	$ 40,000	$ 40,000
Salary	15,000	25,000
	25,000	15,000
Pension contribution (25% of salary)	3,750	6,250
Net corporate earnings	$ 21,250	$ 8,750
Corporate income tax (15%)	3,188	1,313
Retained earnings—available for investment	$ 18,062	$ 7,437
Income if invested in common and preferred stocks yielding 8%	$ 1,445	$ 595
Tax-free dividends (70% dividend exclusion)	1,012	417
Salary (single)	$ 15,000	$ 25,000
Less exemption ($2,450) and standard deduction ($3,800)	− 6,250	− 6,250
Net taxable income	$ 8,750	$ 18,750
Personal income tax	$ 1,316	$ 2,816
Corporate tax	3,188	1,313
Total taxes	$ 4,504	$ 4,129

	$15,000 Salary	$25,000 Salary
Salary (married)	$ 15,000	$ 25,000
Less exemptions ($4,900) and standard deduction ($6,350)	− 11,250	− 11,250
Net taxable income	$ 3,750	$ 13,750
Personal income tax	$ 566	$ 2,066
Corporate tax	3,188	1,313
Total taxes	$ 3,754	$ 3,379

There is no hard-and-fast formula to follow in this area; there are too many individual considerations. Are you single? Are you married? Does your spouse work? How many exemptions do you have? Do you itemize or take the standard deduction? How much money can you keep in your corporation to earn 70 percent tax-free dividends? Discuss these trade-offs with your lawyer and accountant and get their advice. Whatever you decide, recognize that no salary decision must be permanent and inflexible. Your salary can be raised or lowered as long as such provisions are spelled out neatly in the bylaws of your corporation, which will be dealt with at length in Chapter 2, "Getting Ready."

SHOULD YOUR SPOUSE INCORPORATE?

Most certainly, if your spouse is self-employed, and for the same reasons that you should incorporate. Furthermore, if at all possible, your spouse should form his or her own corporation, rather than incorporating with you. Yes, once more it's more paperwork keeping two separate sets of corporate records, but there's a compelling reason to do it this way. Since a corporation can accumulate $150,000/$250,000 at minimum tax rates whether the corporation has one shareholder or 100, incorporating as two separate corporations permits the two of you to accumulate double that amount, or $300,000/$500,000.

THE TAXMAN COMETH

If you are a one-person corporation, as I am, the IRS may scrutinize your return very carefully, with an eye toward ruling that your corporation was created to avoid taxes and is therefore illegal. Here are some important arguments you can use to disprove the IRS's claim:

1. Incorporation gives you greater ease in doing business and frequently offers special corporate accounts and discounts.
2. Incorporation increases the attractiveness of your business to new or future employees.
3. Incorporation provides insurance benefits (e.g., workers' compensation) that may not be available to self-employed persons.
4. Incorporation offers greater medical benefits.
5. Incorporation permits limited—rather than unlimited—liability.

But the most important test of whether a corporation is valid depends on how much business activity is being conducted by the corporation. Normally, if the corporation is clearly operating a business and earning income, there would be no reason for the IRS not to accept it as a valid corporation; it would be very difficult for the IRS to attack the corporation as a sham.

THE "HIDDEN EMPLOYEE" TRAP

As Fortune 500 companies have been firing executives en masse and rehiring them as free-lancers and consultants, the IRS and many state and local governments have raised an important question: are these people truly free-lancers—independent contractors—or are they employees in disguise? There's a serious financial issue here: if the IRS or your state can prove that you're really an employee, it can disqualify your corporation and stick your employer for Social Security and unemployment taxes and worker's compensation and disability insurance payments.

Here are the 20 factors that the IRS uses to determine whether an individual is someone's employee or an independent contractor:*

1. *Instructions.* An employee must comply with instructions about when, where, and how to work. Even if no instructions are given, the control factor is present if the employer has the right to give instructions.

2. *Training.* An employee is trained to perform services in a particular manner. Independent contractors ordinarily use their own methods and receive no training from the purchasers of their services.

3. *Integration.* An employee's services are integrated into the business operations because the services are important to the success or continuation of the business. This shows that the employee is subject to direction and control.

4. *Services rendered personally.* An employee renders services personally. This shows that the employer is interested in the methods as well as the results.

5. *Hiring assistants.* An employee works for an employer who hires, supervises, and pays assistants. An independent contractor hires, supervises, and pays assistants under a contract that requires him or her to provide materials and labor and to be responsible only for the result.

6. *Continuing relationship.* An employee has a continuing relationship with an employer. A continuing relationship may exist where work is performed at frequently recurring although irregular intervals.

7. *Set hours of work.* An employee has set hours of work established by an employer. An independent contractor is the master of his or her own time.

8. *Full-time work.* An employee normally works full time for an employer. An independent contractor can work when and for whom he or she chooses.

*Source: IRS Publication 937, *Business Reporting,* p. 3.

9. *Work done on premises.* An employee works on the premises of an employer, or works on a route or at a location designated by an employer.

10. *Order or sequence set.* An employee must perform services in the order or sequence set by an employer. This shows that the employee is subject to direction and control.

11. *Reports.* An employee submits reports to an employer. This shows that the employee must account to the employer for his or her actions.

12. *Payments.* An employee is paid by the hour, week, or month. An independent contractor is paid by the job or on a straight commission.

13. *Expenses.* An employee's business and travel expenses are paid by an employer. This shows that the employee is subject to regulation and control.

14. *Tools and materials.* An employee is furnished significant tools, materials, and other equipment by an employer.

15. *Investment.* An independent contractor has a significant investment in the facilities he or she uses in performing services for someone else.

16. *Profit or loss.* An independent contractor can make a profit or suffer a loss.

17. *Works for more than one person or firm.* An independent contractor gives his or her services to two or more unrelated persons or firms at the same time.

18. *Offers services to general public.* An independent contractor makes his or her services available to the general public.

19. *Right to fire.* An employee can be fired by an employer. An independent contractor cannot be fired so long as he or she produces a result that meets the specifications of the contract.

20. *Right to quit.* An employee can quit his or her job at any time without incurring liability. An independent contractor usually agrees to complete a specific job and is responsible for its satisfactory completion, or is legally obligated to make good for failure to complete it.

Obviously, the key factor is control: Do *you* determine the hours you work and where you work? And the easiest factors to satisfy to prove that you are an independent contractor—and therefore able to incorporate—are numbers 7, 8, and 17 in this list: *you* choose *when* to work, *you* choose for whom to work, and *you* choose *how many clients* you wish to work for.

> **As long as you work for at least two clients—even if one provides 75 percent of your income—you have satisfied the IRS independent contractor test.**

THE PERSONAL-HOLDING-CORPORATION TRAP

However, even if your corporation is deemed valid by the IRS, there is still another pitfall to avoid: you do not want to be considered a personal holding corporation. A personal holding corporation is a corporation in which 60 percent or more of corporate income is derived from investments and less than 40 percent comes from actual operation of the business. This situation is to be avoided because personal holding corporations are subject to special heavy taxes and do not enjoy the preferential tax treatment of general business corporations and professional corporations.

In the past, some people who had a great deal of money incorporated and took their investments into the corporation, since, by incorporating, 85 percent of their preferred and common stock dividend income would not be taxed.* These people weren't really conducting a business, they were just managing their investments and collecting dividends. It was a tax loophole.

The personal-holding-corporation regulations, which were designed by the IRS to close this tax loophole and to prevent further tax inequities, provide that if a corporation is held to be

---

*The Tax Reform Act of 1986 reduced this dividend exclusion to 80 percent, and the Revenue Act of 1987 reduced it further, to 70 percent. It remains a very valuable benefit of incorporation.

a personal holding corporation—and obviously this can vary from year to year depending on annual earned income versus annual dividend income—the personal-holding-company income must be distributed to its shareholders. If it is a one-person corporation, then the shareholder will be taxed on the dividend income as though he or she owned the stocks personally and not the corporation. If there are several shareholders, they will be taxed on the income as though they themselves owned the stocks and not the corporation.

But there are ways around even this problem. Let's assume that your corporation has a portfolio of $100,000, which yields 7.5 percent, or $7,500 in dividend income, and that for some reason your corporation earned only $5,000. Because the dividend income represents 60 percent—the crucial figure—of total income, your corporation is regarded as a personal holding corporation for that year.

To avoid this problem, sell one of the stocks before the final quarterly dividend is paid to avoid reaching the $7,500 figure. Since many corporations pay dividends in December, all you have to do is make certain that your corporation sells the stock before the record date for payment of the dividend.

Then, depending on your financial situation, you might either invest the proceeds of the sale of the stock in a lower-yielding "growth" stock to reduce your dividend income below the 60 percent figure or buy municipal bonds, whose income is not counted by the IRS in making personal-holding-company determinations.

Tax-free dividends are but one of the many benefits of incorporating. The next chapters will show you how to set up your corporation to start taking advantage of them.

2
GETTING READY

Both incorporating and dissolving your corporation later, either when you are ready to retire or earlier, are especially easy if you are the only stockholder and officer. This is legal in every state.

Once you decide to incorporate, the first, crucial step is creating a corporate name.

WHAT TO NAME YOUR "BABY"

If I had a specialty catering company, I'd be tempted to call it Just Desserts. And if I were starting an upmarket cleaning service, I'd probably want to call it Maid in Heaven. Both with an "Inc." after them—all corporations must have a word like *Company, Corporation, Incorporated,* or their abbreviations in their titles. Wit and memorability can turn your corporate name into a valuable asset: your clients and potential clients will remember it easily.

Another strategy, naming your company after yourself, has two other advantages. First, business contacts will link you to your company more easily; it's brand recognition. Second, if you have an unusual name or your name has an unusual spelling, you may be able to avoid making a corporate name search when you *Inc. Yourself.* In fact, after I checked the New York City phone directories for a Judith McQuown and found no others, I decided that I was safe in skipping the corporate-search step when I incorporated.

If you plan to do business primarily in your own state, and perhaps deal with clients in other states occasionally, a name search in just your own state will suffice. All states will do a name search free; most charge $10 to $50 for reserving your corporate name for two to six months.

However, if you plan to set up your business in more than one state, you have some work to do in order to ensure that the corporate name you have chosen is available for you to use in each of those states.

Just one horror story should persuade you to treat this process carefully. A company retained a public relations expert to create a new corporate name and symbol. They loved the new name and set up an advertising program to promote it. When a young company lawyer looked into the legal ramifications of adopting the new name, he discovered that the proposed name, for which the company had paid $8,000, wasn't available anywhere. It was already being used nationally by another company.

The probability of finding your corporation's name to be available will decrease geometrically as your company's business expands into additional states. Therefore, if you plan to set up your business in three or more states or eventually franchise your operation, hire professionals to perform your name search. It will be faster, more accurate, and less expensive in the long run.

The CT Corporation System, one of the largest search companies, will perform a name search for $15 per state* and reserve a name for $35 per state.* However, the company works directly only for lawyers.

---

*Plus disbursements.

FILING THE FORMS

Now you're ready to apply to the IRS for an Employer Identification Number: you will not be able to open corporate savings or checking accounts without it.

If you already have an Employer Identification Number (e.g., for your Keogh plan account), it's no good—you'll need to apply for another one in the corporate name—even if you're just adding "Inc." to your own name. In the eyes of the IRS, the corporation is a separate "person" and must have a separate number. Think of your Employer Identification Number as your corporation's Social Security number.

Getting an Employer Identification Number is much easier and faster now than it was several years ago. Just call 1-800-829-1040 and you'll be given your EIN over the phone. Then you must file Form SS-4, "Application for Employer Identification Number" with the IRS immediately. (See page 25.)

As soon as you receive your Employer Identification Number, apply *immediately* for Subchapter S status if you decide that an S corporation is the right choice for you (see Chapter 7, "How to Profit from Your S Corporation")* by filing IRS Form 2553, "Election by a Small Business Corporation" (see pages 79–80). This form must be postmarked no later than the fifteenth day of the third month of your corporation's existing tax year. If your corporation is on a calendar year, your deadline is March 15. The IRS will accept no excuses for even one day's lateness: your corporation will not receive S corporation treatment until the following year.

When you are filing these first forms that are crucial to your corporation's existence, it is a good idea to employ the good old "belt-and-suspenders" strategy of dealing with the IRS. Send all forms by certified mail, return receipt requested, so that you will have proof that you filed them before the deadline. Enclose a copy of the form, a self-addressed stamped envelope, and a note asking that your form be stamped "Received" by the IRS and

*It's called an S corporation, but you still choose *Subchapter* S status.

| Form **SS-4** (Rev. December 1993) Department of the Treasury Internal Revenue Service | **Application for Employer Identification Number** (For use by employers, corporations, partnerships, trusts, estates, churches, government agencies, certain individuals, and others. See instructions.) | EIN OMB No. 1545-0003 Expires 12-31-96 |

Please type or print clearly.

1 Name of applicant (Legal name) (See instructions.)
J. ENTREPRENEUR + Co., INC.

2 Trade name of business, if different from name in line 1

3 Executor, trustee, "care of" name
J. ENTREPRENEUR

4a Mailing address (street address) (room, apt., or suite no.)
123 EASY STREET

5a Business address, if different from address in lines 4a and 4b

4b City, state, and ZIP code
NEW YORK, NY 10021

5b City, state, and ZIP code

6 County and state where principal business is located
NEW YORK, NY

7 Name of principal officer, general partner, grantor, owner, or trustor—SSN required (See instructions.) ▶
J. ENTREPRENEUR 123-45-6789

8a Type of entity (Check only one box.) (See instructions.)
☐ Sole Proprietor (SSN) _____
☐ REMIC
☐ State/local government ☐ National guard
☐ Other nonprofit organization (specify) _____
☐ Other (specify) ▶ _____

☐ Estate (SSN of decedent) _____
☐ Plan administrator-SSN _____
☑ Personal service corp.
☐ Other corporation (specify) _____
☐ Federal government/military ☐ Church or church controlled organization
(enter GEN if applicable) _____
☐ Trust
☐ Partnership
☐ Farmers' cooperative

8b If a corporation, name the state or foreign country (if applicable) where incorporated ▶
State NEW YORK | Foreign country

9 Reason for applying (Check only one box.)
☑ Started new business (specify) ▶ 1/2/96
☐ Hired employees
☐ Created a pension plan (specify type) ▶ _____
☐ Banking purpose (specify) ▶ _____
☐ Changed type of organization (specify) ▶ _____
☐ Purchased going business
☐ Created a trust (specify) ▶ _____
☐ Other (specify) ▶ _____

10 Date business started or acquired (Mo., day, year) (See instructions.)
1/2/96

11 Enter closing month of accounting year. (See instructions.)
DECEMBER

12 First date wages or annuities were paid or will be paid (Mo., day, year). **Note:** If applicant is a withholding agent, enter date income will first be paid to nonresident alien. (Mo., day, year) . . . . ▶ JANUARY 31, 1996

13 Enter highest number of employees expected in the next 12 months. **Note:** If the applicant does not expect to have any employees during the period, enter "0." . . . . ▶

	Nonagricultural	Agricultural	Household
	1	0	0

14 Principal activity (See instructions.) ▶ COMPUTER PROGRAMMING

15 Is the principal business activity manufacturing? . . . . ☐ Yes ☑ No
If "Yes," principal product and raw material used ▶

16 To whom are most of the products or services sold? Please check the appropriate box. ☐ Business (wholesale)
☐ Public (retail) ☑ Other (specify) ▶ SMALL BUSINESSES + PROFESSIONALS ☐ N/A

17a Has the applicant ever applied for an identification number for this or any other business? . . . . ☐ Yes ☑ No
Note: If "Yes," please complete lines 17b and 17c.

17b If you checked the "Yes" box in line 17a, give applicant's legal name and trade name, if different than name shown on prior application.

Legal name ▶ | Trade name ▶

17c Enter approximate date, city, and state where the application was filed and the previous employer identification number if known.

Approximate date when filed (Mo., day, year)	City and state where filed	Previous EIN

Under penalties of perjury, I declare that I have examined this application, and to the best of my knowledge and belief, it is true, correct, and complete.
Business telephone number (include area code)

Name and title (Please type or print clearly.) ▶ J. ENTREPRENEUR, PRESIDENT (212) 555-0000

Signature ▶ Date ▶ 1/2/96

Note: Do not write below this line. For official use only.

Please leave blank ▶	Geo.	Ind.	Class	Size	Reason for applying

For Paperwork Reduction Act Notice, see attached instructions. Cat. No. 16055N Form **SS-4** (Rev. 12-93)

returned to you. Paranoid? Maybe. But anyone who has ever had problems proving to the IRS that forms were sent on time will agree that being supercautious is better than being sorry.

Order your corporate stationery and business cards now so that you will have them on hand before January 1. You may wish to have cards printed and sent to your clients and customers announcing that on January 1 your business or profession will be conducted under your new corporate name:

As of January 1, 1996
J. ENTREPRENEUR
Will Be Doing Business As
J. ENTREPRENEUR & CO., INC.
123 EASY STREET
NEW YORK, NEW YORK 10021

Now you're ready for the big step: applying for your Certificate of Incorporation. This is a procedure that varies from state to state; the different state requirements, forms, and fees are shown in Appendix A. In any case, your first step would be writing to the secretary of state or appropriate department or agency for your state, as shown on the chart.

For purposes of illustration, in this chapter I will walk you through the procedure of incorporation, using New York State laws, procedures, and forms. (Many of the states will differ in detail, but New York State is fairly representative.)

In New York State, the Certificate of Incorporation forms can be bought for approximately $1 each at most commercial stationers. Ask for Form A 234—Certificate of Incorporation, Business Corporation Law § (Section) 402, and get several blanks. You'll be sending one copy to Albany, you'll want a duplicate for your files, and you may want one or two forms to practice on.

Following is a sample Certificate of Incorporation. Of course, the purpose of your corporation may be different from the one shown; for the wording you need, consult §§ (Sections) 202 and 402 of the Business Corporation Law. For most small corporations, the broad language already on the form revised in late 1987 and shown here is all that is necessary.*

In New York State, this form is sent to New York State Division of Corporations, 162 Washington Avenue, Albany, New York 12231, along with a money order or bank cashier's check for $135. Unless you are a lawyer, New York State will not accept your personal check.

CHOOSING A FISCAL YEAR

You will note that the IRS Request for Employer Identification Number and the New York State Certificate of Incorporation both ask for your fiscal year.

In the first five editions of *Inc. Yourself,* the recommendations made were very different from the suggestions many tax experts are making now. Back then, the KISS (Keep It Simple, Sweetheart) strategy, which recommended electing a calendar year in order to file fewer tax forms during the first year of incorporation, outweighed the benefits of choosing a different fiscal year in order to implement more sophisticated tax planning.

Since 1987, though, it's quite clear that the highly profitable deferral strategies available through choosing a fiscal year that differs from the calendar year make it well worth the few hours of extra paperwork in your corporation's first year of life.

Choosing a fiscal year that ends on January 31 will give you the maximum tax-deferral advantage. If your corporation pays your salary annually or semiannually, it can pay you a good part—or all—of your salary in January 1996. The corporation takes its salary deduction for fiscal 1995, which ends on January 31, 1996. But since you, as an individual, are on a calendar year, you will not owe income tax on the salary you received in Janu-

*For the purpose of this book, I have transferred the material on my original Certificate of Incorporation to this new form.

Certificate of Incorporation

of

JUDITH H. McQUOWN & CO., INC.

under Section 402 of the Business Corporation Law

Filed By: Judith H. McQuown & Co., Inc.

Office and Post Office Address

134 Franklin Avenue
Staten Island, NY 10301

A 234—Certificate of Incorporation
Business Corporation Law §402: 1-89

© 1975 BY JULIUS BLUMBERG
PUBLISHER, NYC 1C   27

Certificate of Incorporation of

JUDITH H. McQUOWN & CO., INC.

under Section 402 of the Business Corporation Law

T IS HEREBY CERTIFIED THAT:

(1) The name of the proposed corporation is   JUDITH H. McQUOWN & CO., INC.

(2) The purpose or purposes for which this corporation is formed, are as follows, to wit:
To engage in any lawful act or activity for which corporations may be organized under the Business Corporation Law. The corporation is not formed to engage in any act or activity requiring the consent or approval of any state official, department, board, agency or other body.*

The corporation, in furtherance of its corporate purposes above set forth, shall have all of the powers enumerated in Section 202 of the Business Corporation Law, subject to any limitations provided in the Business Corporation Law or any other statute of the State of New York.

*If specific consent or approval is required delete this paragraph, insert specific purposes and obtain consent or approval prior to filing.

(3) The office of the corporation is to be located in the County of Richmond
   State of New York.

(4) The aggregate number of shares which the corporation shall have the authority to issue is

   One Hundred (100) no par

(5) The Secretary of State is designated as agent of the corporation upon whom process against it may be served. The post office address to which the Secretary of State shall mail a copy of any process against the corporation served upon him is

134 Franklin Avenue, Staten Island, New York 10301

(6) A director of the corporation shall not be liable to the corporation or its shareholders for damages for any breach of duty in such capacity except for

(i) liability if a judgment or other final adjudication adverse to a director establishes that his or her acts or omissions were in bad faith or involved intentional misconduct or a knowing violation of law or that the director personally gained in fact a financial profit or other advantage to which he or she was not legally entitled or that the director's acts violated BCL § 719, or

(ii) liability for any act or omission prior to the adoption of this provision.

The undersigned incorporator, or each of them if there are more than one, is of the age of eighteen years or over.

IN WITNESS WHEREOF, this certificate has been subscribed on December 20, 19 76 by the undersigned who affirm(s) that the statements made herein are true under the penalties of perjury.

Judith H. McQuown
Type name of incorporator _____ Signature

134 Franklin Avenue, Staten Island, NY 10301
Address

_____ _____
Type name of incorporator   Signature

_____
Address

_____ _____
Type name of incorporator   Signature

_____
Address

ary 1996 until April 1997. That's a fifteen-month deferral for some people. If you are paying estimated taxes, the actual deferral time may be shorter, but you will still have fifteen months to do your tax planning.

Unfortunately, the Tax Reform Act of 1986 made it very difficult for certain personal service corporations—defined as those whose principal function is "services in the fields of law, health, engineering, architecture, accounting, actuarial science, performing arts, or consulting"—to elect a fiscal year other than a calendar year. Now, personal service corporations, like S corporations, partnerships, and sole proprietorships, must use a calendar year.

Unless your corporation receives special permission, granted by the District Director of the Internal Revenue Service, to use a fiscal year. Here's how to try for it:

You need a clear, documented business reason. If your corporation makes gingerbread houses and most of its income is received in January for sales made in December, you have an excellent business reason for choosing a January fiscal year so that your corporation's income and expenses will fall in the same year.

Even if your services aren't as seasonal as those of a maker of gingerbread houses, you may still have a good chance of convincing the Internal Revenue Service if you can show that a good chunk of your income is received in January. Here's an argument that may work:

"My corporation gets paid in January for work it has done in the preceding year. I have to wait until my clients receive their Christmas bonuses and pay their bills before I know the corporation's income for the year, how many full or partial payments are coming in, and so on. In fact, nearly half of my corporation's income is received in January. Accordingly, it makes both economic and tax sense not to separate the time period in which the income was received from the time period in which the work was done."

Obviously, this line of reasoning is perfectly logical. You may find that you'll need a more sophisticated argument—consult your accountant or tax lawyer—and up-to-date books whose receivables prove your point if the IRS ever comes knocking at your door; but this argument is the core, and it may very well work for you.

To apply for a fiscal year, file IRS Form 1128 in triplicate (shown on pages 35–38) and cross your fingers. You should receive an answer in six to eight weeks.

The Revenue Act of 1987 gave these personal service corporations another alternative, which may be a better choice for some owners. Under certain circumstances, it may be advantageous—and permissible—to elect a fiscal year that gives you up to a three-month deferral—that is, a September 30 fiscal year. Consult your tax adviser for details and specific advice. Ask about the "enhanced estimated tax payments" system.

PAR-VALUE VERSUS NO-PAR-VALUE STOCK

Most states' Certificate of Incorporation forms ask whether the corporation plans to issue par-value stock or no-par-value stock, as in the preceding illustration. Par value (sometimes called face value) means the value or price at which the corporation's stock is issued; if a share of stock has a par value of $10, there must be $10 in the treasury to back it when the stock is initially sold or transferred. An entering stockholder would have to pay $1,000 for 100 shares, and the $1,000 would go into the corporate treasury to back the shares of stock ($10 per share).

No-par-value stock has no money behind the shares; no stockholder investment is necessary. Usually, in an ongoing sole proprietorship, the assets and liabilities of the proprietorship are transferred to the corporation in exchange for the corporation's stock.

Generally, if you are offered the option, issue no-par-value stock, rather than par-value stock. No-par-value stock is easier to set up, cheaper, and requires less paperwork. Some states assess taxes based on the par value of the issued and outstanding stock; if you have 100 shares of $100 par-value stock issued and outstanding, your total par value is $10,000; if those 100 shares have no par value, your total par value is $0.

In most states, corporations that deal in services can choose either par-value or no-par-value stock; it is just those businesses that use a great deal of capital (e.g., manufacturing), which may not be given the choice and would have to issue par-value stock so that the corporation would start with substantial cash assets.

YOUR CORPORATE RECORDS

If you incorporate in New York State, shortly after you submit your Certificate of Incorporation and cashier's check or money order for $135 to the Division of Corporations, you will receive a filing receipt. Now you are able to proceed to the next step: ordering a set of corporate records and a corporation seal at a commercial stationer; both of these are required by law.* Depending on where you live, it may take one to three weeks for you to receive your order. You must present your filing receipt to the stationer, or your order will not be accepted.

The simplest and cheapest corporate record set is a loose-leaf binder (approximately $85, including corporation seal) that contains stock certificates, a stock transfer ledger in which the shareholders' names and addresses are recorded, pages to which you attach the filing receipt and a copy of the Certificate of Incorporation, and sample minutes of meetings and bylaws that are set up so that you can just fill in the blanks. (A sample set of corporate minutes and bylaws is shown in Appendix B.) Even if you are the sole stockholder, officer, and employee of your corporation, alas, it is necessary to go through this paperwork. Or, if you put a higher value on your time than on your money, you can have your lawyer set up your corporation.

However, as lawyers' going rate for setting up a one- or two-person corporation is $500 to over $1,000 and you can fill out all

*While some states no longer require a corporate seal, virtually all banks and brokerage houses still require your corporate seal on documents.

Form **1128**

(Rev. June 1993)
Department of the Treasury
Internal Revenue Service

Application To Adopt, Change, or Retain a Tax Year

▶ **Instructions are separate.**

OMB No. 1545-0134
Expires 5-31-96

Before completing Form 1128, see the instructions to determine if this form must be filed.

Form 1128 consists of three parts:

- **Part I** must be completed by all applicants.
- **Part II** must be completed only by applicants requesting approval on a change or retention of a tax year under an expeditious approval rule. See the **Expeditious Approval Rules** in the instructions to determine who qualifies.
- **Part III,** Section A must be completed by all applicants requesting a ruling from the IRS National Office on a change, adoption, or retention of their tax year. For this type of application, a user fee must be attached. In addition to completing Section A, corporations, S corporations, partnerships, controlled foreign corporations, tax-exempt organizations, estates, and passive foreign investment companies must also complete the specific section in Part III that applies to the particular entity.

Check one of the boxes below:

- ☐ Individual
- ☐ Partnership
- ☐ Estate
- ☑ Corporation
- ☐ S Corporation
- ☐ Personal Service Corporation
- ☐ Cooperative (Sec. 1381(a))
- ☐ Tax-Exempt Organization
- ☐ Controlled Foreign Corporation (Sec. 957)
- ☐ Foreign Personal Holding Company (Sec. 552)
- ☐ Specified Foreign Corporation (Sec. 898)
- ☐ Passive Foreign Investment Company (Sec. 1296)
- ☐ Other Foreign Corporation
- ☐ Other _____
  (Specify entity and applicable Code section)

Part I **All Applicants** (See page 4 for required signature(s)).

Name of applicant (If joint return is filed, also give spouse's name.) **WONDERFUL CORPORATION**	Identifying number (See instructions.) **13-0000000**
Number, street, and room or suite no. (If a P.O. box, see page 2 of instructions.) **123 EASY STREET**	Service center where income tax return will be filed **HOLTSVILLE, NY**
City or town, state, and ZIP code **NEW YORK, NY 10021**	Applicant's area code and telephone number/Fax number **(212) 555-0000 ( )**
Name of person to contact (If not applicant, attach power of attorney.) **I.M. WONDERFUL**	Contact person's area code and telephone number/Fax number ( ) ( )

Please Type or Print

1 Is Form 2848, Power of Attorney and Declaration of Representative, attached to this application? . ▶ ☐ Yes ☑ No

2 Enter amount of **User Fee** attached to this application. (See instructions for Part I.) . . . . . ▶ $ **NOT APPLICABLE**

3a Approval is requested to (check one):

- ☑ Adopt a tax year ending ▶ **1|31|96** ....
  (Partnerships and personal service corporations: Go to Part III after completing Part I.)
- ☐ Change to a tax year ending ▶ ....

- ☐ Retain a tax year ending ▶ ....

b If changing a tax year, indicate the date the present tax year ends ▶ ....

c If adopting or changing a tax year, indicate the short period return that will be required to be filed for the tax year
beginning ▶ _____ , 19 ____ , and ending ▶ _____ , 19 ____ .

4 Nature of applicant's business or principal source of income:

DESIGN STUDIO

5 Indicate the applicant's overall method of accounting:

- ☑ Cash receipts and disbursements method

- ☐ Accrual method

- ☐ Other method (explain) ▶

For Paperwork Reduction Act Notice, see separate instructions. Cat. No. 21115C Form **1128** (Rev. 6-93)

Form 1128 (Rev. 6-93)   Page **2**

		Yes	No

Part II   **Expeditious Approval Rules** (See instructions.)

1 Is the applicant a corporation described in section 4 of Rev. Proc. 92-13, 1992-1 C.B. 665 (as modified and amplified by Rev. Proc. 92-13A, 1992-1 C.B. 668), that is requesting a change in a tax year under Rev. Proc. 92-13? . . . . ▶   ✓ |

2a Is the applicant a partnership, an S corporation, or a personal service corporation that is requesting a tax year under the expeditious approval rules in section 4 of Rev. Proc. 87-32, 1987-2 C.B. 396, **and** that is not precluded from using the expeditious approval rules under section 3 of that revenue procedure? . . . . ▶   ✓

b Is the applicant a partnership, an S corporation, or a personal service corporation that is retaining or changing to a tax year that coincides with its natural business year as defined in section 4.01(1) of Rev. Proc. 87-32, **and** such tax year results in no greater deferral of income to the partners or shareholders than the present tax year? ▶   ✓

c Is the applicant an S corporation whose shareholders own more than 50% of the shares of stock (as of the first day of the tax year to which the request relates) of the corporation **and** have the same tax year that the corporation is retaining or changing to? . . . . ▶   ✓

d Is the applicant an S corporation whose shareholders own more than 50% of the shares of stock (as of the first day of the tax year to which the request relates) of the corporation **and** have requested approval to concurrently change to the tax year that the corporation is retaining or changing to? . . . . ▶   ✓

3 Is the applicant an individual requesting a change from a fiscal year to a calendar year under Rev. Proc. 66-50, 1966-2 C.B. 1260? . . . . ▶   ✓

4 Is the applicant a tax-exempt organization requesting a change under Rev. Proc. 85-58, 1985-2 C.B. 740, or Rev. Proc. 76-10, 1976-1 C.B. 548? . . . . ▶   ✓

If the answer to any of the above questions is "Yes," file this form with the Internal Revenue service center where the income tax return of the applicant is filed. Do **not** file Form 1128 with the National Office and do not include a user fee. See **Where to file** in Part II of the instructions.

Form 1128 (Rev. 6-93)   Page **3**

Part III	Ruling Provisions

(If Part III applies, file Form 1128 with the National Office and attach a user fee. See instructions.)

SECTION A—General Information (See instructions.)

		Yes	No
1	In the last 6 years has the applicant changed or requested approval to change its tax year? . . . . . . ▶		✓
a	If "Yes" and there was a ruling letter issued granting approval to make the change, attach a copy. If a copy of the ruling letter is not available, attach an explanation and give the date the approval was granted. If a ruling letter was not issued, explain the facts and give the date the change was implemented.		
b	If a change in tax year was granted within the last 6 years, attach an explanation discussing why another change in tax year is necessary.		
2	Does the applicant have any accounting method, tax year, ruling, or technical advice request pending with the National Office? . . . . ▶		✓
	If "Yes," attach a statement explaining the type of request (method, tax year, etc.) and the specific issues involved in each request.		
3	Enter the taxable income * or (loss) for the 3 tax years immediately before the short period and for the short period. If necessary, estimate the amount for the short period. First preceding year $ .... Second preceding year $ .... Third preceding year $ .... Short period $ .... *Individuals enter adjusted gross income. Partnerships and S corporations enter ordinary income. Section 501(c) organizations enter unrelated business taxable income. Corporations enter taxable income before net operating loss deduction and special deductions. Estates enter adjusted total income.*		
4	Is the applicant a U.S. shareholder in a controlled foreign corporation (CFC)? . . . . ▶		✓
	If "Yes," attach a statement for each CFC stating the name, address, identifying number, tax year, the percentage of total combined voting power of the applicant, and the amount of income included in the gross income of the applicant under section 951 for the 3 tax years immediately before the short period and for the short period.		
5a	Is the applicant a U.S. shareholder in a passive foreign investment company as defined in section 1296? . ▶		✓
	If "Yes," attach a statement showing the name, address, identifying number and tax year of the passive foreign investment company, the percentage of interest owned by the applicant, and the amount of ordinary earnings and net capital gain from the passive foreign investment company included in the income of the applicant.		
b	Did the applicant elect under section 1295 to treat the passive foreign investment company as a qualified electing fund? ▶		
6	Is the applicant a member of a partnership, a beneficiary of a trust or estate, a shareholder of an S corporation, a shareholder of an Interest Charge Domestic International Sales Corporation (IC-DISC) or a shareholder in a Foreign Sales Corporation (FSC)? . . . . ▶		✓
	If "Yes," attach a statement showing the name, address, identifying number, tax year, percentage of interest in capital and profits, or percentage of interest of each IC-DISC and the amount of income received from each partnership, trust, estate, S corporation, IC-DISC, or FSC for the first preceding year and for the short period. Also indicate the percentage of gross income of the applicant represented by each amount.		
7	State the reasons for requesting the change in tax year. (Attach a separate sheet if more space is needed.) This information is required by Regulations section 1.442-1(b)(1). If the reasons are not provided, the application will be denied. **Note:** *Corporations that want to elect S corporation status should see question 2 in Section B below and the related instructions.* .... BULK OF RECEIPTS FOR PRIOR YEAR'S WORK WILL COME IN THE FOLLOWING JANUARY		

SECTION B—Corporations (other than S corporations and controlled foreign corporations) (See instructions.)

		Yes	No
1	Date of incorporation ▶ 1|2|95		
2	Does the corporation intend to elect to be treated as an S corporation for the tax year immediately following the short period? . . . . ▶		✓
	If "Yes," see the instructions for restrictions on this election.		
3	Is the corporation a member of an affiliated group filing a consolidated return? . . . . ▶		✓
	If "Yes," attach a statement showing (a) the name, address, identifying number used on the consolidated return, the tax year, and the Internal Revenue service center where the applicant files the return, (b) the name, address, and identifying number of each member of the affiliated group, (c) the taxable income (loss) of each member for the 3 years immediately before the short period and for the short period, and (d) the name of the parent corporation.		
4	If the applicant is a personal service corporation, attach a statement showing each shareholder's name, type of entity (e.g., individual, partnership, corporation, etc.), address, identifying number, tax year, and percentage of ownership. NOT APPLICABLE		

Form 1128 (Rev. 6-93)   Page **4**

SECTION C—S Corporations (See instructions.)

		Yes	No
1	Date of S corporation election ▶		
2	Is any shareholder applying for a corresponding change in tax year? . . . . ▶		
3	If the corporation is using a tax year other than the required tax year, indicate how it obtained its fiscal tax year (i.e., "grandfathered," section 444 election, or ruling from the IRS National Office). .... If the corporation received a ruling, indicate the date of the ruling's approval and provide a copy of the ruling letter .... If the corporation made a section 444 election, indicate the date of the election ▶		
4	Attach a statement showing each shareholder's name, type of entity (i.e., individual, estate, trust, or qualified Subchapter S Trust as defined in section 1361(d)(3)), address, identifying number, tax year, and percentage of ownership.		

SECTION D—Partnerships (See instructions.)

		Yes	No
1	Date business began ▶		
2	Is any partner applying for a corresponding change in tax year? . . . . ▶		
3	Attach a statement showing each partner's name, type of partner (e.g., individual, partnership, estate, trust, corporation, S corporation, IC-DISC, etc.), address, identifying number, tax year, and the percentage of interest in capital and profits.		
4	Is any partner a shareholder of a personal service corporation as defined in Temporary Regulations section 1.441-4T(d)(1)? . . . . ▶		
	If "Yes," attach a statement providing the name, address, identifying number, tax year, percentage of interest in capital and profits, and the amount of income received from each personal service corporation for the first preceding year and the short period.		

SECTION E—Controlled Foreign Corporations (See instructions.)

Attach a statement for each U.S. shareholder (as defined in section 951(b)) stating the name, address, identifying number, tax year, percentage of total combined voting power, and the amount of income included in gross income under section 951 for the 3 tax years immediately before the short period and for the short period.

SECTION F—Tax-Exempt Organizations

		Yes	No
1	Form of organization: ☐ Corporation ☐ Trust ☐ Other (specify) ▶		
2	Date of organization ▶		
3	Code section under which the organization is exempt ▶		
4	Is the organization required to file an annual return on Form 990, 990-C, 990-PF, 990-T, 1120-H, or 1120-POL? . . . . ▶		
5	Date exemption was granted ▶................................ Attach a copy of the ruling letter granting exemption. If a copy of the letter is not available, attach explanation.		
6	If a private foundation, is the foundation terminating its status under section 507? . . . . ▶		

SECTION G—Estates

1 Date estate was created ▶

2 Attach a statement showing:

a Name, identifying number, address, and tax year of each beneficiary and each person who is an owner or treated as an owner of any portion of the estate.

b Based on the adjusted total income of the estate entered in Part III, Section A, line 3, show the distribution deduction and the taxable amounts distributed to each beneficiary for the 2 tax years immediately before the short period and for the short period.

SECTION H—Passive Foreign Investment Company

Attach a statement showing each U.S. shareholder's name, address, identifying number, and the percentage of interest owned.

Signature—All Applicants (See instructions.)

Under penalties of perjury, I declare that I have examined this application, including accompanying schedules and statements, and to the best of my knowledge and belief it is true, correct, and complete. Declaration of preparer (other than applicant) is based on all information of which preparer has any knowledge.

WONDERFUL CORPORATION   11/1/95
Applicant's name   Date

                                                              PRESIDENT
Signature (officer of parent corporation, if applicable)   Title

I. M. WONDERFUL   11/1/95
Signing official's name (print or type)   Date

_____   _____
Signature of individual or firm (other than applicant) preparing the application   Date

_____
Firm or preparer's name

*U.S. Government Printing Office: 1993 — 343-034/80156

the forms in a couple of hours, wouldn't you rather do it yourself and "pay" yourself $250 to $500 an hour?

YOUR CORPORATE BANK ACCOUNTS

After you receive your new Employer Identification Number and your corporate seal, you will be able to open your new corporate bank accounts; I find it best to keep both a savings account and a checking account. Both types of accounts require the impression of your corporate seal.

Start your corporate checks with high numbers, like 626 or 340. It makes your corporation look as though it's been established for years. In fact, I recently heard of a California health-food store which will not accept checks numbered lower than 500.

Following is a typical commercial bank checking-account corporate resolution, to which you would sign and affix the corporate seal; since a savings bank corporate resolution is much less detailed, a sample is not given.

TRANSFERRING ASSETS TO YOUR NEW CORPORATION

On the date on which you begin corporate life, you can either cut off your sole proprietorship and start afresh or transfer the proprietorship's assets and liabilities to the new corporation. Note that these are assets and liabilities, such as office equipment and accounts receivable and payable, not earnings and profits from the proprietorship. In general, a corporation's assumption of the proprietorship's liabilities is beneficial; a dentist who had

$\mathcal{B}$USINESS
&$\mathcal{P}$ROFESSIONAL
$\mathcal{B}$ANKING

Certificate of Authorization of Corporation
to Open and Maintain Accounts at
The   Bank

I, the undersigned, Secretary of _____

_____

a corporation duly organized and existing under the laws of the State of _____ (hereinafte
referred to as the "Corporation") hereby certify to The   Bank that at a meeting of the Board of Directors o
the Corporation duly called and held on the _____ day of _____, 19_____, at which a quorum fo
the transaction of business was present and acting throughout, the following resolutions were duly adopted:

RESOLVED, that The   Bank, a New York banking organization, (hereinafter referred to as the "Bank")
be and it hereby is designated a depository of the Corporation and that the officers and agents of the Corporation be and each o
them is hereby authorized to open and maintain deposit accounts with the Bank at any of its banking offices and to deposit the funds
of the Corporation in any of such accounts, and it is further

RESOLVED, that except as otherwise specifically agreed by the Corporation and the Bank in writing, any deposit account opened
and maintained with the Bank by the Corporation shall be governed by all provisions of these resolutions as well as by the rules and
regulations and any deposit account agreement of the Bank from time to time applicable to such account and shall be subject to
such maintenance and service charges as the Bank shall from time to time establish, and it is further

RESOLVED, that the Bank be and it hereby is authorized to receive, collect and deposit into any account of the Corporation
maintained with the Bank all money and all checks, drafts, notes, bills of exchange, acceptances and other writings containing a promise
of or order for the payment of money drawn, payable or endorsed to bearer, to the name or order of the Corporation or otherwise,
tendered for deposit to the credit of the Corporation, and all such items drawn, payable or endorsed to the name or order of the
Corporation shall be deemed to have been unqualifiedly endorsed by the Corporation, whether or not actually so endorsed, and i
is further

RESOLVED, that the Bank is hereby authorized and directed to honor, pay and charge to the accounts of the Corporation maintained
with the Bank, without inquiry to or responsibility for the application of the proceeds thereof and regardless of the circumstances,
all checks, drafts, notes, bills of exchange, acceptances or other orders for the payment, withdrawal or transfer of funds deposited
in the accounts or to the credit of the Corporation, including any check, draft, note, bill of exchange, acceptance or other order that
may cause any overdraft, and to execute any instructions with regard thereto, when signed, drawn, accepted, endorsed or given on
behalf of the Corporation by actual or facsimile signature of any one of _____

_____
(Indicate titles of authorized persons)

(each such person is hereinafter referred to as an "Authorized Signer"), even if drawn to the individual order of or payable to or for
the benefit of an Authorized Signer or payable to the Bank or others for an Authorized Signer's account, provided, however, the Bank
may execute any instructions given by an Authorized Signer for the transfer of funds between different accounts of the Corporation
maintained with the Bank, whether such instructions are written or oral or are conveyed by telephone or electronic means, and it is further

RESOLVED, that the Corporation assumes full responsibility and agrees to indemnify and hold the Bank harmless of, from and
against all liabilities, costs and expenses (including, but not limited to attorneys' fees and disbursements) for refusing to honor any
signatures not provided to the Bank, and, also, for any and all payments made or other actions taken by the Bank in reliance upon
the original or facsimile signature of any Authorized Signer, notwithstanding that the use of a facsimile signature may have been unlawful
or uauthorized and regardless of by whom or by what means the actual or purported facsimile signature may have been affixed to
any instrument, if such facsimile signature reasonably resembles the facsimile specimen of an Authorized Signer designated in the
most recent resolutions of the Corporation accepted by and on file with the Bank, and it is further

RESOLVED, that any one of the Authorized Signers is hereby authorized to borrow money and receive advances of credit from
the Bank on behalf of and in the name of the Corporation, on any terms, and for any sum so borrowed or credit received, to pledge
any one or more of the accounts of the Corporation maintained with the Bank, and to execute and deliver to the Bank such documents
and agreements, which shall be binding on the Corporation, as the Bank shall require to evidence and secure such borrowings or
advances of credit, and it is further

RESOLVED, that any one of the Authorized Signers is hereby authorized to act for the Corporation in all other matters and
transactions relating to any of its accounts with the Bank, including, but not limited to, the issuance or cancellation of any stop payment
instruction with respect to any item drawn on any such account and the execution and delivery of any agreement with respect to any
account of the Corporation or any item deposited therein or drawn thereon, and it is further

RESOLVED, that the Secretary of the Corporation be and (s)he hereby is authorized to certify to the Bank the names of the present fficers of the Corporation and other persons empowered to act as Authorized Signers and the offices respectively held by them, any, together with specimens of their signatures (including the facsimile signature of each Authorized Signer, if any), and, in the ase of any change as to the holder of any office or any other person empowered to act as an Authorized Signer, the fact of such hange and the names of any new officers or persons so empowered and the offices respectively held by them, if any, together with pecimens of their signatures (including the facsimile signature of each such new officer or other person empowered as an Authorized igner, if any), and it is further

RESOLVED, that the authority given under these resolutions be and it shall be deemed retroactive and any and all acts performed ursuant thereto prior to the adoption of these resolutions be and they are hereby ratified and approved, and it is futher

RESOLVED, that the Secretary of the Corporation be and (s)he hereby is authorized to certify to the Bank that the board of directors f the Corporation has adopted these resolutions; that each of such resolutions remains in full force and effect, has not been rescinded, evoked or modified in any way and that none of such resolutions or any action taken or to be taken by the Corporation or its officers, mployees or agents pursuant thereto violates, or will result in any violation of, any applicable law or regulation, the certificate or articles f incorporation or by-laws of the Corporation or any instrument, agreement or document to which the Corporation is a party or by hich the Corporation or any of the assets of the Corporation is bound, and the Bank be and it hereby is authorized to rely on the ontinuing full force and effect of these resolutions as so certified to it by the Secretary of the Corporation until it shall have received ritten notice from the Corporation of the rescision, revocation, or modification thereof by further resolutions adopted by the board f directors of the Corporation together with the certification of the Secretary of the Corporation as to the adoption of such further esolutions and the Bank shall have had a reasonable opportunity to act upon such notice, and it is further

RESOLVED, that the resolutions hereby adopted be and they shall supercede and replace all prior resolutions heretofore adopted y the board of directors of the Corporation and on file with the Bank.

I hereby further certify that the foregoing resolutions, as of the date hereof, have not been rescinded, revoked or modified in any ay and remain in full force and effect, and that neither any of such resolutions nor any action taken or to be taken by the Corporation r its officers, employees or agents pursuant thereto violates, or will result in a violation of, any law or regulation, the certificate or rticles of incorporation or by-laws of the Corporation or any instrument, agreement or document to which the Corporation is a party r by which the Corporation or any of the assets of the Corporation is bound.

I hereby further certify that the individual(s) whose name(s) appear below has/have been duly elected or appointed to hold the ffice(s) of the Corporation indicated opposite his/her/their name(s); that he/she/they presently hold such offices as of the date hereof; nd that the signature(s) appearing next to his/her/their name(s) is/are his/her/their genuine original signature(s), and, that appearing elow the original signature of each named individual is a specimen of any facsimile signature that is authorized for use in substitution ereof.

Name	Title	Signature
_____	_____	_____
		_____
_____	_____	_____
		_____
_____	_____	_____
		_____
_____	_____	_____
		_____

☐ I further certify that I am the sole owner of all the issued and outstanding stock of the Corporation; that I am the sole officer f the Corporation and hold the offices of both President and Secretary thereof; and, that neither the laws of the state under which e Corporation is organized and existing nor the certificate or articles of incorporation or by-laws of the Corporation require that the ffices of President and Secretary of the Corporation be held by different individuals.

ate: _____, 19____   _____

Name: _____

Title: Secretary

____
Initial if applicable

ordered silver would rather have the corporation pay the bill than pay it out of his own pocket.

When partners in a partnership decide to incorporate, there are theoretically three ways in which the incorporation may take place. Therefore it seems advisable, where substantial sums are involved, that the partners either seek professional advice or use the simplest method. Under this method, the partnership transfers all its assets to the newly formed corporation in exchange for all the outstanding stock of the corporation. The partnership would then terminate, distributing all the stock to its partners in proportion to their partnership interests.

The only danger—in terms of federal tax—is transferring more liabilities than assets, which can lead to unnecessary taxes. This situation can be avoided fairly easily; you can always throw in a personal asset to equalize the balance, even if it's only another chair for your office or a few more reams of paper.

The asset/liability balance is probably a question of magnitude. If the liabilities exceed the assets by $50, it is unlikely that the IRS would bother with your case; if they exceed the assets by $5,000, that's another story. Just to be on the safe side, though, get your accountant's advice; theoretically, even a difference of $100 could get you in trouble with the IRS.

SEED MONEY

Whether you transfer your sole proprietorship's assets and liabilities to your new corporation or close down everything and start from scratch, there will probably be a period of a month or two in which the corporation will need some kind of seed money until funds start coming into the corporation. This would usually be money for new stationery, petty cash, one month's operating capital, and similar expenses.

Of course, the simplest—but also the most expensive—route would be taking out a 30-, 60-, or 90-day bank loan. But it is possible for you to lend the corporation money as long as the amount of money you are lending the corporation is not too great and as long as the corporation repays you within a short period of time. The IRS suggests that if you choose to lend money to the corporation for start-up expenses, you should limit the loan to no more than about $10,000 and the corporation should repay you within three to six months.

Whether you should charge your corporation interest on the loan or make it an interest-free loan depends on several considerations. Your decision will probably involve less than $300 in interest (a maximum of $10,000 × 12% × 3 months), so it really isn't crucial. Among the factors you should consider are whether your corporation will be very successful in its first year, your income from other sources, and whether you need interest income to offset interest you are paying on loans or on your margin account at a brokerage house.

The IRS points out some possible pitfalls in your lending money to the corporation. If the loan is on the corporation's books for an extended period of time and if there is no provision for interest, the IRS could maintain that this money is not really a loan, that instead it is equity capital (money that the corporation must have to stay alive). If the IRS can prove that you need all that money for a fairly long time to keep your business afloat, then, whether or not you call it a loan, the IRS will hold that the money is equity capital.

If the IRS does establish that the loan is really equity capital, then when the loan is repaid, it may be deemed to be a dividend (and therefore taxable to you), rather than a repayment of the loan: you would be distributing part of that equity capital to yourself, and such a distribution is considered a dividend.

However, this is generally a problem that affects only companies which need a great deal of capital; small business and professional corporations can usually stay within the loan-size and repayment-time limitations that satisfy the IRS.

When I incorporated, I had to handle the problem of seed money for my corporation. Because I had to wait for my Employer Identification Number, I paid some corporate expenses with personal checks and then reimbursed myself when the corporate checking account was activated. I delayed paying myself salary until corporate income could be transferred to the checking account and then paid myself back salary and reimbursed expenses in two large lump-sum checks: one for salary, and one for expenses. This procedure might well work for you and your new corporation.

HOW MUCH SEED MONEY WILL YOU NEED?

	One-time Cost	One Month	Three Months
Corporate filing fees (see Appendix A)	$ _____		
Corporate record book	_____		
Stationery, business cards	_____		
Rent		$ _____	$ _____
Phone		_____	_____
Utilities		_____	_____
Postage/Xerox/Fax		_____	_____
Car		_____	_____
Travel & entertainment		_____	_____
Your salary (if any)		_____	_____
Employees' salary (if any)		_____	_____
Insurance		_____	_____
Taxes	_____		_____
Other expenses (list)			
_____	_____	_____	_____
_____	_____	_____	_____
	_____	_____	_____
Totals	$	$	$

Do you have enough money for the first three months?

Shortly after you incorporate, you will have to decide whether you want an S corporation and/or whether you want to issue §1244 stock. These are independent choices; you may choose either, both, or neither. *Do not make either decision without consulting a lawyer and/or an accountant.*

LIMITED LIABILITY COMPANIES (LLCS)

Limited Liability Companies (LLCs) have spread dramatically since the seventh edition of *Inc. Yourself,* and are now covered in the new Chapter 6. The LLC is a *noncorporate* form that combines the limited liability of the corporation with the flow-through tax treatment of the partnership. LLCs require at least two members, as their owners are called, so if you are a single entrepreneur or professional, you may wish to form an S corporation instead.

S CORPORATIONS

The Revenue Act of 1987 had a dramatic impact on some entrepreneurs' and professionals' decisions to choose Subchapter S as their corporate form. In an S corporation, profits and losses flow through to the individual shareholder(s) and profits are taxed as personal income. In a C (general business) corporation, *you* choose whether corporate profits remain in your corporation or are paid to you.

The key provision of the 1987 act—that "certain personal service corporations" (most professional corporations and corporations whose chief source of income is consulting or the performing arts) would be taxed at a flat 34 percent instead of the graduated rates of 15 percent for income under $50,000 and 25 percent for income between $50,000 and $75,000—has made Subchapter S election even more attractive to many people than the 1986 act had made it. By forming an S corporation, professionals, consultants, and performers whose net income is $50,000 would be in the 15 percent bracket for part of their income and 21 percent for the remainder, rather than the mandated 34 percent.

As a result of the 1986 and 1987 acts, S corporations have become so important that I have devoted an entire chapter to them. In fact, if you think that your corporation might be one of those "certain personal service corporations," finish this overview section and then skip immediately to Chapter 7, "How to Profit from Your S Corporation." Deciding whether you should choose an S corporation or a C corporation can be the most important business and tax decision that you make for your new corporation. Obviously, you'll want to consult your tax lawyer and/or accountant before choosing between an S corporation and a C corporation.

§1244 STOCK

If the officers of a corporation decide to issue §1244 stock—a decision that must be made and recorded before the stock is issued—any shareholder who subsequently sells or exchanges that stock at a loss can take the loss as an ordinary loss—as opposed to the less favorable capital loss—on his or her personal income tax return. The rules governing this tax shelter are too technical to describe in detail in a general book like this one, and it is very unlikely that small business owners will choose §1244. However, if you feel that issuing §1244 stock might benefit your stockholders and your corporation (usually only if you think that at some point outsiders may buy your stock), you should consult your lawyer and/or your accountant.

MINUTES AND BYLAWS

Appendix B consists of a sample set of minutes and bylaws for a corporation registered in New York State. They include minutes of the organizational meeting, the bylaws, minutes of a board of directors' meeting, minutes of a shareholders' meeting, and minutes of a special meeting of the board of directors to elect a January fiscal year. Minutes of a special meeting of the board of directors to approve a medical care reimbursement plan and the plan itself are found in Chapter 11, "Medical Benefits."

3

AND NOW THE PARERWORK

Once you've come this far, the rest is easy. Changing from sole proprietor to corporate status doesn't require vastly more complicated bookkeeping; I find that my routine bookkeeping takes me only ten or fifteen minutes a day, or perhaps an hour or so on Saturday morning.

Your corporate bookkeeping can be very simple; any bookkeeping method that you can walk the IRS through is acceptable. For many people, single-entry bookkeeping is much simpler than double-entry. Your ledger can show what funds came in, what was paid out, what money was left, and how it was allocated.

There are now some excellent computer programs to help you with your bookkeeping and corporate records. For around $50, you can find a very adequate program; for around $200, you'll get some extremely sophisticated programs.

No matter how accurate your records are, the IRS may be somewhat reluctant to accept records written on index cards or stray pieces of paper. From the standpoint of creating a good corporate impression, it may be wise to invest in a ledger and to learn to use it. It increases your credibility and, as always, neatness counts.

The worksheets that follow show two months' books of a one-person corporation. As you can see, the ledger is quite simple to prepare. Note, too, that many corporate expenses are fully deductible from pretax income. They are only partly deductible in a sole proprietorship.

47

November 1995

Nov	3	CLIENT A	3750 —	Nov	2	Dr. A. BACKSTRETCH CHIROPRACTOR (#371)	50 —
Nov	7	CLIENT B	485 —			HEALTH INSURANCE PLAN	
		CLIENT C	11550			OF GREATER NY (#372)	393 —
Nov	13	CLIENT D	85 —	Nov	9	Dr. A. BACKSTRETCH (#373)	50 —
						Dr. I. PULLEM, DDS (#374)	200 —
Nov	17	CLIENT B	17780				
				Nov	16	Dr. A. BACKSTRETCH (#375)	50 —
Nov	19	CLIENT E	30360				
		CLIENT F	125 —	Nov	23	Dr. A. BACKSTRETCH (#376)	50 —
Nov	23	CLIENT B	80 —	Nov	30	Dr. A. BACKSTRETCH (#377)	50 —
		CLIENT D	444 —			NYNEX (#378)	85 —
						I.M. WONDERFUL	
Nov	28	CLIENT C	19075			Mo. SALARY 2,000 200 IRS -453 153 SS 100 NYS+NYC 453 (#379)	1547 —
		CLIENT B	75 —				
Nov	30	CLIENT G	246 —			IRS (200+306 SS)(#380)	506 —
			607765			NYS INCOME TAX BUREAU (#381)	100 —
							3081 —

DECEMBER 1995

DEC	1	CLIENT B	250 —	DEC	6	DR. A. BACKSTRETCH (#382)	50 —
DEC	7	CLIENT B	16250	DEC	13	DR. A. BACKSTRETCH (#383)	50 —
DEC	10	CLIENT A	621 —	DEC	20	DR. A. BACKSTRETCH (#384)	50 —
						ICU OPTOMETRISTS (#385)	250 —
DEC	18	CLIENT B	595 —				
				DEC	27	DR. A. BACKSTRETCH (#386)	50 —
DEC	27	CLIENT C	145 —			DR. I. PULLGMDDS (#387)	200 —
		CLIENT D	550 —			OFFICE DEPOT (#388)	6585
			2 3 2 3 50			NYNEX (#389)	7507
						AIRLINE MASTERCARD (#390)	14751

DEC 29 I.M. WONDERFUL

SALARY 2,000
200 IRS −453
153 SS
100 NYS+NYC
453

(#391)   1547 —

IRS (200+306SS)(#392)   506 —

NYS INCOME TAX BUREAU (#393)   100 —

3091 43

Getting down to specifics, always remember that you and your corporation are two separate, distinct legal entities. The corporation is now your employer and should pay your salary regularly, just as any other employer would. It will also withhold taxes from your salary and send them to the appropriate government agencies.

Your corporation will send out all the bills, and all income must now go into corporate bank accounts. I prefer using both a money-market account and a NOW checking account: all income goes directly into a corporate money-market account that earns interest; when money is needed to pay salary and bills, it is transferred from the money-market account to the NOW account.

Paying bills is a little more complicated now than it used to be. As an individual proprietor, your personal check paid for all expenses—personal and business; it was only at the end of the year that you had to figure out what part of a check to a credit-card company covered business expenses and what part represented personal items. Now you will have to make these calculations in advance and pay many bills with two checks: corporate and personal. There is a bonus, though: when you come to the end of the year, your business and personal expenses will already have been segregated, and tax preparation of these items will take no time at all.

You may find it simpler to use one credit card for business only; many people use their American Express or Diner's Club cards for corporate expenditures and their MasterCard or VISA for personal ones.

Paying office bills isn't difficult, but it deserves a chapter all its own; mortgages, rent, phone, and utilities are covered in the next chapter.

TAX CALENDAR FOR YOUR NEW CORPORATION

The calendar below shows you how simple your tax recordkeeping can be—only eight to eleven dates per year.

January 31	Deadline for issuing Form 1099s to independent contractors. Deadline for Form 941, employee withholding and FICA return, and Form 940, FUTA (unemployment), unless you made timely deposit of taxes; deadline is then February 10. Deadline for W-2s to employees.
February 28	Deadline for Form 1099s to IRS. Deadline for Form W-2 "A" copies to Social Security Administration and Forms W-2G and 1099-R "A" copies to IRS.
March 15	Original deadline for filing Form 1120, 1120A, or 1120S corporate income-tax return OR Deadline for filing Form 7004 for automatic extension of time to file return.
April 15	Deadline for filing Form 1040 personal income-tax return OR Deadline for filing Form 4868 to request automatic four-month extension. Deadline for Form 1040-ES, first installment of estimated taxes (not necessary if your withholding is adequate).
April 30	Deadline for Form 941, withholding, and FICA tax return for first quarter.

June 15   Deadline for Form 1040-ES, second installment of estimated taxes (not necessary if your withholding is adequate).

July 31   Deadline for Form 941, withholding, and FICA tax return for second quarter.

August 15   Deadline for filing additional Form 4868 to request additional extension for filing Form 1040, if desired.

September 15   Deadline for Form 1040-ES, third installment of estimated taxes (not necessary if your withholding is adequate).

October 31   Deadline for Form 941, withholding, and FICA tax return for third quarter.

January 15   Deadline for Form 1040-ES, last installment of estimated taxes (not necessary if your withholding is adequate).

4
YOUR OFFICE

Home or Away?

If you have been renting an office as an individual proprietor, corporate status doesn't mean much of a change: from the date of incorporation, you'll be paying your rent and office expenses with company checks instead of personal checks, as you were doing when you were an individual proprietor.

If your office is at home, the 1995 Job Creation and Wage Enhancement Act, passed by the House in April 1995 and likely to be passed by the Senate by the fall of 1995, will greatly expand the availability of the home-office deduction. Under this law, after 1995, a home office will qualify as the principal place of business if (1) your essential administrative and management activities are regularly conducted there; and (2) your home office is necessary because no other location is available. The home-office deduction for inventory charge will now include storage of your samples, if you are in sales, as well as inventory storage. If you work out of a vehicle—e.g., trucking, sales, or the professional trades—you will now also qualify for the home-office deduction.

(Happily, this law nullifies the 1993 Supreme Court case *Commissioner* v. *Soliman*, which gutted the home-office deduction for many professionals and entrepreneurs. In this case, an anesthesiologist was not permitted to claim a home-office deduction for case management and billing, even though none of the hospitals where he worked provided him with an office. Though he spent far more time on studying his cases before surgery and doing

53

paperwork at home, his work in the hospital operating room far outweighed the paperwork in terms of *relative importance*.)

So, having been spared this nasty trap, if your office is at home—one or more rooms of an apartment or a house that you rent—you would now use a corporate check to pay for the rent on that portion of the apartment or the house that you use as an office. If your rent is $800 a month for a four-room apartment and you use one room of the apartment exclusively as an office, you would now pay the rent with two checks: a corporate check for $200 for the office portion of your apartment, and a personal check for the personal living portion of your apartment. *Make sure you get your landlord's permission in writing.* Similarly, using these proportions, you would send the electric utility company a corporate check for 25 percent of your electric bill and a personal check for 75 percent of it. Or you might be able to make a convincing case for a larger share to be allocated to your office—a word processor and lights in constant use, perhaps—and write off 33 or 40 percent as a corporate office expense and 67 or 60 percent for personal use.

In some cases, where your landlord would look askance at your running a business from your second bedroom, it will be more prudent to pay your rent with one single personal check and have your corporation reimburse you monthly with its share of the rent. In this example, you would pay the entire rent of $800 and your corporation would reimburse you $200, or an annual lump sum of $2,400, which might be easier. Your net rent would still be $600 a month.

Actually, even if you have an S.O.B. for a landlord, it may pay for you to check whether rent or zoning regulations bar you from working at home. For example, in New York City, which has tough regulations, many business and professional people are permitted to work at home. The occupational use must be secondary to the residential use and limited to the greater of 500 square feet or 25 percent of the space. The person offering the service or product must live there and is permitted only one nonresident employee. About fifteen enterprises are banned, the most significant of which are public relations or advertising agency, beauty parlor, interior decorating office, real estate, or insurance office.

Check your lease, too, to see whether it contains a clause specifying residential use. New York's Court of Appeals ruled that a psychologist who partitioned an apartment to create an office and saw more than twenty clients a week significantly violated such a clause.

Your telephone bill is a bit more complicated. If you have a separate business phone, the bill gets paid with a corporate check, of course, and your private phone bill gets paid with a personal check. If your home office has only one phone, you will have to prorate business and personal use and pay the appropriate shares with corporate and personal checks. Be especially careful to allocate long-distance calls properly; you should be able to document business long-distance calls if the IRS audits your tax return.

Still more complicated is the situation where your office is part of a house, cooperative apartment, or condominium you own and live in. In this case, in order to preserve the separation between your corporation and you, one accountant suggests that the corporation rent its office space from you, the shareholder, in an arm's-length transaction. You may wish to have a lease and corporate resolutions approving the lease—see pages 56–58 to document the arm's-length nature of the transaction. In this kind of transaction, it is clear that there are two separate entities and that there is no favoritism shown—for example, if you would not rent anyone else office space at $10 per month, you must not rent space to the corporation at this price.

You can even profit from this transaction: as the stockholder, you could take the position that the fair rental value of the corporate offices is higher than the proportionate share of the mortgage and the real estate tax payments you have to make. For example, if your mortgage and tax payments total $1,000 a month and your corporation uses two rooms of your eight-room house, you could conceivably and reasonably argue that $500 a month (rather than the $250 that would be the proportionate share) is a reasonable rent for a two-room office in your neighborhood. Then, as the homeowner (or cooperative or condominium owner), you would be able to take 100 percent of all the deductions on your individual tax return: interest amortization, real estate taxes, etc. You would have to report the rent your corporation pays you as income, but this way you are withdrawing funds from your corporation that will be deductible by the corporation: sales, rentals, anything but dividends, since dividends would be taxed twice.

MINUTES OF A SPECIAL MEETING OF SHAREHOLDERS OF WONDERFUL CORPORATION

MINUTES of a special meeting of shareholders held at 123 Easy Street, New York City, in the State of New York, on the second day of January 1996, at nine o'clock in the forenoon.

The meeting was duly called to order by the President and sole stockholder, who stated the object of the meeting.

On motion duly made, amended, and unanimously carried, the following resolution was adopted:

WHEREAS, there has been presented to and considered by this meeting a proposed lease from I. M. Wonderful, as Lessor, to this corporation, as Lessee, covering the premises known as 123 Easy Street; and

WHEREAS, said proposed lease is for a term of two years, commencing January 2, 1996, at the annual rental of $6,000.00 (six thousand dollars);

NOW, THEREFORE, BE IT RESOLVED, that the terms and conditions of the proposed lease presented to and considered by this meeting be and the same hereby are approved.

FURTHER RESOLVED, that the President and Secretary of this corporation be and they hereby are authorized to execute said lease in the name of and on behalf of this corporation and in substantially the form approved at this meeting.

There being no further business, the meeting was adjourned. Dated the second day of January, 1996.

_____

Secretary

_____

President

In fact, there are some excellent reasons to have your corporation pay you as high a rent as is comfortable for your corporation to pay on an annual or biannual basis and that is consistent with neighborhood office-space rents. First, payment of a high rent removes cash from your corporation. In doing so, it slows down the accumulation of retained earnings and may even lower your corporation's tax bracket. Second, as compared with salary, neither you nor your corporation pays Social Security tax on rent, although there is a trade-off: the higher your salary, the higher your pension contribution and your eventual pension— but the higher your Social Security and income taxes. Third, the rent payments you receive can be offset by depreciation, repairs, cleaning, and other real estate expenses.

Check whether your locality imposes a commercial rent tax on rents over a certain figure. (In New York City it's a generous $31,000 per year rising to $40,000 after June 1, 1996.) You can avoid the tax by paying yourself less rent.

As you can see, the corporation is defraying a larger part of your home's expenses than the proportion of the actual physical space it is using, and yet the $500-a-month rent, in this example, is quite reasonable and not likely to be questioned by the IRS.

The key is what the IRS considers reasonable. No matter what comparable office space might cost, the IRS will probably question rent that comes within $100 or so of your house's monthly mortgage payment or coop's or condominium's monthly main-

This Lease, dated the SECOND   day of JANUARY   1996

Between

Parties

I.M. WONDERFUL   hereinafter referred to as the Landlord, and

WONDERFUL CORPORATION

hereinafter referred to as the Tenant,

WITNESSETH: That the Landlord hereby demises and leases unto the Tenant, and the Tenant hereby hires and takes from the Landlord for the term and upon the rentals hereinafter specified, the premises described as follows, situated in the CITY   of NEW YORK

County of NEW YORK   and State of NEW YORK

Premises

OFFICE SPACE AT 123 EASY STREET, NEW YORK, NY 10001

Term

The term of this demise shall be for TWO YEARS
beginning JANUARY 2,   1996 and ending JANUARY 1,   1998.

Rent

The rent for the demised term shall be TWELVE THOUSAND DOLLARS
($12,000 —), which shall accrue at the yearly rate of
SIX THOUSAND DOLLARS ($6,000 —).

The said rent is to be payable monthly in advance on the first day of each calendar month for the term hereof, in instalments as follows:

Payment of Rent

FIVE HUNDRED DOLLARS ($500 —) PER MONTH.

at the office of
or as may be otherwise directed by the Landlord in writing.

THE ABOVE LETTING IS UPON THE FOLLOWING CONDITIONS:

Peaceful Possession

First.—The Landlord covenants that the Tenant, on paying the said rental and performing the covenants and conditions in this Lease contained, shall and may peaceably and quietly have, hold and enjoy the demised premises for the term aforesaid.

Second.—The Tenant covenants and agrees to use the demised premises as u

Purpose

and agrees not to use or permit the premises to be used for any other purpose without the prior written consent of the Landlord endorsed hereon.

Default in Payment of Rent

Third.—The Tenant shall, without any previous demand therefor, pay to the Landlord, or its agent, the said rent at the times and in the manner above provided. In the event of the non-payment of said rent, or any instalment thereof, at the times and in the manner above provided, and if the same shall remain in default for ten days after becoming due, or if the Tenant shall be dispossessed for non-payment of rent, or if the leased premises shall be deserted or vacated, the

IN WITNESS WHEREOF, the said Parties have hereunto set their hands and seals the day and year first above written.

Witness: ___I. M. Wonderful_____(SEAL)
                                              Landlord

_____   By _I. M. Wonderful_____

_____   _Wonderful Corporation___(SEAL)
                                                   Tenant
                                  By I. M. Wonderful,

Because the lease is between you and your corporation, as long as you renew it and your company pays fair market value, you can file the form and forget it.

tenance charge. Still, *without your being greedy,* these basic guidelines allow a great deal of flexibility. Depending on your office space, its percentage of your total house or apartment space, your monthly rent, maintenance, or mortgage payment, and, to a great extent, your corporation's income, you should be able to charge your corporation rent of anywhere from $400 to $1,000 a month (sometimes more) and still fall within the IRS guidelines of reasonable rent.

Schedule E on the following page shows corporate rental of a portion of a $200,000 apartment. Although the rent is $500 per month—$6,000 per year—in income to the owner, note that less than one-third of the $6,000 rental—$1,800—is actual taxable income.

Be aware, though, that if you do rent part of your home or apartment to your corporation, when you sell your home or apartment, you'll have to pay tax on the same percentage of any gain as the percentage of the home or apartment you rented to your corporation as well as tax on the recaptured depreciation. Good tax advice can help minimize the bite.

To avoid any problems on qualifying for a complete rollover or favorable capital-gains treatment when you plan to sell your house or apartment, ask your accountant the current period of time when you should not use your residence for business purposes (your renting office space to your corporation) in order to "deconsecrate" it and return it to 100 percent residential use. Then have your corporation rent office space elsewhere for that time. It's extra work, but you'll save thousands of dollars in taxes.

SCHEDULE E (Form 1040) Department of the Treasury Internal Revenue Service (O)	**Supplemental Income and Loss** (From rental real estate, royalties, partnerships, S corporations, estates, trusts, REMICs, etc.) ▶ Attach to Form 1040 or Form 1041. ▶ See Instructions for Schedule E (Form 1040).	OMB No. 1545-0074 19**94** Attachment Sequence No. **13**

Name(s) shown on return I. M. WONDERFUL	Your social security number 000 : 00 : 0000

Part I   **Income or Loss From Rental Real Estate and Royalties**   Note: *Report income and expenses from your business of renting personal property on **Schedule C** or **C-EZ** (see page E-1). Report farm rental income or loss from **Form 4835** on page 2, line 39.*

				Yes	No
1	Show the kind and location of each **rental real estate property:**	2	For each rental real estate property listed on line 1, did you or your family use it for personal purposes for more than the greater of 14 days or 10% of the total days rented at fair rental value during the tax year? (See page E-1.)		
A	123 EASY STREET, NYC - OFFICE SPACE		A		✓
B					
C			B		
			C		

Income:			**Properties**			**Totals**
			A	**B**	**C**	(Add columns A, B, and C.)
3	Rents received	3	6,000 —			3	6,000 —
4	Royalties received	4				4	0

Expenses:

5	Advertising	5					
6	Auto and travel (see page E-2) .	6					
7	Cleaning and maintenance . . .	7	600 —				
8	Commissions	8					
9	Insurance	9					
10	Legal and other professional fees	10	500 —				
11	Management fees	11					
12	Mortgage interest paid to banks, etc. (see page E-2)	12				12	0
13	Other interest	13					
14	Repairs	14					
15	Supplies	15					
16	Taxes	16					
17	Utilities . . . . . ▶	17	600 —				
18	Other (list) ▶ DEPRECIATION BASIS: $200,000-5% VALUE OF LAND= $190,000÷4 (1 ROOM OF 4 RM APT) = $47,500÷19 YEARS = $2500 PER YR. (PLACED IN SERVICE 1984)	18					
19	Add lines 5 through 18	19	1,700 —			19	1,700 —
20	Depreciation expense or depletion (see page E-2)	20	2,500 —			20	2,500 —
21	Total expenses. Add lines 19 and 20	21	4,200 —				
22	Income or (loss) from rental real estate or royalty properties. Subtract line 21 from line 3 (rents) or line 4 (royalties). If the result is a (loss), see page E-2 to find out if you must file **Form 6198**. . .	22	1,800 —				
23	Deductible rental real estate loss. **Caution:** *Your rental real estate loss on line 22 may be limited. See page E-3 to find out if you must file **Form 8582**. Real estate professionals must complete line 42 on page 2*	23	(	)(	)(	)	

24	**Income.** Add positive amounts shown on line 22. **Do not** include any losses	24	1,800 —
25	**Losses.** Add royalty losses from line 22 and rental real estate losses from line 23. Enter the total losses here .	25	( )
26	Total rental real estate and royalty income or (loss). Combine lines 24 and 25. Enter the result here. If Parts II, III, IV, and line 39 on page 2 do not apply to you, also enter this amount on Form 1040, line 17. Otherwise, include this amount in the total on line 40 on page 2	26	1,800 —

For Paperwork Reduction Act Notice, see Form 1040 instructions.   Cat. No. 11344L   Schedule E (Form 1040) 1994

5
YOUR BUSINESS PLAN:

Preparing for Success

Actually, all entrepreneurs and professionals need at least one business plan: one for themselves, and one if they intend to borrow money or sell a portion of their corporation to outside investors.

The popular perception is that successful entrepreneurs or independent professionals are mavericks, ego-driven macho types (regardless of their sex), flying by the seats of their pants. That perception, shared unfortunately by many entrepreneurs, is only about half accurate. Many are ego-driven mavericks; that part is true. But the most successful of them have a plan, even if it's informal and unwritten.

YOUR OWN BUSINESS PLAN

Think of your own private business plan as a road map; if you don't know where you're going, you won't know how to get there and you won't know whether you've arrived. Unwritten plans have their value, especially for one-person corporations that depend more on brains and a good Rolodex than on bricks and mortar (e.g., "This year I want my corporation to bill $100,000"). But a written plan, no matter how rough or brief, has the advantage of crystallizing your thoughts. A written plan will help you fine-tune your dreams and thereby achieve them.

61

"Sales Doctor" Brian Azar suggests the following informal broad-based business plan:

I Making a Situation Analysis
   A. Identify yourself and your market
      1. Where are you now and where do you want to be _____ years from now?
      2. What are your strong points? Weak points?
      3. What is unique about your product or service?
      4. Who are your clients? (Demographics: age, sex, income, education, etc.) What kind of clients do you wish to attract?
      5. Where is your business located? Is it located where it can take advantage of your clients' demographics?
      6. Do you have the financial resources to sustain a marketing program?
   B. Examining Your Market
      1. The competition
         (a) What fees do they charge?
         (b) What products or services do they offer? What are their strengths? Weaknesses?
         (c) How do they promote their products or services?
         (d) Where are they located?
      2. Economic conditions (national and regional)
      3. Industry conditions
II Positioning Your Product or Service
   A. What is unique about your product or service?
   B. How can you reposition an existing product or service?
   C. How can you concentrate on market segments?
   D. How can you fill a customer's need or needs?
III Setting Your Objectives
   A. Build a $_____ practice within one year.
   B. Attract _____ new customers/clients/patients each month (or year).

C. Achieve _____ % awareness in the community within one year.

D. Maintain _____ % market share.

E. Achieve _____ % increase in profitability.

After working on this broad-based plan, it's a good idea to write down some brief shorter-term objectives—for example, "I will make at least three cold calls and three follow-up calls every Friday morning" or "I will ask every client for a new project and for referrals as soon as I complete the original project."

YOUR FORMAL BUSINESS PLAN

If you plan to borrow money from banks or the Small Business Administration or similar agencies, or to sell some of your corporation's stock to investors, you will need a more formal business plan. Most entrepreneurs—especially high-tech inventors—make the mistake of preparing a lengthy technical tome, more suitable as a doctoral dissertation than a business proposal. They also err by using poor-quality paper and type, and by not packaging their business plan attractively. It's true that Einstein walked around wearing a rumpled, tobacco-stained sweater. But if you—as a fledgling Einstein—present a rumpled, tobacco-stained proposal to a banker or investment group, you will almost certainly be turned down. In all probability, your plan won't even be read. Business plans are very much like résumés. The people with the power receive hundreds of them every week. If your plan isn't neat, clean, and packaged attractively, it won't even be looked at; it will go right into the wastebasket.

George Auxier, national director, Entrepreneurial Advisory Services, for the Big Six accounting firm of Coopers & Lybrand L.L.P., offers these excellent suggestions for creating a winning business plan:

- Be brief, but include everything important to the business. A proposal of seven to ten typewritten pages, double-spaced, is often ideal. Leave secondary issues and information for discussion at a later meeting.
- Avoid highly technical descriptions of your products, processes, and operations. Use layman's terms. Keep it simple and complete.
- Be realistic in making estimates and assessing market and other potentials.
- Discuss your company's business risks. Your credibility can be damaged seriously if existing risks and problems are discovered by outside parties on their own.
- Don't make vague or unsubstantiated statements. For example, don't just say that sales will double in the next two years or that you are adding new product lines. Be specific. Substantiate your statements with underlying data and market information.
- Internal business plans and budgets normally are more detailed than those presented to external users. Accordingly, internal documents should be summarized and properly structured to facilitate review by outside parties.
- Enclose your proposal/business plan with an attractive but not overdone cover.
- Provide extra copies of your plan to speed the review process.

Make sure that you answer these questions:

- What is the company's business? While this may seem obvious, many plans tell the reader on page 20 what business it's in, and with some plans you're never certain.
- What are the company's objectives?
- What are the strategy and tactics that will enable the company to reach those objectives?
- How much money will the company need, over what period, and how will the funds be used?
- When and how will the money be paid back?

To make it easier for your lenders or investors to read your business plan, Coopers & Lybrand L.L.P. recommends beginning with a summary of no more than two pages, including a brief discussion of:

- The market potential
- The product and technology you expect to capitalize on
- The track record and depth of your management team
- Abbreviated financial forecasts
- The desired financing

Then briefly describe your company, its products or services, and industry, including:

- Your company's operating history, present ownership, and future objectives
- Your product's function and uniqueness
- The technology involved
- Your company's role within your industry and the trends in that industry

Assess Your Market Potential. Market potential is where financiers separate the inventors from the entrepreneurs. Many good products are never successfully commercialized because their inventors don't stop to analyze the market potential or assemble the management team necessary to capitalize on the opportunity.

This section of your plan will be scrutinized carefully. Your market analysis should therefore be as specific as possible, focusing on believable, reasonable, and obtainable projections, including:

- The size of the potential market and market niche you are pursuing
- The market share you anticipate achieving
- The competition—who and what
- The marketing channels you expect to use

- The potential customers—who, where, how many
- The pricing of your product, compared with competitive products

Independent studies are valuable in verifying the potential of certain markets or market niches. In addition to their credibility, they can show both you and your bankers or backers the size and scope of your potential market.

Specify Your Marketing Strategy. The ability to market your product successfully is just as important as your product's development. In presenting your marketing strategy, therefore, be sure to include a discussion of:

- The specific marketing techniques you plan to use—that is, how you plan to identify, contact, and sell to potential customers
- Your pricing plans—demonstrating the value added to the customer, versus the price paid
- Your planned sales force and selling strategies for various accounts, areas, and markets
- Your customers—how many there are and where they are located
- Your customer service—which markets will be covered by the direct sales force, which by distributors, representatives, or resellers
- Your specific approaches for capitalizing on each channel and how they compare with other practices within your industry
- Your advertising and promotional plans

Present Your Product Development. In broad, fairly nontechnical terms, present the status of your product development, so as to allow someone reasonably familiar with the technology or industry to conclude whether you are dealing with a concept, prototype, or product ready for market. Points to cover in this section include:

- The extent of invention or development required to complete your projects successfully
- The track record of key people in developing similar products
- The proprietary aspects of your technology
- The reasons why your product is more advanced or better than the existing technology, products, or services

Outline Your Operations. Outline your plans for operations within various time frames. For instance, development, early manufacture, market development, and first product installation—as well as facilities, work force by job category, extent of subcontracting, sources of supply, and warranty and service strategy.

Your work-force analysis should represent a head count by function or department (or both) for a specified time period. This analysis not only will allow you to better plan your hiring, but also will demonstrate to potential investors the sensitivity of your plans to the hiring of key personnel.

Describe Your Management Team. Financiers invest in people— people who have run or are likely to run successful operations— so potential investors will look closely at the members of your management team. Your team should have experience and talents in the most important management disciplines, such as research and development, marketing and sales, and manufacturing and finance. This section of the business plan should therefore introduce the members of your management team, highlighting their track records. Detailed résumés should be included in an appendix.

Provide a Financial Summary. Detailed financial forecasts also should appear in an appendix, but within your business plan— condensed to about a page—you should include a financial summary of your company, income statement, cash-flow analysis, and balance sheet. Be sure this information addresses the extent of investment you'll need and provides the basis for a financier to decide on the potential future value of the investment.

The following thorough outline lists everything that bankers and investors want to know:

1. Introduction and summary of business plan
   - Purpose of the plan
   - Business and history of the company
   - Major customers
   - Summary of comparative income statement results
   - Address and telephone number
2. The company—its industry and objectives
   - Industry background
   - Corporate short- and long-term objectives
   - Company size; market share
   - Expected rate of profitability goals
   - Strategies to reach objectives
3. Products and services
   - Principal products or services
   - Proprietary position and potential
   - Product development
   - Trademarks and royalty agreements
4. Market
   - Assessment of market size, history, market segments, and product position in the market
   - Costs/benefits of the product
   - Market pricing: company's strategy
   - Evaluation of competition, type of competition, customer service, lead time, price, terms, location, product quality
   - Marketing strategy defined; how and why sales will be made
   - Description of type and size of customer base; relationship and percent of total sales with major customers; stability; special terms
   - Product distribution and sales force

- Advertising and promotion approach
- Product or product-line profitability and markups

5. Manufacturing
    - Plant locations and description of facilities
    - Description of manufacturing process if unique
    - Capital equipment requirements
    - Labor force
    - Cost and quality control
    - Backup sources of supply

6. R&D and engineering
    - Status of product line; what remains to be done, how, time required, at what cost
    - Product life cycle, technical obsolescence
    - Plans to meet competition and/or obsolescence
    - Needs for manufacturing and applications engineering
    - Proprietary and patent position

7. Management
    - Management team, responsibilities, skills
    - Identification of principal owner-managers
    - Human-resource projections and plans
    - Supporting external advisers and relationships, attorneys, accountants, investors, and lenders
    - Board of directors

8. Historical financials
    - Latest balance sheet plus income statement for past two to three years
    - Brief explanation of major operating variances
    - Consideration of sales and cost of sales data by product line if significant

9. Financial plan and forecast
    - Profit and loss/cash flow forecast, by month or quarter for first year, and by year for years two and three
    - Forecasted balance sheets at year-ends
    - Summary of all significant assumptions used in forecasts considering sales plan, changes in customer base,

selling-price increases, margin improvements, material and labor and other operating-cost increases, capital expenditures required, changes in receivable collection patterns, inventory lead time and turnover, trade credit terms and availability, and the effects of income taxes

10. Proposed financing
   - Desired financing
   - Use of proceeds
   - Securities or debt instruments offered, terms
   - Payback and collateral

11. The future
   - Commentary and summary on where the company is going.

   In planning for "start-up," new ventures, new product lines and additional plants, the following should be considered:
   - Identify the critical events or actions that must occur in order for you to achieve your objectives—for example, opening of a pilot operation to test a new product or service or approval on a patent application.
   - Identify and assess the key assumptions on which the new venture's success depends.
   - Set out events which must take place in a necessary sequence. For example, the sequence may be:
     - Completion of concept
     - Product testing
     - Prototype developed
     - Pilot operation opened
     - Market tests
     - Production start-up
     - Initial key sales
   - Develop a graphic presentation of the aforementioned sequence of key events by dates and by expenditures, if appropriate.

Your business plan can also work as a management tool. It's a corporate and sometimes a personal self-appraisal. Performing this assessment is important for any new or ongoing venture, even when outside financing is not a factor.

After you draft your business plan, put it away for a day or two. Then go over it with a thesaurus in one hand and a red pencil in the other. Make sure that you choose the most dramatic, colorful, and precise words—and always write in the active voice. Don't be afraid of making two or three drafts. A successful business plan will help your new company obtain the financing it needs to grow.

6

LIMITED LIABILITY COMPANIES (LLCs):

The Newest
Business Entity

Strictly speaking, limited liability companies (LLCs) should not be included in this book because they are not corporations. Essentially, they are partnerships that give their owners the protection of limited liability that is one of the most valuable advantages of incorporation. However, because LLCs have sprung up in the last five years, and every state has enacted or proposed LLC statutes, some brief coverage is warranted now.

The most important limitation of LLCs is that they are required to have at least two members (as LLC owners are called) in order to ensure partnership tax treatment. This restriction prevents their use by single entrepreneurs and professionals. (If these individuals desire partnership tax treatment, they should form S corporations, as discussed in Chapter 7.)

For federal tax purposes, LLCs are usually treated as partnerships if they *lack* at least two of the four standard corporate characteristics:

- limited liability
- limited life
- central management
- free transferability of interest

To comply, when members set up an LLC, they file Articles of Organization or a Certificate of Formation (similar to a corporation's Certificate of Incorporation) with the Secretary of State. This document usually states that the LLC will have a limited life (many states restrict an LLC's life to thirty years and require it to dissolve upon the death, retirement, resignation, expulsion, bankruptcy, or dissolution of a member) and will restrict the transferability of interests.

LLCs are particularly useful in real estate because they provide liability protection for their investors while enabling them to take advantage of tax benefits offered by real estate projects, especially the use of nonrecourse financing to enhance their tax basis, leverage, and potential profits.

According to Coopers & Lybrand L.L.P.'s monograph, *Choosing a Business Entity in the 1990's,* LLCs are especially attractive for the following businesses:

Start-Up Businesses. "New operations can easily be formed as LLCs. The pass-through of losses to members makes the LLC form attractive for new businesses. Later, if desirable, it is easy to convert the LLC to a corporation."

High-Tech Companies. "The LLC form may be attractive to companies conducting high-risk research or marketing high-risk products. LLCs permit pass-through of initial losses and research expenses and use of preferred equity interests, compensation of employees with special ownership interests, and joint venturing with other high-tech companies."

Venture Capital. "The LLC can be used by venture capitalists as a vehicle for members to participate in investment activities without exposure to personal liability. As long as the LLC is classified as a partnership, the venture capital fund can make special allocations of investment earnings to its members. The LLC can invest in a large number of corporations and partnerships. Ownership can be structured to provide different member interests to lenders, underwriters, employees and other investors."

In fact, according to the monograph, "One of the most attractive characteristics of the LLC is the ability to make special allocations of income, gains, losses, deductions and credit among members. If the allocations satisfy IRS regulations, members generally may structure these allocations to benefit their individual tax situations or to more closely reflect the members' interests in different aspects of the business. For example, profits derived from property contributed by one member can be disproportionately allocated to that member. In comparison, S corporation items of income, gain, loss, deduction, and credit are allocated on a per-share/per-day basis to all shareholders." *There is no flexibility in S corporations, as there is with LLCs.*

In conclusion, while an LLC is probably not a viable choice for at least 80 percent of entrepreneurs and professionals, this chapter will help you and your lawyer and accountant (be sure they are LLC experts) make an informed decision.

7

HOW TO PROFIT FROM YOUR S CORPORATION

In a sense, an S corporation is a hybrid. It is generally treated like a corporation for legal purposes, but like a partnership for income-tax purposes. Think of an S corporation as a conduit: its profits and losses are not taxed. Instead, corporate income or losses flow through and are credited or debited to the shareholders in proportion to their shareholdings. Since the shareholders are treated like partners and the corporation like a partnership for tax purposes, shareholders who are owner-employees may benefit from lower individual income-tax rates.

The Tax Reform Act of 1986 suddenly made Subchapter S election very desirable because, for the first time in U.S. tax history, the maximum corporate income-tax rate became higher than the maximum individual income-tax rate. But now the tide has shifted again. Now the highest maximum corporate income-tax rate is slightly lower than the highest maximum individual rate. More to the point, for lower income levels, the point spread is much more favorable. A net taxable income of $50,000 puts your corporation in the 15 percent bracket, but puts you, the entrepreneur, in the 28 percent bracket, whether you are single or married, a difference of 13 percent.

But for those in the "perilous professions" (see next page), if you can flow earnings through your corporation and have them taxed at a lower rate, you're better off. You are also getting money out without fear of double taxation. In contrast, if you were to let your corporate profits build up in a C corporation and wanted to liquidate it at some future date, you might be taking a chance. You don't know what the tax rules will be when you liquidate. As of mid-1995, there is no special favorable treatment for liquidating your corporation.

There are a few ground rules that are easy to satisfy. An S corporation must be a "small business corporation" with no more than thirty-five shareholders—a husband and wife are treated as a single shareholder—all of whom must be U.S. residents. There must be only one class of stock, and shares cannot be owned by another corporation or a partnership. Some trusts qualify as owners; some don't. You'll need expert legal advice here.*

The mechanics of Subchapter S election are simple. You must file Form 2553, shown on pages 79–80, with the District Director of the Internal Revenue Service before the fifteenth day of the third month of your corporation's taxable year, whether calendar or fiscal. (For a calendar-year corporation, the deadline is March 15.) Your corporate clock starts running from the earliest of these events: (1) the date your corporation began business, (2) the date your corporation issued stock, or (3) the date your corporation owned assets. While not mandatory, it's also a good idea to hold a special meeting of your corporation to declare that you have made a Subchapter S election.

PERILOUS PROFESSIONS, OR, NEVER CALL YOURSELF A CONSULTANT

Electing Subchapter S status has become a complex choice. For many people, there are myriad pros and cons. But some people, those in what I call the perilous professions—defined by the IRS as corporations whose principal function is "services in the field of law, health, engineering, architecture, accounting, actuarial science, performing arts, or consulting"—may have an easier

---

*Features of the more liberal S Corporation Reform Act, expected to be passed in late 1995, include expansion to fifty shareholders and the ability to issue preferred stock.

choice because the Revenue Act of 1987 raised their corporate taxes to a flat 34 percent. This move has forced most people in these professions and arts into choosing an S corporation in order to save as much as 19 percent on their income taxes. However, if you use a great deal of expensive equipment in your professional practice, a C corporation may still be a better choice for you. Read this entire chapter, work out the numbers, and get some expert tax advice.

Be aware of the exceptions. Writers, artists, and their agents and representatives do not fall into this group. Neither do people who provide a number of personal or business services. Consultants who are clever enough to find another job description for their services may also be able to escape this new corporate trap.

ADVANTAGES OF S CORPORATION STATUS

There are five major reasons to elect S corporation status for your new corporation:

1. *Lower taxes if you are a member of the perilous professions.* Let's take someone whose corporate income for 1994 was $50,000. The flat rate of 34 percent means that the corporation's federal income tax for the year is $17,000. But if the corporation's owner elects S corporation status, the $50,000 corporate income flows through to the owner and is taxed at his or her individual rate. Assuming that there is no other income and that the standard deduction is used, the tax is $9,300 for single taxpayers, or $5,917 for married taxpayers—a substantial savings.

However, if you are not a member of the perilous professions, *you can achieve even greater tax savings by using the income-splitting feature of a C corporation,* paying yourself a $25,000 salary and retaining $25,000 in your corporation. (For simplicity's sake, I won't even deduct a permissible $6,250 pension contribution from the corporate profits in making these calculations.) Your corporate income tax is $3,750. Your personal income tax, assuming that you had no other income and that you took the standard deduction, is $2,816 if you are single, or

$2,066 if you are married—or total taxes of $6,566 and $5,816, respectively. These totals are far lower than the taxes under S corporation election—especially for single taxpayers.

2. Because corporate profits flow through to the shareholders, *the IRS can never claim that owner-shareholders are receiving excessive compensation and that some of the compensation is really a dividend* and must be treated as such. Thus *the specter of double taxation cannot rear its frightful head.*

3. Because corporate profits are taxed every year whether or not they are distributed, *there is no buildup of corporate assets,* as there frequently is in a C corporation. *This simplifies matters when you are ready to liquidate your corporation* at some future date. It also removes a great deal of uncertainty because *no one knows how favorably corporate liquidations will be taxed several years down the road.* At present, corporate liquidations do not have attractive tax-exempt provisions.

4. *Perhaps the greatest advantage is that any losses that are not passive* that your corporation incurs can flow through to you, as an individual taxpayer, to the extent of the basis of the stock in the corporation* (see pages 81 and 98) *to offset income from other sources immediately, rather than being carried forward from year to year on your C corporation return until they are finally offset by corporate profits.* You must be an active shareholder to deduct losses. But if you are a passive shareholder, you can use passive losses to offset passive income.

There's another significant but subtle advantage, too: corporate tax-loss dollars are worth more when they are used to offset personal-income dollars. For example, $1,000 of corporate-loss carryforward offsets the first $1,000 of corporate income. At current corporate-tax rates, since the first $1,000 of corporate income is taxed at 15 percent, the corporate-loss carryforward is worth only $150.

However, suppose that the $1,000 corporate-loss carryforward flows through to you as a single individual and is used to reduce your investment income and stock-trading profits from

*Real estate investing has its own rules. You'll need professional help here.

Form **2553** (Rev. September 1993) Department of Treasury Internal Revenue Service	**Election by a Small Business Corporation** (Under section 1362 of the Internal Revenue Code) ▶ For Paperwork Reduction Act Notice, see page 1 of instructions. ▶ See separate instructions.	OMB No. 1545-0146 Expires 8-31-96

Notes: 1. This election, to be an "S corporation," can be accepted only if all the tests are met under Who May Elect on page 1 of the instructions; all signatures in Parts I and III are originals (no photocopies); and the exact name and address of the corporation and other required form information are provided.

2. Do not file Form 1120S, U.S. Income Tax Return for an S Corporation, until you are notified that your election is accepted.

Part I | **Election Information**

Please Type or Print	Name of corporation (see instructions) NEW S COMPANY, INC.	**A** Employer identification no.(EIN) 13-0000000
	Number, street, and room or suite no. (If a P.O. box, see instructions.) 123 ENTREPRENEURIAL ROW	**B** Date incorporated 1/2/95
	City or town, state, and ZIP code NEW YORK, NY 10021	**C** State of incorporation NEW YORK

D Election is to be effective for tax year beginning (month, day, year) .... ▶ 1/2/95

E Name and title of officer or legal representative who the IRS may call for more information
SAM SMART
PRESIDENT

F Telephone number of officer or legal representative
(212) 999-9970

G If the corporation changed its name or address after applying for the EIN shown in **A** , check this box .... ▶

H If this election takes effect for the first tax year the corporation exists, enter month, day, and year of the **earliest** of the following: (1) date the corporation first had shareholders, (2) date the corporation first had assets, or (3) date the corporation began doing business .... ▶ 1/2/95

I Selected tax year: Annual return will be filed for tax year ending (month & day)▶ 12/95

If the tax year ends on any date other than December 31, except for an automatic 52–53–week tax year ending with reference to the month of December, you **must** complete Part II on page 2. If the date you enter is the ending date of an automatic 52–53–week tax year, write "52–53–week year" to the right of the date. See Temporary Regulations section 1.441–2T(e)(3).

J Name and address of each share- holder, shareholder's spouse having a community property interest in the corporation's stock, and each tenant in common, joint tenant, and tenant by the entirety. (A husband and wife (and their estates) are counted as one share- holder in determining the number of shareholders without regard to the manner in which the stock is owned.)	**K** Shareholders' Consent Statement. Under penalties of perjury, we declare that we consent to the election of the above-named corporation to be an "S corporation" under section 1362(a) and that we have examined this consent statement, including accompanying schedules and statements, and to the best of our knowledge and belief, it is true, correct, and complete. (Shareholders sign and date below.)		**L** Stock owned		**M** Social security number or employer identification number (see instructions)	**N** Share- holder's tax year ends (month and day)
	Signature	Date	Number of shares	Dates acquired		
SAM SMART 123 ENTREPRENEURIAL ROW	Sam Smart	1/2/95	85	1/2/95	000-00-0000	12/31
JANET SMART 123 ENTREPRENEURIAL ROW	Janet Smart	1/2/95	10	1/2/95	000-00-0000	12/31
SAM SMART, JR. 123 ENTREPRENEURIAL ROW	Sam Smart Jr	1/2/95	5	1/2/95	000-00-0000	12/31

For this election to be valid, the consent of each shareholder, shareholder's spouse having a community property interest in the corporation's stock, and each tenant in common, joint tenant, and tenant by the entirety must either appear above or be attached to this form. (See instructions for Column K if a continuation sheet or a separate consent statement is needed.)

Under penalties of perjury, I declare that I have examined this election, including accompanying schedules and statements, and to the best of my knowledge and belief, it is true, correct, and complete.

Signature of officer ▶ Sam Smart   Title ▶ PRESIDENT   Date ▶ 1/2/95

See Parts II and III on page 2.   Form **2553** (Rev. 9-93)

733   255312   NTF 2510

Form 2553 (Rev. 9–93)   Page

| **Part II** | **Selection of Fiscal Tax Year (All corporations using this part must complete item O and one of items P, Q, or R.)** |

O   Check the applicable box below to indicate whether the corporation is:

   1. ☑ A new corporation adopting the tax year entered in item I, Part I.

   2. ☐ An existing corporation retaining the tax year entered in item I, Part I.

   3. ☐ An existing corporation changing to the tax year entered in item I, Part I.

P   Complete item P if the corporation is using the expeditious approval provisions of Revenue Procedure 87–32, 1987–2 C.B. 396, to request: **(1)** a natural business year (as defined in section 4.01(1) of Rev. Proc. 87–32), or **(2)** a year that satisfies the ownership tax year test in section 4.01(2) of Rev. Proc. 87–32. Check the applicable box below to indicate the representation statement the corporation is making as required under section 4 of Rev. Proc. 87–32.

   1. Natural Business Year ▶ ☐ I represent that the corporation is retaining or changing to a tax year that coincides with its natural business year as defined in section 4.01(1) of Rev. Proc. 87–32 and as verified by its satisfaction of the requirements of section 4.02(1) of Rev. Proc. 87–32. In addition, if the corporation is changing to a natural business year as defined in section 4.01(1), I further represent that such tax year results in less deferral of income to the owners than the corporation's present tax year. I also represent that the corporation is not described in section 3.01(2) of Rev. Proc. 87–32. (See instructions for additional information that must be attached.)

   2. Ownership Tax Year ▶ ☑ I represent that shareholders holding more than half of the shares of the stock (as of the first day of the tax year to which the request relates) of the corporation have the same tax year or are concurrently changing to the tax year that the corporation adopts, retains, or changes to per item I, Part I. I also represent that the corporation is not described in section 3.01(2) of Rev. Proc. 87–32.

Note: If you do not use item P and the corporation wants a fiscal tax year, complete either item Q or R below. Item Q is used to request a fiscal tax year based on a business purpose and to make a back-up section 444 election. Item R is used to make a regular section 444 election.

Q   Business Purpose — To request a fiscal tax year based on a business purpose, you must check box Q1 and pay a user fee. See instructions for details. You may also check box Q2 and/or box Q3.

   1. Check here ▶ ☐ if the fiscal year entered in item I, Part I, is requested under the provisions of section 6.03 of Rev. Proc. 87–32. Attach to Form 2553 a statement showing the business purpose for the requested fiscal year. See inst. for additional information that must be attached.

   2. Check here ▶ ☐ to show that the corporation intends to make a back-up section 444 election in the event the corporation's business purpose request is not approved by the IRS. (See instructions for more information.)

   3. Check here ▶ ☐ to show that the corporation agrees to adopt or change to a tax year ending December 31 if necessary for the IRS to accept this election for S corporation status in the event: (1) the corporation's business purpose request is not approved and the corporation makes a back-up section 444 election, but is ultimately not qualified to make a section 444 election, or (2) the corporation's business purpose request is not approved and the corporation did not make a back-up section 444 election.

R   Section 444 Election — To make a section 444 election, you must check box R1 and you may also check box R2.

   1. Check here ▶ ☐ to show the corporation will make, if qualified, a section 444 election to have the fiscal tax year shown in item I, Part I. To make the election, you must complete **Form 8716**, Election To Have a Tax Year Other Than a Required Tax Year, and either attach it to Form 2553 or file it separately.

   2. Check here ▶ ☐ to show that the corporation agrees to adopt or change to a tax year ending December 31 if necessary for the IRS to accept this election for S corporation status in the event the corporation is ultimately not qualified to make a section 444 election.

| **Part III** | **Qualified Subchapter S Trust (QSST) Election Under Section 1361(d)(2)**** |

Income beneficiary's name and address	Social security number
Trust's name and address	Employer identification number

Date on which stock of the corp. was transferred to the trust (month, day, year) ▶

In order for the trust named above to be a QSST and thus a qualifying shareholder of the S corporation for which this Form 2553 is filed, I hereby make the election under section 1361(d)(2). Under penalties of perjury, I certify that the trust meets the definitional requirements of section 1361(d)(3) and that all other information provided in Part III is true, correct, and complete.

Signature of income beneficiary or signature & title of legal rep./other qualified person making election   Date

** Use of Part III to make the QSST election may be made only if stock of the corporation has been transferred to the trust on or before the date on which the corporation makes its election to be an S corporation. The QSST election must be made and filed separately if stock of the corporation is transferred to the trust after the date on which the corporation makes the S election.

H733 **2553 2** NTF 2511

$85,000 to $84,000. Since your income places you in the 31 percent federal bracket, that $1,000 corporate-loss carryforward is worth $310 in actual tax dollars and probably even more when state and local income taxes are calculated.

5. *When the assets of an S corporation are eventually sold, there is no double taxation of any profits generated.* However, C corporation owners can avoid double taxation by making judicious use of stripping out corporate assets.

To see the advantages of Subchapter S election in action, look at the sample tax returns on pages 82–97. In each, a successful investor has profits of $30,000 but losses of $20,000 in his new design company. In the first example, he has an S corporation; in the second, he doesn't. Our S corporate head is entitled to have his corporation's loss flow through to his own personal tax return to offset his trading profits. As a result, he paid only $566 in federal income taxes in 1994.

The second corporate head can use his corporation's loss only to offset past or future corporate profits. He derives no real immediate benefit and would have paid $3,756 in personal federal income tax in 1994—$3,190 more than our first executive. In fact, as you can see, one of the major advantages of an S corporation is its ability to pass on its losses to an individual shareholder who has great income from other sources—interest, dividends, rents, stock-market profits, and the like.

RAISING THE BASIS OF YOUR STOCK

Because owner-shareholders are not permitted to deduct losses in excess of the basis of their stock, this is a good time to discuss the basis of your stock: what it is and how to raise it.

The basis of your stock is a dollar figure that consists of the assets (property, etc.) that the shareholder contributes to the corporation both at its inception and throughout its life. Even if your corporation is a service corporation, you can still make contributions to it: at its inception, you might give the corporation some office equipment and furniture and a library. These

Form **1120S**		U.S. Income Tax Return for an S Corporation		OMB No. 1545-0130

Form **1120S**

Department of the Treasury
Internal Revenue Service

U.S. Income Tax Return for an S Corporation

▶ Do not file this form unless the corporation has timely filed
Form 2553 to elect to be an S corporation.
▶ See separate instructions.

OMB No. 1545-0130

19**94**

For calendar year 1994, or tax year beginning _____ , 1994, and ending _____ , 19 ____

A Date of election as an S corporation	Use IRS label. Other- wise, please print or type.	C Employer identification number

A Date of election as an S corporation
1/2/94

B Business code no. (see Specific Instructions)
8999

Use IRS label. Other-wise, please print or type.

Name
NEW CONSULTING, INC.

Number, street, and room or suite no. (If a P.O. box, see page 9 of the instructions.)
123 EASY STREET

City or town, state, and ZIP code
NEW YORK, NY 10021

C Employer identification number
13:0000000

D Date incorporated
1/2/94

E Total assets (see Specific Instructions)
$ 16,000 —

F Check applicable boxes: (1) ☑ Initial return (2) ☐ Final return (3) ☐ Change in address (4) ☐ Amended return
G Check this box if this S corporation is subject to the consolidated audit procedures of sections 6241 through 6245 (see instructions before checking this box) . ▶ ☐
H Enter number of shareholders in the corporation at end of the tax year . . . . ▶

Caution: *Include* **only** *trade or business income and expenses on lines 1a through 21. See the instructions for more information.*

Income	**1a** Gross receipts or sales 10,000 — **b** Less returns and allowances 0 **c** Bal ▶	**1c**	10,000	—
	2 Cost of goods sold (Schedule A, line 8)	**2**		
	3 Gross profit. Subtract line 2 from line 1c	**3**		
	4 Net gain (loss) from Form 4797, Part II, line 20 *(attach Form 4797)* . . .	**4**		
	5 Other income (loss) (see instructions) *(attach schedule)*	**5**		
	6 **Total income (loss).** Combine lines 3 through 5 . . . . . . ▶	**6**	10,000	—
Deductions (See instructions for limitations.)	**7** Compensation of officers	**7**		
	8 Salaries and wages (less employment credits)	**8**		
	9 Repairs and maintenance.	**9**		
	10 Bad debts	**10**		
	11 Rents	**11**	15,000	—
	12 Taxes and licenses.	**12**		
	13 Interest	**13**		
	14a Depreciation (see instructions) . . . **14a**			
	b Depreciation claimed on Schedule A and elsewhere on return . **14b**			
	c Subtract line 14b from line 14a	**14c**		
	15 Depletion **(Do not deduct oil and gas depletion.)**	**15**		
	16 Advertising	**16**	10,000	—
	17 Pension, profit-sharing, etc., plans	**17**		
	18 Employee benefit programs	**18**		
	19 Other deductions (see instructions) *(attach schedule)* . . .	**19**	5,000	—
	20 **Total deductions.** Add the amounts shown in the far right column for lines 7 through 19 . ▶	**20**	30,000	—
	21 Ordinary income (loss) from trade or business activities. Subtract line 20 from line 6 . . .	**21**	(20,000	—)
Tax and Payments	**22** **Tax: a** Excess net passive income tax *(attach schedule)*. . . **22a**			
	b Tax from Schedule D (Form 1120S) **22b**			
	c Add lines 22a and 22b (see instructions for additional taxes) . .	**22c**	0	
	23 **Payments: a** 1994 estimated tax payments and amount applied from 1993 return **23a**			
	b Tax deposited with Form 7004 . . . . . **23b**			
	c Credit for Federal tax paid on fuels *(attach Form 4136)* . . **23c**			
	d Add lines 23a through 23c	**23d**	0	
	24 Estimated tax penalty (see instructions). Check if Form 2220 is attached. . . . . ▶☐	**24**	0	
	25 **Tax due.** If the total of lines 22c and 24 is larger than line 23d, enter amount owed. See instructions for depositary method of payment . . . . ▶	**25**	0	
	26 **Overpayment.** If line 23d is larger than the total of lines 22c and 24, enter amount overpaid ▶	**26**	0	
	27 Enter amount of line 26 you want: **Credited to 1995 estimated tax** ▶ | **Refunded** ▶	**27**	0	

Please Sign Here

Under penalties of perjury, I declare that I have examined this return, including accompanying schedules and statements, and to the best of my knowledge and belief, it is true, correct, and complete. Declaration of preparer (other than taxpayer) is based on all information of which preparer has any knowledge.

▶ Signature of officer [signature] Date 3/15/95 ▶ Title PRESIDENT

Paid Preparer's Use Only	Preparer's signature ▶	Date	Check if self-employed ▶ ☐	Preparer's social security number
	Firm's name (or yours if self-employed) and address ▶		E.I. No. ▶	
			ZIP code ▶	

For Paperwork Reduction Act Notice, see page 1 of separate instructions.   Cat. No. 11510H   Form **1120S** (1994)

Form 1120S (1994)   Page **2**

Schedule A	Cost of Goods Sold (See instructions.)

1	Inventory at beginning of year	**1**	
2	Purchases	**2**	
3	Cost of labor	**3**	
4	Additional section 263A costs (see instructions) *(attach schedule)*	**4**	
5	Other costs *(attach schedule)*	**5**	
6	**Total.** Add lines 1 through 5	**6**	
7	Inventory at end of year	**7**	
8	**Cost of goods sold.** Subtract line 7 from line 6. Enter here and on page 1, line 2	**8**	N/A

9a Check all methods used for valuing closing inventory:
 (i) ☐ Cost
 (ii) ☐ Lower of cost or market as described in Regulations section 1.471-4
 (iii) ☐ Writedown of "subnormal" goods as described in Regulations section 1.471-2(c)
 (iv) ☐ Other (specify method used and attach explanation) ▶ ....

 b Check if the LIFO inventory method was adopted this tax year for any goods *(if checked, attach Form 970)*. . . . . . . ▶ ☐
 c If the LIFO inventory method was used for this tax year, enter percentage (or amounts) of closing
 inventory computed under LIFO . . . . **9c** |
 d Do the rules of section 263A (for property produced or acquired for resale) apply to the corporation? . . . . ☐ Yes ☐ No
 e Was there any change in determining quantities, cost, or valuations between opening and closing inventory? . . ☐ Yes ☐ No
 If "Yes," attach explanation.

Schedule B	Other Information

		Yes	No
1	Check method of accounting: **(a)** ☑ Cash **(b)** ☐ Accrual **(c)** ☐ Other (specify) ▶		
2	Refer to the list in the instructions and state the corporation's principal: **(a)** Business activity ▶ .... **(b)** Product or service ▶ EDITORIAL SERVICES......		
3	Did the corporation at the end of the tax year own, directly or indirectly, 50% or more of the voting stock of a domestic corporation? (For rules of attribution, see section 267(c).) If "Yes," attach a schedule showing: **(a)** name, address, and employer identification number and **(b)** percentage owned.		✓
4	Was the corporation a member of a controlled group subject to the provisions of section 1561?		✓
5	At any time during calendar year 1994, did the corporation have an interest in or a signature or other authority over a financial account in a foreign country (such as a bank account, securities account, or other financial account)? (See instructions for exceptions and filing requirements for Form TD F 90-22.1.) . . . . If "Yes," enter the name of the foreign country ▶		✓
6	Was the corporation the grantor of, or transferor to, a foreign trust that existed during the current tax year, whether or not the corporation has any beneficial interest in it? If "Yes," the corporation may have to file Forms 3520, 3520-A, or 926		✓
7	Check this box if the corporation has filed or is required to file **Form 8264,** Application for Registration of a Tax Shelter . . . . ▶ ☐		
8	Check this box if the corporation issued publicly offered debt instruments with original issue discount . . ▶ ☐ If so, the corporation may have to file **Form 8281,** Information Return for Publicly Offered Original Issue Discount Instruments.		
9	If the corporation: **(a)** filed its election to be an S corporation after 1986, **(b)** was a C corporation before it elected to be an S corporation **or** the corporation acquired an asset with a basis determined by reference to its basis (or the basis of any other property) in the hands of a C corporation, and **(c)** has net unrealized built-in gain (defined in section 1374(d)(1)) in excess of the net recognized built-in gain from prior years, enter the net unrealized built-in gain reduced by net recognized built-in gain from prior years (see instructions) . . . . ▶ $		
10	Check this box if the corporation had subchapter C earnings and profits at the close of the tax year (see instructions) . . . . ▶ ☐		

Designation of Tax Matters Person (See instructions.)

Enter below the shareholder designated as the tax matters person (TMP) for the tax year of this return:

Name of
designated TMP ▶ J. FOX ENTREPRENEUR

Identifying
number of TMP ▶ 000-00-0000

Address of
designated TMP ▶ 123 EASY STREET, NEW YORK, NY 10021

Form 1120S (1994)   Page **3**

Schedule K   Shareholders' Shares of Income, Credits, Deductions, etc.

	(a) Pro rata share items		(b) Total amount
Income (Loss)	1 Ordinary income (loss) from trade or business activities (page 1, line 21)	**1**	(20,000 —)
	2 Net income (loss) from rental real estate activities *(attach Form 8825)*	**2**	
	3a Gross income from other rental activities **3a**		
	b Expenses from other rental activities *(attach schedule)*. . **3b**		
	c Net income (loss) from other rental activities. Subtract line 3b from line 3a	**3c**	
	4 Portfolio income (loss):		
	a Interest income	**4a**	
	b Dividend income	**4b**	
	c Royalty income	**4c**	
	d Net short-term capital gain (loss) *(attach Schedule D (Form 1120S))*	**4d**	
	e Net long-term capital gain (loss) *(attach Schedule D (Form 1120S))*	**4e**	
	f Other portfolio income (loss) *(attach schedule)*	**4f**	
	5 Net gain (loss) under section 1231 (other than due to casualty or theft) *(attach Form 4797)*	**5**	
	6 Other income (loss) *(attach schedule)*	**6**	
Deductions	7 Charitable contributions (see instructions) *(attach schedule)*	**7**	
	8 Section 179 expense deduction *(attach Form 4562)*.	**8**	
	9 Deductions related to portfolio income (loss) (see instructions) (itemize) . . .	**9**	
	10 Other deductions *(attach schedule)*	**10**	
Investment Interest	11a Interest expense on investment debts	**11a**	
	b (1) Investment income included on lines 4a, 4b, 4c, and 4f above	**11b(1)**	
	(2) Investment expenses included on line 9 above	**11b(2)**	
Credits	12a Credit for alcohol used as a fuel *(attach Form 6478)*	**12a**	
	b Low-income housing credit (see instructions):		
	(1) From partnerships to which section 42(j)(5) applies for property placed in service before 1990	**12b(1)**	
	(2) Other than on line 12b(1) for property placed in service before 1990. . .	**12b(2)**	
	(3) From partnerships to which section 42(j)(5) applies for property placed in service after 1989	**12b(3)**	
	(4) Other than on line 12b(3) for property placed in service after 1989	**12b(4)**	
	c Qualified rehabilitation expenditures related to rental real estate activities *(attach Form 3468)* .	**12c**	
	d Credits (other than credits shown on lines 12b and 12c) related to rental real estate activities (see instructions).	**12d**	
	e Credits related to other rental activities (see instructions)	**12e**	
	13 Other credits (see instructions)	**13**	
Adjustments and Tax Preference Items	14a Depreciation adjustment on property placed in service after 1986	**14a**	
	b Adjusted gain or loss	**14b**	
	c Depletion (other than oil and gas)	**14c**	
	d (1) Gross income from oil, gas, or geothermal properties	**14d(1)**	
	(2) Deductions allocable to oil, gas, or geothermal properties	**14d(2)**	
	e Other adjustments and tax preference items *(attach schedule)*	**14e**	
Foreign Taxes	15a Type of income ▶...		
	b Name of foreign country or U.S. possession ▶................................		
	c Total gross income from sources outside the United States *(attach schedule)* . . .	**15c**	
	d Total applicable deductions and losses *(attach schedule)*	**15d**	
	e Total foreign taxes (check one): ▶ ☐ Paid ☐ Accrued	**15e**	
	f Reduction in taxes available for credit *(attach schedule)*	**15f**	
	g Other foreign tax information *(attach schedule)*	**15g**	
Other	16a Total expenditures to which a section 59(e) election may apply	**16a**	
	b Type of expenditures ▶...		
	17 Tax-exempt interest income	**17**	
	18 Other tax-exempt income	**18**	
	19 Nondeductible expenses	**19**	
	20 Total property distributions (including cash) other than dividends reported on line 22 below	**20**	
	21 Other items and amounts required to be reported separately to shareholders (see instructions) *(attach schedule)*		
	22 Total dividend distributions paid from accumulated earnings and profits	**22**	
	23 **Income (loss).** (Required only if Schedule M-1 must be completed.) Combine lines 1 through 6 in column (b). From the result, subtract the sum of lines 7 through 11a, 15e, and 16a	**23**	

Form 1120S (1994)   Page **4**

Schedule L	Balance Sheets	Beginning of tax year		End of tax year	
	Assets	**(a)**	**(b)**	**(c)**	**(d)**
1	Cash				6,000
2a	Trade notes and accounts receivable			5,000	
b	Less allowance for bad debts				5,000
3	Inventories				
4	U.S. Government obligations				
5	Tax-exempt securities		INITIAL		
6	Other current assets (attach schedule)		RETURN		
7	Loans to shareholders				
8	Mortgage and real estate loans				
9	Other investments (attach schedule)				5,000
10a	Buildings and other depreciable assets				
b	Less accumulated depreciation				
11a	Depletable assets				
b	Less accumulated depletion				
12	Land (net of any amortization)				
13a	Intangible assets (amortizable only)				
b	Less accumulated amortization				
14	Other assets (attach schedule)				
15	Total assets				16,000
	Liabilities and Shareholders' Equity				
16	Accounts payable				4,000
17	Mortgages, notes, bonds payable in less than 1 year				
18	Other current liabilities (attach schedule)				
19	Loans from shareholders				5,000
20	Mortgages, notes, bonds payable in 1 year or more				
21	Other liabilities (attach schedule)				
22	Capital stock				27,000
23	Paid-in or capital surplus				
24	Retained earnings				(20,000)
25	Less cost of treasury stock		( )		( )
26	Total liabilities and shareholders' equity				16,000

Schedule M-1	**Reconciliation of Income (Loss) per Books With Income (Loss) per Return** (You are not required to complete this schedule if the total assets on line 15, column (d), of Schedule L are less than $25,000.)

1	Net income (loss) per books	5	Income recorded on books this year not included on Schedule K, lines 1 through 6 (itemize):
2	Income included on Schedule K, lines 1 through 6, not recorded on books this year (itemize):	a	Tax-exempt interest $ ....
	....		....
3	Expenses recorded on books this year not included on Schedule K, lines 1 through 11a, 15e, and 16a (itemize):	6	Deductions included on Schedule K, lines 1 through 11a; 15e, and 16a, not charged against book income this year (itemize):
a	Depreciation $	a	Depreciation $ ....
b	Travel and entertainment $		....
	....	7	Add lines 5 and 6
4	Add lines 1 through 3	8	Income (loss) (Schedule K, line 23). Line 4 less line 7

Schedule M-2	**Analysis of Accumulated Adjustments Account, Other Adjustments Account, and Shareholders' Undistributed Taxable Income Previously Taxed** (See instructions.)

		(a) Accumulated adjustments account	(b) Other adjustments account	(c) Shareholders' undistributed taxable income previously taxed
1	Balance at beginning of tax year	0		
2	Ordinary income from page 1, line 21			
3	Other additions			
4	Loss from page 1, line 21	(20,000)		
5	Other reductions	( )	( )	
6	Combine lines 1 through 5	(20,000)		
7	Distributions other than dividend distributions			
8	Balance at end of tax year. Subtract line 7 from line 6	(20,000)		

*U.S.GPO:1994-375-315

Form **1040**   Department of the Treasury—Internal Revenue Service
U.S. Individual Income Tax Return (O) **19**94   IRS Use Only—Do not write or staple in this space.

For the year Jan. 1–Dec. 31, 1994, or other tax year beginning _____ , 1994, ending _____ , 19 ___   OMB No. 1545-0074

Label

(See instructions on page 12.)

Use the IRS label. Otherwise, please print or type.

Your first name and initial: J. Fox   Last name: ENTREPRENEUR   Your social security number: 000 00 0000

If a joint return, spouse's first name and initial _____ Last name _____   Spouse's social security number

Home address (number and street). If you have a P.O. box, see page 12.: 123 EASY STREET   Apt. no.: PH

City, town or post office, state, and ZIP code. If you have a foreign address, see page 12.: NEW YORK, NY 10021

For Privacy Act and Paperwork Reduction Act Notice, see page 4.

Presidential Election Campaign
(See page 12.)

Do you want $3 to go to this fund? . . . .   Yes [ ] No [✓]
If a joint return, does your spouse want $3 to go to this fund? . . . . .   Yes [ ] No [ ]

Note: *Checking "Yes" will not change your tax or reduce your refund.*

Filing Status
(See page 12.)
Check only one box.

1 [✓] Single
2 [ ] Married filing joint return (even if only one had income)
3 [ ] Married filing separate return. Enter spouse's social security no. above and full name here. ▶ _____
4 [ ] Head of household (with qualifying person). (See page 13.) If the qualifying person is a child but not your dependent, enter this child's name here. ▶ _____
5 [ ] Qualifying widow(er) with dependent child (year spouse died ▶ 19 ___). (See page 13.)

Exemptions
(See page 13.)

6a [ ] **Yourself.** If your parent (or someone else) can claim you as a dependent on his or her tax return, **do not** check box 6a. But be sure to check the box on line 33b on page 2 ▶

b [ ] Spouse . . . .

No. of boxes checked on 6a and 6b: 1

c Dependents:

(1) Name (first, initial, and last name)	(2) Check if under age 1	(3) If age 1 or older, dependent's social security number	(4) Dependent's relationship to you	(5) No. of months lived in your home in 1994

If more than six dependents, see page 14.

No. of your children on 6c who:
• lived with you: 0
• didn't live with you due to divorce or separation (see page 14): 0
Dependents on 6c not entered above: 0

d If your child didn't live with you but is claimed as your dependent under a pre-1985 agreement, check here ▶ [ ]
e Total number of exemptions claimed . . . .

Add numbers entered on lines above ▶ 1

Income

Attach Copy B of your Forms W-2, W-2G, and 1099-R here.

If you did not get a W-2, see page 15.

Enclose, but do not attach, any payment with your return.

7 Wages, salaries, tips, etc. Attach Form(s) W-2 . . . .   **7** | 0
8a **Taxable** interest income (see page 15). Attach Schedule B if over $400 . .   **8a** | 0
b **Tax-exempt** interest (see page 16). DON'T include on line 8a | 8b | _____
9 Dividend income. Attach Schedule B if over $400 . . . .   **9** | 0
10 Taxable refunds, credits, or offsets of state and local income taxes (see page 16) .   **10** | 0
11 Alimony received . . . .   **11** | 0
12 Business income or (loss). Attach Schedule C or C-EZ . . . .   **12** | 0
13 Capital gain or (loss). If required, attach Schedule D (see page 16) . . .   **13** | 30,000 —
14 Other gains or (losses). Attach Form 4797 . . . .   **14** | 0
15a Total IRA distributions . | 15a | b Taxable amount (see page 17)   **15b** | 0
16a Total pensions and annuities | 16a | b Taxable amount (see page 17)   **16b** | 0
17 Rental real estate, royalties, partnerships, S corporations, trusts, etc. ~~Attach Schedule E~~ 1120S ATTACHED   **17** | (20,000) —
18 Farm income or (loss). Attach Schedule F . . . .   **18** | 0
19 Unemployment compensation (see page 18) . . . .   **19** | 0
20a Social security benefits | 20a | b Taxable amount (see page 18)   **20b** | 0
21 Other income. List type and amount—see page 18 _____   **21** | 0
22 Add the amounts in the far right column for lines 7 through 21. This is your **total income** ▶   **22** | 10,000 —

Adjustments to Income

Caution: See instructions . . ▶

23a Your IRA deduction (see page 19) . . . | 23a |
b Spouse's IRA deduction (see page 19) . . . | 23b |
24 Moving expenses. Attach Form 3903 or 3903-F . . . | 24 |
25 One-half of self-employment tax . . . . . . | 25 |
26 Self-employed health insurance deduction (see page 21) | 26 |
27 Keogh retirement plan and self-employed SEP deduction | 27 |
28 Penalty on early withdrawal of savings . . . . | 28 |
29 Alimony paid. Recipient's SSN ▶ _____ | 29 |
30 Add lines 23a through 29. These are your **total adjustments** . . . . . . ▶   **30** | 0

Adjusted Gross Income

31 Subtract line 30 from line 22. This is your **adjusted gross income.** If less than $25,296 and a child lived with you (less than $9,000 if a child didn't live with you), see "Earned Income Credit" on page 27 ▶   **31** | 10,000 —

Cat. No. 11320B   Form **1040** (1994)

Form 1040 (1994)   Page **2**

Tax Compu- tation (See page 23.)	**32**	Amount from line 31 (adjusted gross income)	**32**	10,000 —
	33a	Check if: ☐ **You** were 65 or older, ☐ Blind; ☐ **Spouse** was 65 or older, ☐ Blind. Add the number of boxes checked above and enter the total here . . . . ▶ **33a**		
	b	If your parent (or someone else) can claim you as a dependent, check here . ▶ **33b** ☐		
	c	If you are married filing separately and your spouse itemizes deductions or you are a dual-status alien, see page 23 and check here . . . . . ▶ **33c** ☐		
	34	Enter the larger of your: **Itemized deductions** from Schedule A, line 29, **OR** **Standard deduction** shown below for your filing status. **But if you checked any box on line 33a or b,** go to page 23 to find your standard deduction. If you checked **box 33c,** your standard deduction is zero. • Single—$3,800 • Head of household—$5,600 • Married filing jointly or Qualifying widow(er)—$6,350 • Married filing separately—$3,175	**34**	3,800 —
	35	Subtract line 34 from line 32	**35**	6,200 —
	36	If line 32 is $83,850 or less, multiply $2,450 by the total number of exemptions claimed on line 6e. If line 32 is over $83,850, see the worksheet on page 24 for the amount to enter .	**36**	2,450 —
If you want the IRS to figure your tax, see page 24.	**37**	**Taxable income.** Subtract line 36 from line 35. If line 36 is more than line 35, enter -0-	**37**	3,750 —
	38	Tax. Check if from **a** ☑ Tax Table, **b** ☐ Tax Rate Schedules, **c** ☐ Capital Gain Tax Work-sheet, or **d** ☐ Form 8615 (see page 24). Amount from Form(s) 8814 ▶ **e** _____	**38**	566 —
	39	Additional taxes. Check if from **a** ☐ Form 4970 **b** ☐ Form 4972	**39**	0
	40	Add lines 38 and 39 . . . . ▶	**40**	566 —
Credits (See page 24.)	**41**	Credit for child and dependent care expenses. Attach Form 2441	**41** 0	
	42	Credit for the elderly or the disabled. Attach Schedule R .	**42** 0	
	43	Foreign tax credit. Attach Form 1116	**43** 0	
	44	Other credits (see page 25). Check if from **a** ☐ Form 3800 **b** ☐ Form 8396 **c** ☐ Form 8801 **d** ☐ Form (specify)____	**44** 0	
	45	Add lines 41 through 44	**45**	0
	46	Subtract line 45 from line 40. If line 45 is more than line 40, enter -0- . ▶	**46**	566 —
Other Taxes (See page 25.)	**47**	Self-employment tax. Attach Schedule SE	**47**	0
	48	Alternative minimum tax. Attach Form 6251	**48**	0
	49	Recapture taxes. Check if from **a** ☐ Form 4255 **b** ☐ Form 8611 **c** ☐ Form 8828 .	**49**	0
	50	Social security and Medicare tax on tip income not reported to employer. Attach Form 4137 .	**50**	0
	51	Tax on qualified retirement plans, including IRAs. If required, attach Form 5329 . .	**51**	0
	52	Advance earned income credit payments from Form W-2	**52**	0
	53	Add lines 46 through 52. This is your **total tax** . . . . . ▶	**53**	566 —
Payments Attach Forms W-2, W-2G, and 1099-R on the front.	**54**	Federal income tax withheld. If any is from Form(s) 1099, check ▶ ☐	**54** 0	
	55	1994 estimated tax payments and amount applied from 1993 return .	**55** 0	
	56	**Earned income credit.** If required, attach Schedule EIC (see page 27). Nontaxable earned income: amount ▶ _____ and type ▶	**56** 0	
	57	Amount paid with Form 4868 (extension request)	**57** 0	
	58	Excess social security and RRTA tax withheld (see page 32) .	**58** 0	
	59	Other payments. Check if from **a** ☐ Form 2439 **b** ☐ Form 4136	**59** 0	
	60	Add lines 54 through 59. These are your **total payments** . . . . . . ▶	**60**	0
Refund or Amount You Owe	**61**	If line 60 is more than line 53, subtract line 53 from line 60. This is the amount you **OVERPAID.** ▶	**61**	0
	62	Amount of line 61 you want **REFUNDED TO YOU.** . . . . . ▶	**62**	0
	63	Amount of line 61 you want **APPLIED TO YOUR 1995 ESTIMATED TAX** ▶ **63**		
	64	If line 53 is more than line 60, subtract line 60 from line 53. This is the **AMOUNT YOU OWE.** For details on how to pay, including what to write on your payment, see page 32 . . .	**64**	566 —
	65	Estimated tax penalty (see page 33). Also include on line 64 **65**		

Sign Here Keep a copy of this return for your records.	Under penalties of perjury, I declare that I have examined this return and accompanying schedules and statements, and to the best of my knowledge and belief, they are true, correct, and complete. Declaration of preparer (other than taxpayer) is based on all information of which preparer has any knowledge.

Your signature _J. F. E_____	Date 4/15/95	Your occupation EXECUTIVE
Spouse's signature. If a joint return, BOTH must sign.	Date	Spouse's occupation

Paid Preparer's Use Only	Preparer's signature ▶	Date	Check if self-employed ☐	Preparer's social security no.
	Firm's name (or yours if self-employed) and address ▶		E.I. No.	
			ZIP code	

♻ *Printed on recycled paper*   *U.S. Government Printing Office: 1994 — 375-188

SCHEDULE D	**Capital Gains and Losses**	OMB No. 1545-0074

SCHEDULE D
(Form 1040)

Department of the Treasury
Internal Revenue Service (O)

Capital Gains and Losses

▶ Attach to Form 1040.   ▶ See Instructions for Schedule D (Form 1040).
▶ Use lines 20 and 22 for more space to list transactions for lines 1 and 9.

OMB No. 1545-0074

19**94**

Attachment
Sequence No. **12**

Name(s) shown on Form 1040   J. FOX ENTREPRENEUR

Your social security number   000 : 00 : 0000

Part I   Short-Term Capital Gains and Losses—Assets Held One Year or Less

	(a) Description of property (Example: 100 sh. XYZ Co.)	(b) Date acquired (Mo., day, yr.)	(c) Date sold (Mo., day, yr.)	(d) Sales price (see page D-3)	(e) Cost or other basis (see page D-3)	(f) LOSS If (e) is more than (d), subtract (d) from (e)	(g) GAIN If (d) is more than (e), subtract (e) from (d)
1				OPTIONS TRADES			30,000 —

2	Enter your short-term totals, if any, from line 21	2	
3	**Total short-term sales price amounts.** Add column (d) of lines 1 and 2 . . .	3	
4	Short-term gain from Forms 2119 and 6252, and short-term gain or (loss) from Forms 4684, 6781, and 8824	4	0 ... 0
5	Net short-term gain or (loss) from partnerships, S corporations, estates, and trusts from Schedule(s) K-1	5	0 ... 0
6	Short-term capital loss carryover. Enter the amount, if any, from line 9 of your 1993 Capital Loss Carryover Worksheet	6	0
7	Add lines 1, 2, and 4 through 6, in columns (f) and (g)	7	(0) ... 30,000 —
8	**Net short-term capital gain or (loss).** Combine columns (f) and (g) of line 7 . . . . ▶	8	30,000 —

Part II   Long-Term Capital Gains and Losses—Assets Held More Than One Year

9							

10	Enter your long-term totals, if any, from line 23	10	
11	**Total long-term sales price amounts.** Add column (d) of lines 9 and 10 . . .	11	
12	Gain from Form 4797; long-term gain from Forms 2119, 2439, and 6252; and long-term gain or (loss) from Forms 4684, 6781, and 8824	12	
13	Net long-term gain or (loss) from partnerships, S corporations, estates, and trusts from Schedule(s) K-1	13	
14	Capital gain distributions	14	
15	Long-term capital loss carryover. Enter the amount, if any, from line 14 of your 1993 Capital Loss Carryover Worksheet	15	
16	Add lines 9, 10, and 12 through 15, in columns (f) and (g)	16	( )
17	**Net long-term capital gain or (loss).** Combine columns (f) and (g) of line 16 . . . . . ▶	17	0

Part III   Summary of Parts I and II

18	Combine lines 8 and 17. If a loss, go to line 19. If a gain, enter the gain on Form 1040, line 13. **Note:** If both lines 17 and 18 are gains, see the **Capital Gain Tax Worksheet** on page 25 . .	18	30,000 —
19	If line 18 is a (loss), enter here and as a (loss) on Form 1040, line 13, the **smaller** of these losses:		
a	The (loss) on line 18; **or**		
b	($3,000) or, if married filing separately, ($1,500)	19	( )
	Note: See the **Capital Loss Carryover Worksheet** on page D-3 if the loss on line 18 exceeds the loss on line 19 **or** if Form 1040, line 35, is a loss.		

For Paperwork Reduction Act Notice, see Form 1040 instructions.   Cat. No. 11338H   Schedule D (Form 1040) 1994

Schedule D (Form 1040) 1994   Attachment Sequence No. **12**   Page **2**

Name(s) shown on Form 1040. Do not enter name and social security number if shown on other side. | **Your social security number**

| **Part IV** | Short-Term Capital Gains and Losses—Assets Held One Year or Less *(Continuation of Part I)* | | | | | |

(a) Description of property (Example: 100 sh. XYZ Co.)	(b) Date acquired (Mo., day, yr.)	(c) Date sold (Mo., day, yr.)	(d) Sales price (see page D-3)	(e) Cost or other basis (see page D-3)	(f) LOSS If (e) is more than (d), subtract (d) from (e)	(g) GAIN If (d) is more than (e), subtract (e) from (d)
20						
	OPTIONS TRADES (CONT.)					

21 Short-term totals. Add columns (d), (f), and (g) of line 20. Enter here and on line 2 .   **21**

Part V	Long-Term Capital Gains and Losses—Assets Held More Than One Year *(Continuation of Part II)*					
22						

23 Long-term totals. Add columns (d), (f), and (g) of line 22. Enter here and on line 10 .   **23**

SCHEDULE E (Form 1040) Department of the Treasury Internal Revenue Service (O)	**Supplemental Income and Loss** (From rental real estate, royalties, partnerships, S corporations, estates, trusts, REMICs, etc.) ▶ **Attach to Form 1040 or Form 1041.** ▶ **See Instructions for Schedule E (Form 1040).**	OMB No. 1545-0074 19**94** Attachment Sequence No. **13**

Name(s) shown on return   J. Fox ENTREPRENEUR   Your social security number 000 00 0000

Part I **Income or Loss From Rental Real Estate and Royalties** Note: *Report income and expenses from your business of renting personal property on* **Schedule C** *or* **C-EZ** *(see page E-1). Report farm rental income or loss from* **Form 4835** *on page 2, line 39.*

1	Show the kind and location of each **rental real estate property:**	2	For each rental real estate property listed on line 1, did you or your family use it for personal purposes for more than the greater of 14 days or 10% of the total days rented at fair rental value during the tax year? (See page E-1.)		Yes	No
A	....			A		
B	....			B		
C	....			C		

Income:			Properties			Totals
			A	B	C	(Add columns A, B, and C)
3	Rents received	3				3
4	Royalties received	4				4
Expenses:						
5	Advertising	5				
6	Auto and travel (see page E-2) .	6				
7	Cleaning and maintenance . . .	7				
8	Commissions	8				
9	Insurance	9				
10	Legal and other professional fees	10				
11	Management fees.	11				
12	Mortgage interest paid to banks, etc. (see page E-2)	12				12
13	Other interest	13				
14	Repairs	14				
15	Supplies	15				
16	Taxes	16				
17	Utilities	17				
18	Other (list) ▶............	18				
19	Add lines 5 through 18	19				19
20	Depreciation expense or depletion (see page E-2)	20				20
21	Total expenses. Add lines 19 and 20	21				
22	Income or (loss) from rental real estate or royalty properties. Subtract line 21 from line 3 (rents) or line 4 (royalties). If the result is a (loss), see page E-2 to find out if you must file **Form 6198**. . .	22				
23	Deductible rental real estate loss. **Caution:** *Your rental real estate loss on line 22 may be limited. See page E-3 to find out if you must file* **Form 8582**. *Real estate professionals must complete line 42 on page 2*	23	(	)(	)(	)
24	**Income.** Add positive amounts shown on line 22. **Do not** include any losses				24	
25	**Losses.** Add royalty losses from line 22 and rental real estate losses from line 23. Enter the total losses here .				25	( )
26	Total rental real estate and royalty income or (loss). Combine lines 24 and 25. Enter the result here. If Parts II, III, IV, and line 39 on page 2 do not apply to you, also enter this amount on Form 1040, line 17. Otherwise, include this amount in the total on line 40 on page 2				26	0

For Paperwork Reduction Act Notice, see Form 1040 instructions.   Cat. No. 11344L   Schedule E (Form 1040) 1994

HOW TO PROFIT FROM YOUR S CORPORATION 91

Name(s) shown on return. Do not enter name and social security number if shown on other side.   **Your social security number**

Note: *If you report amounts from farming or fishing on Schedule E, you must enter your gross income from those activities on line 41 below. Real estate professionals must complete line 42 below.*

Part II   Income or Loss From Partnerships and S Corporations   Note: *If you report a loss from an at-risk activity, you MUST check either column (e) or (f) of line 27 to describe your investment in the activity. See page E-4. If you check column (f), you must attach Form 6198.*

27	(a) Name	(b) Enter **P** for partnership; **S** for S corporation	(c) Check if foreign partnership	(d) Employer identification number	(e) All is at risk	(f) Some is not at risk
A	NEW CONSULTING, INC.	S		13-0000000	✓	
B						
C						
D						
E						

	Passive Income and Loss		Nonpassive Income and Loss		
	(g) Passive loss allowed (attach **Form 8582** if required)	(h) Passive income from **Schedule K-1**	(i) Nonpassive loss from **Schedule K-1**	(j) Section 179 expense deduction from **Form 4562**	(k) Nonpassive income from **Schedule K-1**
A			(20,000 –)		
B					
C					
D					
E					
28a Totals					
b Totals			(20,000 –)		

29 Add columns (h) and (k) of line 28a . . .   **29**   0
30 Add columns (g), (i), and (j) of line 28b . . .   **30** (20,000 –)
31 Total partnership and S corporation income or (loss). Combine lines 29 and 30. Enter the result here and include in the total on line 40 below . . .   **31** (20,000 –)

Part III   Income or Loss From Estates and Trusts

32	(a) Name	(b) Employer identification number
A		
B		

	Passive Income and Loss		Nonpassive Income and Loss	
	(c) Passive deduction or loss allowed (attach **Form 8582** if required)	(d) Passive income from **Schedule K-1**	(e) Deduction or loss from **Schedule K-1**	(f) Other income from **Schedule K-1**
A				
B				
33a Totals				
b Totals				

34 Add columns (d) and (f) of line 33a . . .   **34**
35 Add columns (c) and (e) of line 33b . . .   **35** ( )
36 Total estate and trust income or (loss). Combine lines 34 and 35. Enter the result here and include in the total on line 40 below . . .   **36**

Part IV   Income or Loss From Real Estate Mortgage Investment Conduits (REMICs)—Residual Holder

37	(a) Name	(b) Employer identification number	(c) Excess inclusion from **Schedules Q**, line 2c (see page E-4)	(d) Taxable income (net loss) from **Schedules Q**, line 1b	(e) Income from **Schedules Q**, line 3b

38 Combine columns (d) and (e) only. Enter the result here and include in the total on line 40 below   **38**

Part V   Summary

39 Net farm rental income or (loss) from **Form 4835**. Also, complete line 41 below . . .   **39**
40 TOTAL income or (loss). Combine lines 26, 31, 36, 38, and 39. Enter the result here and on Form 1040, line 17 ▶   **40** (20,000 –)

41 **Reconciliation of Farming and Fishing Income.** Enter your **gross** farming and fishing income reported on Form 4835, line 7; Schedule K-1 (Form 1065), line 15b; Schedule K-1 (Form 1120S), line 23; and Schedule K-1 (Form 1041), line 13 (see page E-4) . . .   **41**

42 **Reconciliation for Real Estate Professionals.** If you were a real estate professional (see page E-3), enter the net income or (loss) you reported anywhere on Form 1040 from all rental real estate activities in which you materially participated under the passive activity loss rules . .   **42**

Printed on recycled paper   *U.S. Government Printing Office: 1994 — 375-205

Form **1120-A**	**U.S. Corporation Short-Form Income Tax Return**	OMB No. 1545-0890
Department of the Treasury Internal Revenue Service	See separate instructions to make sure the corporation qualifies to file Form 1120-A. For calendar year 1994 or tax year beginning ...., 1994, ending.............., 19.....	**1994**

A Check this box if the corp. is a personal service corp. (as defined in Temporary Regs. section 1.441-4T—see instructions) ▶ ☐

Use IRS label. Otherwise, please print or type.

Name **REARGUARD DESIGNS, INC.**

Number, street, and room or suite no. (If a P.O. box, see page 6 of instructions.) **999 EASY STREET**

City or town, state, and ZIP code **NEW YORK, NY 10021**

B Employer identification number **13 : 0000000**

C Date incorporated **1 | 2 | 94**

D Total assets (see Specific Instructions) $ **16,000 |—**

E Check applicable boxes: (1) ☑ Initial return (2) ☐ Change of address

F Check method of accounting: (1) ☑ Cash (2) ☐ Accrual (3) ☐ Other (specify) . ▶

Income

1a	Gross receipts or sales	10,000 —	**b** Less returns and allowances	0	**c** Balance ▶	1c	10,000 —
2	Cost of goods sold (see instructions)				2	
3	Gross profit. Subtract line 2 from line 1c				3	
4	Domestic corporation dividends subject to the 70% deduction				4	
5	Interest				5	
6	Gross rents				6	
7	Gross royalties				7	
8	Capital gain net income (attach Schedule D (Form 1120))				8	
9	Net gain or (loss) from Form 4797, Part II, line 20 (attach Form 4797)				9	
10	Other income (see instructions)				10	
11	**Total income.** Add lines 3 through 10 . . . . ▶				11	10,000 —

Deductions (See instructions for limitations on deductions.)

12	Compensation of officers (see instructions)	12	
13	Salaries and wages (less employment credits)	13	
14	Repairs and maintenance	14	
15	Bad debts	15	
16	Rents	16	15,000 —
17	Taxes and licenses	17	
18	~~Interest~~ ADVERTISING	18	10,000 —
19	Charitable contributions (see instructions for 10% limitation)	19	
20	Depreciation (attach Form 4562) 20		
21	Less depreciation claimed elsewhere on return . . . 21a	21b	
22	Other deductions (attach schedule)	22	5,000 —
23	**Total deductions.** Add lines 12 through 22 . . . . ▶	23	30,000 —
24	Taxable income before net operating loss deduction and special deductions. Subtract line 23 from line 11	24	(20,000 -)
25	**Less: a** Net operating loss deduction (see instructions) 25a 0		
	b Special deductions (see instructions) 25b 0	25c	0
26	**Taxable income.** Subtract line 25c from line 24	26	(20,000 -)
27	**Total tax** (from page 2, Part I, line 7) . . . . ▶	27	0

Tax and Payments

28	**Payments:**		
a	1993 overpayment credited to 1994 28a		
b	1994 estimated tax payments . 28b		
c	Less 1994 refund applied for on Form 4466 28c ( ) Bal ▶	28d	
e	Tax deposited with Form 7004	28e	
f	Credit from regulated investment companies (attach Form 2439) .	28f	
g	Credit for Federal tax on fuels (attach Form 4136). See instructions	28g	
h	**Total payments.** Add lines 28d through 28g	28h	
29	Estimated tax penalty (see instructions). Check if Form 2220 is attached . . . . ▶ ☐	29	
30	**Tax due.** If line 28h is smaller than the total of lines 27 and 29, enter amount owed	30	0
31	**Overpayment.** If line 28h is larger than the total of lines 27 and 29, enter amount overpaid . .	31	
32	Enter amount of line 31 you want: **Credited to 1995 estimated tax** ▶ **Refunded** ▶	32	

Please Sign Here

Under penalties of perjury, I declare that I have examined this return, including accompanying schedules and statements, and to the best of my knowledge and belief, it is true, correct, and complete. Declaration of preparer (other than taxpayer) is based on all information of which preparer has any knowledge.

▶ _(signature)_   Signature of officer   Date **3/15/95**   Title **PRESIDENT**

Paid Preparer's Use Only

Preparer's signature ▶	Date	Check if self-employed ▶ ☐	Preparer's social security number
Firm's name (or yours if self-employed) and address ▶		E.I. No. ▶	
		ZIP code ▶	

For Paperwork Reduction Act Notice, see page 1 of the instructions.   Cat. No. 11456E   Form **1120-A** (1994)

Form 1120-A (1994)   Page **2**

Part I   Tax Computation (See instructions.)

1 Income tax. If the corporation is a qualified personal service corporation (see page 14), check here ▶ ☐	**1**	O
2a General business credit. Check if from: ☐ Form 3800 ☐ Form 3468 ☐ Form 5884		
☐ Form 6478 ☐ Form 6765 ☐ Form 8586 ☐ Form 8830 ☐ Form 8826 ☐ Form 8835		
☐ Form 8844 ☐ Form 8845 ☐ Form 8846 ☐ Form 8847 . . . . . **2a**		
b Credit for prior year minimum tax (attach Form 8827) **2b**		
3 **Total credits.** Add lines 2a and 2b	**3**	
4 Subtract line 3 from line 1	**4**	
5 Recapture taxes. Check if from: ☐ Form 4255 ☐ Form 8611	**5**	
6 Alternative minimum tax (attach Form 4626)	**6**	
7 **Total tax.** Add lines 4 through 6. Enter here and on line 27, page 1	**7**	O

Part II   Other Information (See instructions.)

1 Refer to page 19 of the instructions and state the principal:

  a Business activity code no. ▶ .8999..................

  b Business activity ▶.....................................

  c Product or service ▶ GRAPHIC DESIGN..............

2 Did any individual, partnership, estate, or trust at the end of the tax year own, directly or indirectly, 50% or more of the corporation's voting stock? (For rules of attribution, see section 267(c).) . . . .   ☑ Yes   ☐ No

⌐REARDON J. ENTREPRENEUR. 999 EASY STREET. NY C10021. 000-00-
If "Yes," attach a schedule showing name and identifying number. 0000

3 Enter the amount of tax-exempt interest received or accrued during the tax year . . . . ▶ $ O

4 Enter amount of cash distributions and the book value of property (other than cash) distributions made in this tax year . . . . ▶ $ O

5a If an amount is entered on line 2, page 1, see the worksheet on page 12 for amounts to enter below:

  (1) Purchases . . . . . .

  (2) Additional sec. 263A costs (see instructions—attach schedule) .

  (3) Other costs (attach schedule) .

  b Do the rules of section 263A (for property produced or acquired for resale) apply to the corporation? . . . . . ☐ Yes ☐ No

6 At any time during the 1994 calendar year, did the corporation have an interest in or a signature or other authority over a financial account in a foreign country (such as a bank account, securities account, or other financial account)? If "Yes," the corporation may have to file Form TD F 90-22.1 . . . . ☐ Yes ☑ No
If "Yes," enter the name of the foreign country ▶ ....

Part III   Balance Sheets

		(a) Beginning of tax year		(b) End of tax year	
Assets 1	Cash			6,000	-
2a	Trade notes and accounts receivable . .			5,000	-
b	Less allowance for bad debts	(	)	(	)
3	Inventories				
4	U.S. government obligations				
5	Tax-exempt securities (see instructions) .				
6	Other current assets (attach schedule) . .	INITIAL			
7	Loans to stockholders	RETURN			
8	Mortgage and real estate loans . . .				
9a	Depreciable, depletable, and intangible assets . .				
b	Less accumulated depreciation, depletion, and amortization	(	)	(	)
10	Land (net of any amortization)				
11	Other assets (attach schedule)			5,000	-
12	Total assets			16,000	-
Liabilities and Stockholders' Equity 13	Accounts payable			4,000	-
14	Other current liabilities (attach schedule) .				
15	Loans from stockholders			5,000	-
16	Mortgages, notes, bonds payable . . .				
17	Other liabilities (attach schedule) . . .				
18	Capital stock (preferred and common stock) .			27,000	-
19	Paid-in or capital surplus				
20	Retained earnings			(20,000	-)
21	Less cost of treasury stock	(	)	(	)
22	Total liabilities and stockholders' equity			16,000	-

Part IV   Reconciliation of Income (Loss) per Books With Income per Return (You are not required to complete Part IV if the total assets on line 12, column (b), Part III are less than $25,000.)

1 Net income (loss) per books	6 Income recorded on books this year not included on this return (itemize)	
2 Federal income tax.		
3 Excess of capital losses over capital gains. .	7 Deductions on this return not charged against book income this year (itemize)................	
4 Income subject to tax not recorded on books this year (itemize)		
5 Expenses recorded on books this year not deducted on this return (itemize)	8 Income (line 24, page 1). Enter the sum of lines 1 through 5 less the sum of lines 6 and 7 . .	

⊛ *Printed on recycled paper*   ☆ U.S. GPO: 1994-375-292

INC. YOURSELF

Form **1040**

Department of the Treasury—Internal Revenue Service

U.S. Individual Income Tax Return (O) **1994**

IRS Use Only—Do not write or staple in this space.

For the year Jan. 1–Dec. 31, 1994, or other tax year beginning _____, 1994, ending _____, 19 ___

OMB No. 1545-0074

Label

(See instructions on page 12.)

Use the IRS label. Otherwise, please print or type.

L A B E L   H E R E

Your first name and initial: REARDON J.   Last name: ENTREPRENEUR

Your social security number: 000 00 0000

If a joint return, spouse's first name and initial   Last name

Spouse's social security number

Home address (number and street). If you have a P.O. box, see page 12.: 999 EASY STREET   Apt. no. PH

City, town or post office, state, and ZIP code. If you have a foreign address, see page 12.: NEW YORK, NY 10021

For Privacy Act and Paperwork Reduction Act Notice, see page 4.

Presidential Election Campaign
(See page 12.)

Do you want $3 to go to this fund? . . . .   Yes ☐ No ✓

If a joint return, does your spouse want $3 to go to this fund? . . . .

Note: Checking "Yes" will not change your tax or reduce your refund.

Filing Status

(See page 12.)

Check only one box.

1 ✓ Single

2 ☐ Married filing joint return (even if only one had income)

3 ☐ Married filing separate return. Enter spouse's social security no. above and full name here. ▶

4 ☐ Head of household (with qualifying person). (See page 13.) If the qualifying person is a child but not your dependent, enter this child's name here. ▶

5 ☐ Qualifying widow(er) with dependent child (year spouse died ▶ 19___). (See page 13.)

Exemptions

(See page 13.)

If more than six dependents, see page 14.

6a ✓ **Yourself.** If your parent (or someone else) can claim you as a dependent on his or her tax return, **do not** check box 6a. But be sure to check the box on line 33b on page 2.

b ☐ Spouse

| No. of boxes checked on 6a and 6b | 1 |

c Dependents:

(1) Name (first, initial, and last name)	(2) Check if under age 1	(3) If age 1 or older, dependent's social security number	(4) Dependent's relationship to you	(5) No. of months lived in your home in 1994

No. of your children on 6c who:
- lived with you: 0
- didn't live with you due to divorce or separation (see page 14): 0

Dependents on 6c not entered above: 0

d If your child didn't live with you but is claimed as your dependent under a pre-1985 agreement, check here ▶ ☐

e Total number of exemptions claimed

Add numbers entered on lines above ▶ 1

Income

Attach Copy B of your Forms W-2, W-2G, and 1099-R here.

If you did not get a W-2, see page 15.

Enclose, but do not attach, any payment with your return.

7 Wages, salaries, tips, etc. Attach Form(s) W-2 7

8a **Taxable** interest income (see page 15). Attach Schedule B if over $400 . . . 8a

b **Tax-exempt** interest (see page 16). DON'T include on line 8a | 8b

9 Dividend income. Attach Schedule B if over $400 9

10 Taxable refunds, credits, or offsets of state and local income taxes (see page 16) . . 10

11 Alimony received 11

12 Business income or (loss). Attach Schedule C or C-EZ 12

13 Capital gain or (loss). If required, attach Schedule D (see page 16) . . . 13   30,000 —

14 Other gains or (losses). Attach Form 4797 14

15a Total IRA distributions . | 15a   b Taxable amount (see page 17) 15b

16a Total pensions and annuities | 16a   b Taxable amount (see page 17) 16b

17 Rental real estate, royalties, partnerships, S corporations, trusts, etc. Attach Schedule E 17

18 Farm income or (loss). Attach Schedule F 18

19 Unemployment compensation (see page 18) 19

20a Social security benefits | 20a   b Taxable amount (see page 18) 20b

21 Other income. List type and amount—see page 18 21

22 Add the amounts in the far right column for lines 7 through 21. This is your **total income** ▶ 22   30,000 —

Adjustments to Income

Caution: See instructions . . ▶

23a Your IRA deduction (see page 19) 23a

b Spouse's IRA deduction (see page 19) 23b

24 Moving expenses. Attach Form 3903 or 3903-F . . 24

25 One-half of self-employment tax 25

26 Self-employed health insurance deduction (see page 21) 26

27 Keogh retirement plan and self-employed SEP deduction 27

28 Penalty on early withdrawal of savings . . . 28

29 Alimony paid. Recipient's SSN ▶ | 29

30 Add lines 23a through 29. These are your **total adjustments** . . . . . . ▶ 30   0

Adjusted Gross Income

31 Subtract line 30 from line 22. This is your **adjusted gross income**. If less than $25,296 and a child lived with you (less than $9,000 if a child didn't live with you), see "Earned Income Credit" on page 27 ▶ 31   30,000 —

Cat. No. 11320B

Form **1040** (1994)

Form 1040 (1994)   Page **2**

Tax Compu-tation (See page 23.)	**32**	Amount from line 31 (adjusted gross income)	**32**	30,000
	33a	Check if: ☐ **You** were 65 or older, ☐ Blind; ☐ **Spouse** was 65 or older, ☐ Blind. Add the number of boxes checked above and enter the total here . . . . ▶ 33a		
	b	If your parent (or someone else) can claim you as a dependent, check here . ▶ 33b ☐		
	c	If you are married filing separately and your spouse itemizes deductions or you are a dual-status alien, see page 23 and check here . . . . ▶ 33c ☐		
	34	Enter the larger of your: { **Itemized deductions** from Schedule A, line 29, **OR** **Standard deduction** shown below for your filing status. **But if you checked any box on line 33a or b,** go to page 23 to find your standard deduction. If you checked **box 33c,** your standard deduction is zero. ● Single—$3,800 ● Head of household—$5,600 ● Married filing jointly or Qualifying widow(er)—$6,350 ● Married filing separately—$3,175 }	**34**	3,800
	35	Subtract line 34 from line 32	**35**	26,400
If you want the IRS to figure your tax, see page 24.	**36**	If line 32 is $83,850 or less, multiply $2,450 by the total number of exemptions claimed on line 6e. If line 32 is over $83,850, see the worksheet on page 24 for the amount to enter .	**36**	2,450
	37	**Taxable income.** Subtract line 36 from line 35. If line 36 is more than line 35, enter -0-	**37**	23,950
	38	Tax. Check if from **a** ☑ Tax Table, **b** ☐ Tax Rate Schedules, **c** ☐ Capital Gain Tax Worksheet, or **d** ☐ Form 8615 (see page 24). Amount from Form(s) 8814 ▶ **e** _____	**38**	3,756
	39	Additional taxes. Check if from **a** ☐ Form 4970 **b** ☐ Form 4972	**39**	0
	40	Add lines 38 and 39 . . . . ▶	**40**	3,756
Credits (See page 24.)	**41**	Credit for child and dependent care expenses. Attach Form 2441	**41**		
	42	Credit for the elderly or the disabled. Attach Schedule R . .	**42**		
	43	Foreign tax credit. Attach Form 1116	**43**		
	44	Other credits (see page 25). Check if from **a** ☐ Form 3800 **b** ☐ Form 8396 **c** ☐ Form 8801 **d** ☐ Form (specify) _____	**44**		
	45	Add lines 41 through 44	**45**	0
	46	Subtract line 45 from line 40. If line 45 is more than line 40, enter -0- . . . . ▶	**46**	3,756
Other Taxes (See page 25.)	**47**	Self-employment tax. Attach Schedule SE	**47**		
	48	Alternative minimum tax. Attach Form 6251	**48**		
	49	Recapture taxes. Check if from **a** ☐ Form 4255 **b** ☐ Form 8611 **c** ☐ Form 8828 . .	**49**		
	50	Social security and Medicare tax on tip income not reported to employer. Attach Form 4137	**50**		
	51	Tax on qualified retirement plans, including IRAs. If required, attach Form 5329 . . .	**51**		
	52	Advance earned income credit payments from Form W-2	**52**		
	53	Add lines 46 through 52. This is your **total tax** . . . . ▶	**53**	3,756
Payments Attach Forms W-2, W-2G, and 1099-R on the front.	**54**	Federal income tax withheld. If any is from Form(s) 1099, check ▶ ☐	**54**		
	55	1994 estimated tax payments and amount applied from 1993 return .	**55**	3,500	
	56	**Earned income credit.** If required, attach Schedule EIC (see page 27). Nontaxable earned income: amount ▶ _____ and type ▶	**56**		
	57	Amount paid with Form 4868 (extension request)	**57**		
	58	Excess social security and RRTA tax withheld (see page 32)	**58**		
	59	Other payments. Check if from **a** ☐ Form 2439 **b** ☐ Form 4136	**59**		
	60	Add lines 54 through 59. These are your **total payments** . . . . ▶	**60**	3,500
Refund or Amount You Owe	**61**	If line 60 is more than line 53, subtract line 53 from line 60. This is the amount you **OVERPAID.** ▶	**61**	
	62	Amount of line 61 you want **REFUNDED TO YOU.** . . . . ▶	**62**	
	63	Amount of line 61 you want **APPLIED TO YOUR 1995 ESTIMATED TAX** ▶ 63		
	64	If line 53 is more than line 60, subtract line 60 from line 53. This is the **AMOUNT YOU OWE.** For details on how to pay, including what to write on your payment, see page 32 . . . ▶	**64**	256
	65	Estimated tax penalty (see page 33). Also include on line 64 65		

Sign Here
Keep a copy of this return for your records.

Under penalties of perjury, I declare that I have examined this return and accompanying schedules and statements, and to the best of my knowledge and belief, they are true, correct, and complete. Declaration of preparer (other than taxpayer) is based on all information of which preparer has any knowledge.

Your signature ▶ R ~ J ~ F ~	Date 4/15/95	Your occupation EXECUTIVE
Spouse's signature. If a joint return, BOTH must sign.	Date	Spouse's occupation

Paid Preparer's Use Only

Preparer's signature ▶	Date	Check if self-employed ☐	Preparer's social security no.
Firm's name (or yours if self-employed) and address ▶		E.I. No.	
		ZIP code	

♻ *Printed on recycled paper*   *U.S. Government Printing Office: 1994 — 375-188

SCHEDULE D (Form 1040)	**Capital Gains and Losses**	OMB No. 1545-0074

Department of the Treasury
Internal Revenue Service (O)

▶ Attach to Form 1040. ▶ See Instructions for Schedule D (Form 1040).

▶ Use lines 20 and 22 for more space to list transactions for lines 1 and 9.

1994

Attachment Sequence No. **12**

Name(s) shown on Form 1040

REARDON J. ENTREPRENEUR

Your social security number

000 00 0000

Part I — Short-Term Capital Gains and Losses—Assets Held One Year or Less

(a) Description of property (Example: 100 sh. XYZ Co.)	(b) Date acquired (Mo., day, yr.)	(c) Date sold (Mo., day, yr.)	(d) Sales price (see page D-3)	(e) Cost or other basis (see page D-3)	(f) LOSS If (e) is more than (d), subtract (d) from (e)	(g) GAIN If (d) is more than (e), subtract (e) from (d)
1						
		OPTIONS TRADES				30,000 —

2	Enter your short-term totals, if any, from line 21	2			
3	**Total short-term sales price amounts.** Add column (d) of lines 1 and 2 . .	3			
4	Short-term gain from Forms 2119 and 6252, and short-term gain or (loss) from Forms 4684, 6781, and 8824	4	O		O
5	Net short-term gain or (loss) from partnerships, S corporations, estates, and trusts from Schedule(s) K-1	5	O		
6	Short-term capital loss carryover. Enter the amount, if any, from line 9 of your 1993 Capital Loss Carryover Worksheet . . .	6	O		
7	Add lines 1, 2, and 4 through 6, in columns (f) and (g)	7	(O)		30,000 —
8	**Net short-term capital gain or (loss).** Combine columns (f) and (g) of line 7 . . . . . ▶	8		30,000 —	

Part II — Long-Term Capital Gains and Losses—Assets Held More Than One Year

9					

10	Enter your long-term totals, if any, from line 23	10			
11	**Total long-term sales price amounts.** Add column (d) of lines 9 and 10 . . .	11			
12	Gain from Form 4797; long-term gain from Forms 2119, 2439, and 6252; and long-term gain or (loss) from Forms 4684, 6781, and 8824	12			
13	Net long-term gain or (loss) from partnerships, S corporations, estates, and trusts from Schedule(s) K-1	13			
14	Capital gain distributions	14			
15	Long-term capital loss carryover. Enter the amount, if any, from line 14 of your 1993 Capital Loss Carryover Worksheet	15			
16	Add lines 9, 10, and 12 through 15, in columns (f) and (g)	16	( )		
17	**Net long-term capital gain or (loss).** Combine columns (f) and (g) of line 16 . . . . . ▶	17			

Part III — Summary of Parts I and II

18	Combine lines 8 and 17. If a loss, go to line 19. If a gain, enter the gain on Form 1040, line 13. **Note:** If both lines 17 and 18 are gains, see the **Capital Gain Tax Worksheet** on page 25 . .	18
19	If line 18 is a (loss), enter here and as a (loss) on Form 1040, line 13, the **smaller** of these losses:	
a	The (loss) on line 18; **or**	
b	($3,000) or, if married filing separately, ($1,500)	19 ( )
	Note: See the **Capital Loss Carryover Worksheet** on page D-3 if the loss on line 18 exceeds the loss on line 19 or if Form 1040, line 35, is a loss.	

For Paperwork Reduction Act Notice, see Form 1040 instructions.   Cat. No. 11338H   Schedule D (Form 1040) 1994

Schedule D (Form 1040) 1994   Attachment Sequence No. **12**   Page **2**

Name(s) shown on Form 1040. Do not enter name and social security number if shown on other side. | Your social security number

Part IV   Short-Term Capital Gains and Losses—Assets Held One Year or Less *(Continuation of Part I)*

(a) Description of property (Example: 100 sh. XYZ Co.)	(b) Date acquired (Mo., day, yr.)	(c) Date sold (Mo., day, yr.)	(d) Sales price (see page D-3)	(e) Cost or other basis (see page D-3)	(f) LOSS If (e) is more than (d), subtract (d) from (e)	(g) GAIN If (d) is more than (e), subtract (e) from (d)
		OPTIONS TRADES (CONT.)				

21 Short-term totals. Add columns (d), (f), and (g) of line 20. Enter here and on line 2 . **21**

Part V   Long-Term Capital Gains and Losses—Assets Held More Than One Year *(Continuation of Part II)*

23 Long-term totals. Add columns (d), (f), and (g) of line 22. Enter here and on line 10 . **23**

Printed on recycled paper   *U.S. Government Printing Office: 1994 — 375-201 items are valued at cost, not present value, since the IRS considers current or replacement value irrelevant.

Assets you contribute to your corporation will increase the basis of your stock. Depending on when the shares are issued, you may have shares at varying bases, just as though you had bought stock at varying prices.

TAKING ADVANTAGE OF LOSSES

As mentioned earlier, there's a compelling reason for owner-shareholders of an S corporation to monitor the basis of their stock and to be prepared to raise it: they cannot deduct losses in excess of the basis of their stock. If they want to take full advantage of their corporation's losses to offset their personal income from other sources, their basis must be equal to or greater than their portion of the loss.

In practice, here's how it works: Startup Corporation, your new S corporation in which you are the sole shareholder, is expecting a loss of $10,000 this year. You paid $2,000 for 100 shares (100 percent) of the stock of your new corporation. Your basis in the stock is $2,000. During the year you loaned Startup $5,000. Now you have a basis in debt of $5,000 as well as a basis in stock of $2,000. (Yes, they are two separate accounts.)

If you have a basis in both stock and debt, operating losses are applied first to your basis in stock, then to your basis in debt. In this example, $2,000 of the $10,000 operating loss is applied to your basis in stock and wipes out its value. Then only $5,000 of the remaining $8,000 loss can be used to offset your personal income from other sources because your basis in debt is only $5,000.

In order to make use of the entire $10,000 loss, rather than only $7,000, you'll have to lend Startup $3,000. Next year, when Startup becomes profitable, it can repay you the $3,000.

Your basis changes every year in which Startup has a profit or a loss. When Startup shows a profit, your basis rises by the amount of the profit; if Startup has a loss, your basis is reduced by the amount of the loss. You are taxed on the profit, whether or not it is distributed. When you are taxed, your basis is raised. When the profit is distributed, your basis is reduced by the amount of the distribution.

There is a trap in lending money to your new S corporation, and timing is crucial because the basis changes every year. Discuss with your tax professional whether you receive a greater benefit by accelerating a loss, and whether you are better off repaying loans in a particular year or deferring repayment until the following year. In any case, advises Murray Alter, a tax partner at Coopers & Lybrand L.L.P., "Don't call the money a repayment of loan until the end of the year. Call it an advance or borrowing. Then convert it to a repayment of the loan."

DISADVANTAGES OF S CORPORATIONS

Everything has its price. The price of S corporation election is sacrificing the income-splitting feature of C corporations, which can save thousands of dollars in taxes every year, and giving up lots of juicy fringe benefits.

Not all employee benefits can be deducted by your S corporation as business expenses. The Subchapter S Revision Act differentiates between employee-shareholders owning 2 percent or less of the corporation's stock and those owning *more than 2 percent of the stock*. Obviously, you're in the latter category. Under that legislation, only those benefits received by employee-shareholders owning 2 percent or less of the corporation's stock will be deductible by the corporation as a business expense. Thus, if you elect S corporation status, you'll lose many tax-favored fringe benefits; among them, valuable medical and insurance plans.

You also lose the right to borrow from your pension plan, as employee-shareholders of C corporations are permitted to do. This right can be useful and very profitable to you and to the corporation. Let's say that you want to borrow $50,000 for two years so that you can put a down payment on a house. You can borrow the money at 10 percent for two years, then pay it back with interest. Your pension fund is enriched by $10,000. (But you may not deduct the interest payment on your personal income-tax return.)

STATES' RITES

When you weigh the advantages and disadvantages of electing S corporation status for your new corporation, consider whether the state in which you incorporate recognizes S corporation status. Some states recognize S corporation status; some do not and treat S corporations as C corporations or as unincorporated businesses. Whether your state does or doesn't recognize S corporations can make a big difference in how much you pay in taxes and how many tax returns you must file.

While you probably should consult a tax adviser before electing S corporation status, the following list of states that do and don't recognize S corporations will start you on the right track:

Alabama	Recognizes federal S corporate status. Nonresident shareholders will be taxed on their share of S corporation income from Alabama sources.
Alaska	Recognizes federal S corporation status.
Arizona	Recognizes federal S corporation status.
Arkansas	Recognizes federal S corporation status. Nonresident shareholders will be taxed on their share of S corporation income from Arkansas sources.
California	Recognizes federal S corporation status. S corporations are taxed at a much lower rate than C corporations. Nonresident share-

holders will be taxed on their share of S corporation income from California sources.

Colorado — Recognizes federal S corporation status. Nonresident shareholders will be taxed on their share of S corporation income from Colorado sources. However, the Colorado Court of Appeals has held that distributions of S corporation income to nonresident shareholders are not taxable.

Connecticut — Does not recognize S corporation status. Connecticut S corporations are subject to the state business (income) tax.

Delaware — Recognizes federal S corporation status. However, if on the last day of the corporation's fiscal year any shareholders are nonresidents, the corporation is subject to tax on the percentage of its taxable income equal to the percentage of its stock owned by nonresidents on that day.

District of Columbia — An S corporation is treated as an unincorporated business and pays the District of Columbia unincorporated business franchise (income) tax if its gross income for a tax year is $12,000 or more. If its gross income is less than $12,000, it is treated as a partnership and files an information partnership return. It is exempt from the franchise tax.

If the S corporation has paid

the unincorporated business franchise tax, its shareholders are entitled to a deduction ("modification") on income that has been subject to the franchise tax. But if the corporation has not paid the franchise tax because its gross income was under $12,000, its shareholders are completely taxed on their S corporation income.

Florida   An S corporation is not taxable, except to the extent that it is liable for federal income tax. However, Florida law defines taxable income according to a former Internal Revenue Code Section 1372(b)(1), *prior* to amendment by the Subchapter S Revision Act of 1982.

Georgia   Recognizes federal S corporation status. Nonresident shareholders will be taxed on their share of S corporation income from Georgia sources.

Hawaii   Recognizes federal S corporation status. Nonresident shareholders must file an agreement to pay taxes on their share of S corporation income from Hawaii sources.

Idaho   Recognizes federal S corporation status.

Illinois   Recognizes federal S corporation status, but substitutes a personal property replacement income tax on Illinois net income for S corporations. There are many other intricate modifications. Consult your tax adviser.

Indiana	Recognizes federal S corporation status. Nonresident shareholders will be taxed on their share of S corporation income from Indiana sources.
Iowa	Recognizes federal S corporation status.
Kansas	Recognizes federal S corporation status. Nonresident shareholders will be taxed on their share of S corporation income from Kansas sources.
Kentucky	Recognizes federal S corporation status.
Louisiana	S corporations are taxed as though they were C corporations.
Maine	Recognizes federal S corporation status. Nonresident shareholders will be taxed on their share of S corporation income from Maine sources.
Maryland	Recognizes federal S corporation status. The corporation will be taxed on Maryland income attributable to each nonresident shareholder.
Massachusetts	Recognizes federal S corporation status. However, shareholders are taxed on their distributive share of the S corporation's items of Massachusetts income, loss, or deduction as though they had realized or incurred the item directly from the source, rather

	than through the S corporation. Consult your tax adviser.
Michigan	Michigan S corporations must pay the single business tax. However, S corporations can enjoy a special exemption equal to $12,000 times the number of qualified shareholders, up to a maximum of $48,000, plus a graduated special tax credit. Consult your tax adviser.
Minnesota	Recognizes federal S corporation status.
Mississippi	S corporations are not subject to the Mississippi income tax on corporations, but still must file the regular corporation income-tax return and schedules, as well as partnership returns. Nonresident shareholders will be taxed on their share of S corporation income from Mississippi sources.
Missouri	Recognizes federal S corporation status.
Montana	Recognizes federal S corporation status. Every electing corporation must pay a minimum fee of $10.
Nebraska	Recognizes federal S corporation status. Nonresident shareholders will be taxed on their share of S corporation income from Nebraska sources, but the corporation may pay these taxes for them.
Nevada	No corporate or personal taxes are imposed.

New Hampshire	Does not recognize S corporation status. New Hampshire S corporations are subject to the state business profits tax.
New Jersey	Does not recognize S corporation status. New Jersey S corporations are subject to the corporation business tax.
New Mexico	Recognizes federal S corporation status.
New York	Recognizes federal S corporation status. S corporations are taxed at a much lower rate than C corporations. Nonresident shareholders will be taxed on their share of S corporation income from New York sources. *However, New York City does not recognize S corporation status,* and S corporations are taxed as though they were C corporations.
North Carolina	Recognizes federal S corporation status.
North Dakota	Recognizes federal S corporation status, but an S corporation may elect to be taxed as a C corporation for state income-tax purposes.
Ohio	Recognizes federal S corporation status. Nonresident shareholders may be entitled to claim the nonresident tax credit.
Oklahoma	Recognizes federal S corporation status. Nonresident shareholders will be taxed on their share of S corporation income from Oklahoma sources.

Oregon	Recognizes federal S corporation status. Oregon S corporations must file state corporation income and excise tax returns, but are liable only for the minimum corporate excise tax. Nonresident shareholders will be taxed on their share of S corporation income from Oregon sources.
Pennsylvania	Recognizes federal S corporation status.
Rhode Island	Recognizes federal S corporation status. Rhode Island S corporations are not subject to the state income tax or net worth tax on corporations, but are subject to a franchise tax (minimum $100). Nonresident shareholders will be taxed on their share of S corporation income from Rhode Island sources.
South Carolina	Recognizes federal S corporation status.
South Dakota	Recognizes federal S corporation status, except for financial institutions. No corporate or personal income taxes are imposed.
Tennessee	Does not recognize S corporation status. Tennessee S corporations are subject to the Tennessee excise (income) tax.
Texas	Does not recognize S corporation status. Texas S corporations are subject to the Texas franchise tax. Texas does not impose a personal or corporate income tax.

Utah	Recognizes federal S corporation status.
Vermont	Recognizes federal S corporation status.
Virginia	Recognizes federal S corporation status. Nonresident shareholders will be taxed on their share of S corporation income from Virginia sources.
Washington	Does not recognize S corporation status. Washington S corporations are subject to a franchise tax and gross receipts tax. There are no personal or corporate income taxes.
West Virginia	Recognizes federal S corporation status.
Wisconsin	Recognizes federal S corporation status, with a few minor modifications.
Wyoming	Wyoming imposes a corporate franchise tax, but not an income tax.

TRADE-OFFS

Do the advantages of an S corporation outweigh the disadvantages? It all depends.

You Gain	**You Lose**
• More favorable income-tax rates for members of the "perilous professions."	• Income-splitting strategies. • Right to invest corporate surplus in stocks whose

- Ability to offset personal income with corporate losses.
- Immediate use of corporate funds every year—no buildup of assets to be taxed upon liquidation.*
- Only one tax is paid when money is taken out of the corporation. (In a C corporation, sometimes—but not always—a second tax may have to be paid when money is taken out of the corporation, as in liquidation.)

- dividends paid to your corporation are 70 percent tax-free.
- More generous corporate pension contributions.
- Right to borrow from pension fund.
- Tax-deductible $50,000 group term life insurance.
- Tax-deductible accident and health insurance plans.
- $5,000 death benefit paid to employee-shareholder's estate or beneficiaries.
- Cost of meals or lodging furnished for the convenience of employer.

*However, a C corporation can avoid double taxation by judiciously stripping out corporate assets.

To clarify the pros and cons of electing Subchapter S status, let's look at two stereotypes, one of whom should choose S status and one of whom should not. Your own situation is probably not so clear-cut as these because these examples are weighted heavily in one direction or the other. Nevertheless, these examples should guide you in making a choice. The list is far from complete, but it should point you in the right direction and help you organize questions to ask your tax adviser.

Ideal S Corporation

- Single, few medical expenses that total less than $1,000 per year.

Ideal C Corporation

- Married, heavy medical expenses—orthodontia for one child, psychotherapy for one child. Needs gym and pool memberships and

- Member of a "perilous profession"—faces flat tax rate of 34 percent if doesn't elect S corporation status.
- Needs most of corporate income to live on so doesn't care about income splitting.

- Profession does not require a great deal of expensive equipment.
- Indifferent to borrowing from pension fund, which is prohibited in S corporations.

masseur for bad back. Everyone in family wears contact lenses. Medical expenses total over $10,000 per year.
- Not a member of a "perilous profession." Entitled to corporate tax rate of 15 percent on income under $50,000.
- Does not need most of corporate income to live on—plans to take advantage of income splitting and of investing corporate surplus in stocks whose dividends paid to the corporation are 70 percent tax-free.
- Business requires a great deal of expensive equipment.
- Expects to borrow from pension fund in several years to buy new home.

Fortunately, you can have it both ways. You can start as an S corporation to benefit from the flow-through of your fledgling corporation's losses to offset your personal income and reduce your taxes. When your corporation flourishes and becomes profitable, you can terminate its S status to take advantage of income-splitting strategies, greater pension contributions, medical, dental, and insurance fringe benefits, and corporate investment for dividends that are 70 percent tax-free. Finally, as your corporation matures, if it becomes extremely successful and nets $100,000 a year, you may want to reelect S status so that your corporation doesn't face the Scylla of the accumulated earnings trap (see Chapter 1) or the Charybdis of double taxation of dividends—once as corporate earnings and once as dividends you receive from your corporation.

Because it's easy to elect and to terminate S status but difficult to return to it, this decision should be made in consultation with your tax adviser. You may want to work out some scenarios on a computer—for example, "If I have only $20,000 outside income, it does/doesn't pay to elect S. If my outside income rises to $50,000, it does/doesn't pay to elect S." For most one-person corporations, S status is desirable at some point, and therefore its election and/or termination should be examined every year.

RETURN TO S STATUS

In general, there is a five-year waiting period between terminating and reelecting S corporation status. The major exception to the rule requires the approval of the IRS District Director. How easy is it to get? Do you need a compelling reason?

If there has been a change of ownership of more than 50 percent, the IRS will generally consent to an early return to S corporation status. Similarly, if there has been an inadvertent error,* the IRS will usually permit early reversion to S status.

You will have to apply for IRS approval; if the reversion is approved, the IRS will bill your corporation $250.

HOW TO USE YOUR S CORPORATION AS A FINANCIAL-PLANNING TOOL

Many financial planners are using S corporations as sophisticated long-term tools to achieve not only tax savings but also

---

*For example, the S corporation has the maximum 35 shareholders, including some married couples. When one couple divorces and divides their S corporation shares, there are now 36 shareholders, which is not permitted under S corporation rules. Or, more usually, some tax forms are filed late, triggering an inadvertent reversion to C status.

business and family goals. Because of the impact of state and local income taxes, these can be discussed only generally here and are meant to serve as guidelines and openers for more specific planning with your tax advisers. Here are some problems faced by many successful small businesses and their profitable S solutions:

Problem: How to avoid federal estate tax without loss of the owner's present or future control of the business.

Solution: In general, when a business owner gives or transfers corporate stock to a beneficiary in order to remove the value and growth of the donated stock from his or her gross estate, the donor also creates a potential problem: even a minor block of stock may be sufficient to swing voting control away from the donor, to his or her detriment. However, by structuring or restructuring a company as an S corporation, business owners can create two types of common voting stock (not classes—this distinction is crucial): Type A, with ten or more votes per share; and Type B, with one vote per share. (Or Type B can even be nonvoting stock.) The owners can then give all their Type B stock to children or grandchildren and keep all the Type A stock themselves. Giving away the Type B stock removes it from the owners' taxable estates, which saves current income and eventual estate taxes. But since the Type B stock possesses very little voting power, the business owners can remain secure, in firm control of their corporation.

Problem: How to avoid paying double tax on corporate income while treating family members who work for the company and those who do not equally.

Solution: In family-owned businesses, it's very common for some members to work for the company and for some members not to. These two groups are often at loggerheads over dividends. The family shareholders who don't work for the company want their dividends. The family shareholders who work for the company frequently don't want to receive dividends because it is often difficult for general corporations to pay out corporate earnings to stockholders without incurring a double tax on corporate income. Their refusal may preclude dividends for the other shareholders. An S corporation can solve this problem because corporate earnings are distributed to the shareholders with only one tax on shareholders, as if they were partners.

Problem: How to turn investment income into earned income so that you can qualify for pensions and profit sharing.

Solution: Many people own income-producing securities, but despite the high income taxes they have to pay, they are not entitled to any kind of pension or profit-sharing plan because their dividends and interest are not considered to be earned income. Setting up an S corporation to hold these securities—it could be called "My Investments, Inc."—lets these people receive the same amount as before, but now some of it can be transmuted into salary. The corporations can now pay them a reasonable salary for managing the investments and other concerns of the corporations, and these salaries mean that these people—with no real change in their activities—are now permitted the pension and profit-sharing plans that they were denied earlier.

Furthermore, through their S corporations, these investors are able to make estate-planning gifts of stock to children or grandchildren without loss of control, as in the previous example.

These are only a few ideas to serve as a springboard. S corporations are advantageous, but intricate. To make sure that you belong in one and that you're getting all those benefits, enlist your accountant and lawyer in developing your strategies.

8

ESPECIALLY FOR WOMEN AND MINORITIES:

Taking Advantage of Minority-Supplier Contracts and Business Incubators, and Avoiding a Different "Mommy Trap"

Good news and bad news.

Eighteen years ago, when I wrote this chapter for the first edition of *Inc. Yourself,* women entrepreneurs were still a rarity, and minority business owners other than neighborhood retailers were virtually unheard of. Those eighteen years have brought many changes.

Women- and minority-owned business are now the two fastest-growing sectors of the U.S. economy. According to *Women-Owned Businesses: Breaking the Boundaries,* a recent Dun & Bradstreet Information Services study, the number of women-owned businesses climbed 42 percent between 1991 and 1994—from 5.4 million to 7.7 million companies—and these businesses now hire more workers in the United States (15.5 million) than Fortune 500 companies do globally (11.5 million). The study also found that between 1991 and 1994 employment in women-owned companies grew 11.6 percent, more than double the 5.3 percent rate in all U.S. companies. Nevertheless, with all this good news, one-third of the members of the National Foundation of Women Business Owners reported that they had problems dealing with banks.

Of course, the "glass ceiling" that women bump up against is largely responsible for their deciding on self-employment after working for a larger company or organization for several years. Bernard B. Beal, chairman of M. R. Beal & Company, one of Wall Street's fastest-growing minority-owned investment-banking firms, refers to his experience as a "Lucite ceiling": "It's worse than a glass ceiling because at least you can break glass." Still, as most government agencies and Fortune 500 firms have special affirmative-action programs for doing business with women- and minority-owned suppliers, the glass and Lucite ceilings are much less limiting to entrepreneurs than they were to those same people when they were employees of large firms.

Incorporation brings special benefits to women, too. One talented young *Vogue* photographer puts it this way: "Incorporating sets me apart from a hundred other free-lance photographers. It shows clients and prospective clients that I'm successful and financially sophisticated. It's that extra bit—that extra little touch—that helps them remember *me,* not just my work."

Nowadays, more and more women are self-employed, and with increasing financial sophistication, more women are incorporating. But very often women suffer from the legacy of the past: they are not as knowledgeable about banking and establishing credit as men are, and all too often wives, widows, and divorcées suddenly find that they have no financial history. Quite simply, this means that lenders don't know whether or not to lend them money.

Whether you'll ever use it or not, establish a credit record immediately; you never know when you'll need it. The best way to do this is to open a checking account—*in your own name alone*—and to become known to your bank manager.

Next, ask for a line of credit: overdraft privileges for your checking account. Most banks give this a fancy name—Privilege Checking, Executive Credit, The No-Bounce Check. All it means is that if you overdraw your account, your checks will be honored—but at the same time you will have automatically borrowed money to cover them, at a hefty 10 to 12 percent. Formerly, the traditional advice on establishing credit was: "Take out a loan, make the payments promptly, and pay the final installment a little early." However, if you can show your bank manager that you have assets, you should be granted a line of credit without having to go through the rigmarole of a bank loan that you don't need.

What assets will impress a bank manager? A savings account in your name and property in your name. A savings account is particularly good because it shows that you are not a spendthrift and also that there is money at your disposal even if your income should fluctuate.

A good credit-card or charge-account history will also show that you are fiscally responsible. Like your checking and savings accounts, your credit card and charge plates should also be in your name alone.

Whatever method you use—checking account, line of credit, credit cards—always use your own name alone, even if it involves what seems like duplication and extra service charges. One of my friends who'd worked for twenty years finally decided to go into business for herself and applied for a bank loan to furnish her home office. Alas, the bank manager required her husband to cosign the loan because my friend had never built up an independent credit record—all her accounts were in joint names, and thus all the credit records were in her husband's name.

Now, if you incorporate, there's an additional reason to keep separate accounts: to prove to the IRS that there's no "corporate pocketbook" at work, that you are not lumping together your corporate and personal expenditures.

AVOIDING A DIFFERENT "MOMMY TRAP": WOMEN AS PERSONAL HOLDING CORPORATIONS

In most corporate situations, women experience the same problems as men: setting up a corporation, making it successful, investing corporate surplus profitably, etc. But there is one area in which women (and, incidentally, artists and writers who may produce only one major money-making work every two, three, or more years) are particularly vulnerable.

Because women will often curtail their workload during pregnancy and for a time after their children are born, women who incorporate may frequently have years in which their corporation receives much more dividend income from the stocks the corporation has bought than earned income from the work the corporation has performed for customers and clients, and thus be in danger of being held by the IRS to be a personal holding corporation. This situation would be especially likely if a woman had accumulated around $100,000 in a corporate portfolio that was invested in high-yield stocks paying $7,000 or $8,000 a year at the time of her maternity leave.

As explained earlier, a woman in this position could easily avoid having her corporation deemed a personal holding corporation simply by selling one or more of the corporation's stocks to bring the dividend income down to 59 percent or less of the total corporate income and then by reinvesting the proceeds of the stock sales in either low-yielding growth stocks (but making sure to keep the dividend income down to 59 percent) or municipal bonds (whose income is not counted by the IRS in making these calculations), depending on how aggressive or conservative an investor she is.

When she returns to work full time and her corporation is earning enough so that it is no longer in danger of being classified as a personal holding corporation, she can—and should—reverse the procedure so that her corporation can benefit from the 70 percent tax-free dividend exclusion. She should sell the corporation's municipal bonds or growth stocks and reinvest the proceeds of the sales in high-yielding common or preferred stocks.

SPECIAL PROBLEMS OF WOMEN AND MINORITIES: WHAT TO DO ABOUT THEM

Women and minority entrepreneurs face many of the same problems, according to Carrie L. Clay a partner in Coopers & Lybrand L.L.P.'s Columbus, Ohio, office. Carrie Clay is also Coordinator of Women's Business Activities. Because women and minorities are "new kids on the block," financing and credit can be difficult to obtain. Women and minorities do not seem to have role models, contacts, or resources, but they are slowly building networks and resource groups to overcome these problems. Fortunately for women business owners, nowadays the majority of loan officers are women, so women entrepreneurs and professionals are finding it easier now to obtain bank loans than 10 or 15 years ago.

When trying to obtain financing, be prepared to discuss your financing needs and how you intend to repay the loan. Banks look for two things: whether your corporation's cash flow will repay the loan, and what collateral you can offer.

Before you apply for a loan, get a copy of your credit report. Then you can verify its accuracy and be prepared to explain any errors. As approximately 25 percent of credit reports are inaccurate, Murphy's Law suggests that yours may well be one of them.

If you're short on collateral, there's a Small Business Administration program just for you: the 7A Direct Guarantee Program. Contact your nearest office for details.

The Small Business Administration offers minority programs under Section 8A of the Small Business Act, under which small minority-owned businesses can bid on contracts which provide services to the federal government. In fiscal 1993 contracts awarded under this program came to $4.5 billion. Carrie Clay calls them "a good way for your corporation to get a jump start." Although this program is targeted toward minorities, recently white women have challenged their exclusion from this lucrative sector and have qualified to bid on the contracts, which include construction, manufacturing, professional services (e.g., accounting, architecture, training), and nonprofessional services (e.g., food, maintenance, laundry, landscaping). About the only requirement is that you must be in business for two years. The "economically disadvantaged" requirement is broad: net worth less than $250,000, excluding the value of your home and your business.

> **Federal contracts can be an _undiscovered gold mine_. They are not well advertised. If you think your corporation can provide useful services, make a beeline for your local Small Business Administration office and get some advice. Remember: you're paying their salaries. There are SBA offices located in state capitals as well as many regional offices.**

Melody Borchers, Manager of the Women's Business Resource Program, Ohio Department of Development in Columbus, suggests that Ohio women business owners look at the Ohio Mini Loan program, which targets women entrepreneurs. This program can do start-up financing for projects in the $10,000 to $100,000 range. The program is not tied to the creation of new jobs.

Many states have programs similar to that of Ohio. Contact your state's Small Business Administration or Department of Economic Development.

TAKING ADVANTAGE OF MINORITY-SUPPLIER CONTRACTS

Yes, of course they're quotas! But after all these years when women- and minority-owned businesses have gotten what Marilyn Monroe called "the fuzzy end of the lollipop," it's time to tilt the balance just a bit in their favor through affirmative-action projects.

Melody Borchers offers this advice: "In Ohio [and many other states] there are two ways to sell to the state. One is to register with the state. This is a very regulated procedure, but then you are automatically sent contracts to bid on. A second method is to sell directly to state agencies. It's trickier and harder, but more lucrative, and you can have multiple contracts with one or more agencies. Some contracts are not competitive. Some are set aside for companies that are owned and controlled by minorities or women. The second method is more of a direct sell; it's like cultivating the private-sector marketplace. Bids can be hand-tailored. It's a huge marketplace, and you have to learn who is the decision maker in each agency or department."

HOW INCUBATORS CAN HELP

Just as there are incubators for baby chicks and infants, there are incubators for fledgling businesses. Business incubators are growing nearly as rapidly as new corporations are; ten years ago there were 50, in mid-1995 there were more than 500, and new incubators are opening on the average of one per week, according to Peter R. Collins, Director of National Entrepreneurial Advisory Services at Coopers & Lybrand L.L.P.

Business incubators let a number of new ventures share space, usually in an old, often historic warehouse, factory, or building. Incubators have a manager who facilitates the tenants' business growth and meets with them formally or informally, depending on the structure and house rules of the incubator. Incubators also have a tenant advisory board, often comprised of lawyers, scientific advisers, bankers, accountants, and emerging-business specialists. The board's function is to help business owners who are usually so focused on their products or services that they may have few or no business skills. The board also often helps with marketing, getting the products or services out into the marketplace. The bankers are a welcome source of capital, and it's easy for them to approve the loans because they know the incubator tenants and their businesses. They know that as the tenants grow, they may need to borrow more money for expansion, and the profitable loans will add to the bankers' bottom lines.

There are many other benefits to incubator tenancy. On the profit side, studies have found that 60 percent of all incubator tenants do business with each other. And, because of all the professional guidance, fewer incubator businesses fail, compared to all new-business failures. (However, in all fairness, I should point out that incubator tenants must apply and are chosen by advisory boards, so the tenants are more motivated, more knowledgeable, and better organized than many entrepreneurs.)

On the cost-containment side, being in an incubator is like sharing an apartment. Your rent is lower—usually 75 to 80 percent of market rates, and shared copier, fax machine, and office help result in lower costs. Some incubators have a graduated rent so that each year it becomes progressively less attractive for tenants to stay, a gentle way of easing them out of the nest. Generally new businesses stay in incubators a little less than three years, just long enough for them to get their feet on the ground and get into a real-world business milieu. Research and development ventures may take longer, sometimes five years.

Incubators are sponsored by many different organizations. If you are a member of a minority group, there are incubators targeted to minorities. If you are a scientist, there are high-technology incubators. There are even incubators for industrial subsets, like ceramics. Incubators are designed to fulfill the objectives of their sponsoring organizations and will tell you what they are.

Incubators are funded by various interest groups, such as economic development groups, state organizations, and even local urban-enterprise zones. Colleges and universities are often the most attractive sponsors, says Pete Collins, because they offer the services of laboratories, faculty, and graduate students. "You can't put a dollar value on that."

Some incubators have a combination of sponsors. Science Park in New Haven, Connecticut, is under the joint sponsorship of Yale University, a teaching hospital, and local community and state development groups. It is housed in a group of old buildings donated by Olin Corporation.

Some incubators are housed in unusual surroundings. Three thousand miles away, in Washington state, the Spokane Business Incubator started in what used to be a U.S. Air Force airfield. As the buildings included an airport commissary, the development group started a kitchen incubator that operates 24 hours a day and lets entrepreneurs share a large institutional kitchen without making an enormous cash commitment. The incubator's best-known products are Buckaroo Bagels and gourmet jams and jellies made of fruit from local orchards.

Because incubators are still relatively unknown, it's possible to get into one in a week if there's space and if the board likes you. Think of it as applying to college. Have a business plan. For some incubators your plan can be informal, but you have to convey the likelihood of your venture's success. Collins advises, "The incubator you may be referred to may not take you. It has to have room, and you need to have an elementary business plan to show the admissions committee. You may have a better chance in an incubator that is just starting up."

For more information on incubators, contact:

Mr. Michel Perdreau
Director of Member Services
National Business Incubator Association
20 East Circle Drive
Suite 190
Athens, OH 45701–3751
(614) 593-4331
(614) 593-1996 (fax)

BATORLINK—FOR BETTER INFORMATION

Whether or not you become an incubator tenant, one of the most compelling reasons to join the NBIA (dues are $175 a year for individuals and one-person corporations) is BatorLink, a free on-line networking system. BatorLink software works with IBM-compatible PCs with a Hayes-compatible modem, Macintosh, Windows, DOS, and the Internet, and uses phone lines to connect with a central computer in New York City. Your maximum cost is $9.95 per hour for invaluable information.

Here are some of BatorLink's business-development resources and how they can help you:

• A tie-in with a Federal Laboratory Consortium ombudsman monitors thousands of research teams every day. You can ask, "Who in the FLC is working in a particular area of research?" and BatorLink will provide you with those scientists' names, addresses, and phone numbers. You do not have to reinvent the wheel; you can "leverage off" their information and advice.

• A Small Business Administration ombudsman answers specific questions about business, job training, and financing, and BatorLink will give you names, addresses, and phone numbers of local resources.

• A private "angel" investor group is also represented on BatorLink. Its ombudsman will answer your questions about availability of private investor capital for your business.

• A clearinghouse for strategic alliances, trade, and equity investment that matches incubator companies with potential trading partners and other companies of all sizes for "win-win" partnerships.

OTHER RESOURCES

For volume and excellence of information, here are two of the best:

Most *Crain's* city business magazines publish a "Guide to

Economic Development and Business Assistance Programs" at least once a year, in the fall. The most recent New York/New Jersey guide, published in the September 4, 1995, issue, lists over 100 development and training programs, workshops, advisory and assistance programs, small-business loan sources, women and minority programs, etc.

Coopers & Lybrand L.L.P., the accounting firm with the greatest commitment to entrepreneurs, has Entrepreneurial Advisory Services teams in more than 100 cities in the United States and Puerto Rico. Many of these teams publish *Public Financing Sources,* a brochure detailing city, county, state, and federal financing and tax-abatement programs. Many of them benefit minority- and women-owned corporations.

9

YOUR EMPLOYEES

Up until now, we've been discussing the sometimes-idyllic situation where you are truly a one-man band: in your one-person corporation, you are everything from president down to file clerk.

But what if you have employees? Then it gets more complicated, though not necessarily more expensive.

If your corporation is able to hire what the IRS calls "independent contractors," you will not have to withhold taxes on their pay or cover them for Social Security. At the end of the year, the corporation just sends them an IRS Form 1099, which shows how much you paid them. Obviously, then, your corporation does not have to include independent contractors in its pension or profit-sharing plans because they are not considered to be the corporation's employees. (These independent contractors can set up their own Keogh plans, of course, but that's another subject for another book.)

If your corporation hires part-timers who are held by the IRS to be your employees, unless they give you a W-4 form showing that they are exempt from withholding, you will have to withhold income taxes on their salaries and furnish them with W-2 forms showing the amounts withheld. Depending on how much they earn each quarter, the corporation may or may not have to pay Social Security taxes. State regulations on contributions to workers' compensation and unemployment insurance funds vary too widely to be discussed here. The important point: unless your corporation's part-time employee completes 1,000 hours a year (an average of 20 hours a week), you do not have to include him or her in the corporation's pension or profit-sharing plans.

This means, of course, that your corporation could hire two or three part-timers instead of one full-time employee and save thousands of dollars every year by not having to contribute to employees' plans.

Hiring part-timers has social as well as financial benefits. Very often you can hire more intelligent and qualified people—college students, mothers, retirees—who are unable to work a full week but who perform splendidly on a part-time basis and are often delighted to work flexible hours. (I know from personal experience: I worked my way through college assisting the president of a small legal-services corporation.)

Even if you have full-time employees, though, you may not have to include them in your pension and profit-sharing plans immediately—and there are even ways to exclude them permanently.

First, there is a minimum-age requirement: an employer does not have to include anyone in its pension and profit-sharing plans (1) who is not at least 21 and (2) who has not completed at least one year of service.

Most plans for small corporations which include at least one owner-employee and one staff person are considered "top-heavy," a classification which may change from year to year. Basically, a money-purchase or profit-sharing plan is classified as top-heavy if the defined-contribution pension-plan accounts of "key employees" (generally defined as those earning $60,000 a year or more) are equal to 60 percent or more of total pension-plan assets.

Second, in a top-heavy plan, an employer must start vesting 20 percent of its contributions to an employee pension plan after 2 years and increase vesting by 20 percent each year, so that after 6 years the contributions are 100 percent vested.

> **Calculate service from date of employment so that you can be 100 percent vested in your pension benefits immediately while new employees must undergo the waiting period.**

If your employee leaves before working 2 years, no funds are vested and all the corporation's contributions are used by your corporation to fund subsequent years' contributions. If he or she leaves when partially vested, any of the corporation's contributions that are not vested are similarly applied to future years' contributions.

But don't think that you can hire employees and then fire them just before their 2 years' waiting time is up and they become eligible to vest in your corporation's pension and profit-sharing plans. You may get away with it for the first two 2-year periods. But when the IRS audits your corporation's plan and discovers that your corporation terminates its employees as soon as they become eligible, the IRS may disqualify the plan. The plan then becomes a taxable trust, and the employer really has problems. Besides, this kind of behavior just isn't ethical.

There's still another gimmick, though, for limiting contributions for low-paid employees in pension and profit-sharing plans while increasing the contribution made for you. This plan is called an integrated plan because it is integrated with Social Security. You can choose an integration level that is either the Social Security taxable wage base ($61,200 in 1995), a uniform dollar amount for all participants no greater than $10,000 (or 20 percent of the taxable wage base), or any amount between these two. A plan that used an integration level of $10,000 would let an employer contribute $250 (2.5 percent of $10,000) for each employee plus 5 percent of the employer's compensation over $10,000 for himself or herself.

Another plan lets your corporation contribute as much as

$30,000 a year to your pension-fund account, but as little as $450 for some of your employees. Despite their name and some similarities to defined-benefit plans, target-benefit plans are de-fined-*contribution* plans that are weighted in favor of older participants with long past and future service (i.e., owner-employees). The crucial difference between a target-benefit plan and other defined-contribution plans is that older participants with longer service receive a *higher percentage of pension-fund contributions* than their younger employees.

Dr. Successful is 55 years old and pays herself a salary of $120,000. She has three employees: Nurse Houlihan, age 38, earning $25,000; Receptionist Pierce, age 30, earning $18,000; and Technician O'Reilly, age 25, earning $15,000. Under both a 25 percent money-purchase plan and a target-benefit plan, Dr. Successful's corporation can make a $30,000 contribution to her pension account. But just look at the difference in her corporation's annual pension contributions—*over $12,000*—as a result of *legally reduced employee contributions:*

	Contribution Under 25% Money-Purchase Plan	Contribution Under Target-Benefit Plan
Dr. Successful	$30,000	$30,000
Nurse Houlihan	6,250	1,362
Receptionist Pierce	4,500	564
Technician O'Reilly	3,750	450*
Total	$44,500	$32,376
Amount Contributed for Employees	$14,500	$ 2,376
Percentage Contributed for Dr. Successful	67.4%	92.7%
Amount Saved by Using Target-Benefit Plan		$12,124

*A minimum 3 percent contribution is necessary for top-heavy pension plans.

What are the pros and cons of these two plans? You can set up the integrated plan yourself—it's straight arithmetic—and you can invest the contributions in a choice of investment vehicles. The target-benefit plan must be set up and maintained by actuaries because contributions are based on age. Target-benefit plans will let you contribute more money to your own account, but will cost more to administer. (This is a tax-deductible expense for your corporation, but it's still an expense.) And the assets of a target-benefit plan may not grow as rapidly as the assets of an integrated plan.

In general, if you are more than 15 years older than your employees, consider a target-benefit plan. If the age discrepancy is not as great, it may make more sense to choose an integrated plan.

Both these plans are likely to create top-heavy problems, as are all defined-contribution plans with one or more highly compensated executives and one or two lesser-paid employees.

Closing thought: Consult a lawyer, accountant, or pension professional before you decide how to cover (or not to cover) your employees. Good employees should be rewarded somehow; you *do* want them to stay, don't you?

10

"FREE" INSURANCE

As a key employee of your corporation, you can get "free" life insurance and disability insurance. Workers' compensation, a third form of insurance, is available *only* to employees; sole proprietors are ineligible. By "free" insurance, I mean that the insurance premiums are fully deductible by the corporation and reduce its pretax income, while at the same time they are not treated by the IRS as income to the insured. This "free" insurance may be worth $500 a year.

The "free" life insurance—sometimes called §79 insurance—is limited to one-year renewable term policies of up to $50,000 face value as group insurance in groups of ten people or more. However, smaller groups—including a "group" of one—can qualify for similar renewable term policies that get similar tax treatment from the IRS. It is possible to discriminate on an employee's class basis in choosing the face value for these policies; a common choice would be for officer/employees to have $50,000 policies and for other employees to have $10,000 policies.

If additional life-insurance coverage above $50,000 is desired, the IRS insists that the employee pay taxes on what is called "imputed income." This is a figure per $1,000 of coverage that is based solely on the age of the employee; it is not a percentage of the annual premium. The following table shows annual premiums and imputed income for an additional $50,000 policy as of March 1, 1995. I have indicated comparable 1991 premiums

129

in parentheses simply to demonstrate how remarkably premiums have risen in the past three years.

Age	Approximate Annual Premium for Nonsmokers Per Additional $50,000*	(Comparable 1991 Annual Premium)	Annual Imputed Income Per $50,000
30–34	$ 168	($72)	$ 140
35–39	216	(83)	185
40–44	312	(106)	260
45–49	450	(147)	378
50–54	690	(205)	563
55–59	1,080	(302)	839
60–64	1,572	(422)	1,275

*For dividend-paying insurance company. (Dividends are not guaranteed.) Companies that do not pay dividends may charge somewhat lower premiums.

Sources: For 1991 and 1995 premiums, Leonard Stern, Leonard Stern & Co., Inc. and The Guardian Insurance Co. For imputed income, IRS P S.58 rates.

Since, for all ages, the imputed income is less than the premium for the additional insurance, it pays for the corporation to pay for the additional insurance and for the shareholder/employee to accept the imputed income.

If the imputed income is ever *greater* than the premium for the additional insurance, shareholder/employees should pay for the additional insurance themselves.

But as important as life insurance is, many people worry far more about disability. There are many people who don't need life insurance; they have no family to protect. However, they all need disability insurance: some form of income protection to provide for them if they are unable to work because of illness or injury.

> **If your corporation pays your disability insurance premiums, which are tax-deductible, the benefits the insurance company pays you are subject to income tax. If you pay the premiums, the benefits are tax-free. As a corporate perk, your company can give you the money for the insurance premiums.**

At most ages, temporary or permanent disability is more likely than death for most entrepreneurs and professionals. For example, consider Jay, a 35-year-old commodities trader whose bad luck will keep him out of the silver pit at the New York Metals Exchange for at least a year because he isn't able to stand for long periods of time. Do you remember the movie *Trading Places*? Then you'll recall that commodities trading is almost like football: there's lots of blocking and tackling, broken field running, body checking. Jay can still work on the phone, at a desk, but will lose about half his income because he can't work in the silver pit. He is considered to be disabled: in disability-insurance language, he is unable to perform one or more of his normal work functions. His $5,000 monthly disability policy will help cushion his loss of income.

Employment is rated according to occupational risk. Lawyers and architects usually receive the best ratings because they are the most desirable disability-insurance clients. (They are also the most likely to take out the highest-value policies.) Doctors used to receive top ratings, but have been lowered from Class 4 to Class 3 (Class 1 is the lowest rating) because of heavy malpractice losses. Many companies will not insure surgeons, anesthetists, or emergency-room doctors. Leonard Stern, an expert in the field of disability insurance, recommends getting coverage in your specific occupation or profession. For example, if you are a successful trial lawyer and develop chronic laryngitis, you could still earn a living preparing brilliant briefs. But your income would surely plummet compared to your days of pyrotechnical oratory. If you take out a policy as a trial lawyer, you can make up for some of this loss of income; if you take out a policy as a lawyer, you can't.

Specialist policies are being phased out. By the year 2000, insurance companies probably will no longer offer them.

It makes sense for most professionals and entrepreneurs to get coverage for 50 to 60 percent of their earned income. To reduce the cost of a policy, they can increase the number of days of their elimination period (the time before coverage begins) from 60 days to 90 or even 180 days. Another variable is the length of time over which disability benefits will be paid: 2 years, 5 years, to age 65. Most insurance companies no longer offer lifetime coverage. Jay's policy, for example, which provides benefits of $5,000 per month, provides coverage to age 65 and also covers him in case of accident. His waiting period is 180 days, and his premium costs $2,550 per year.

Some policies still offer an "inflation guard" feature, in which payments are pegged to an inflation index like the Consumer Price Index. However, it costs less and makes more sense to increase coverage periodically. Choose a policy that offers you the option to purchase additional insurance in future years.

Stern advises his clients to choose only noncancellable, guaranteed continuable policies with no change in the premium rate. He also warns that some companies will offer a lowball premium at the beginning in what is called a "step-rated" policy and will increase the premiums every 5 years, so that they may become unaffordable. "A good insurance agent knows the difference between a policy that increases its premiums only once and a policy that increases its premiums every five years," says Stern.

Disability insurance isn't an all-or-nothing proposition. Residual disability features will pay you if your illness or disability limits the number of hours you can work. For instance, if, as the result of a heart attack, you can work only 20 hours per week, you are entitled to 50 percent of your disability benefits. (However, a four-day week is considered full-time employment.)

OVERHEAD EXPENSE INSURANCE

Overhead expense insurance is often connected to disability insurance. It covers office rent, utilities, and employee salaries while you are disabled.

ERRORS & OMISSIONS INSURANCE

Some professionals need Errors & Omissions insurance, frequently abbreviated as E&O, which covers them for any unintentional errors and acts of omission. If an insurance broker fails to place coverage—or the right coverage—and his client sues him, the broker's E&O insurance will cover him. If an accountant misses a tax deadline, the IRS imposes a penalty on her client, and the client turns around and sues her accountant, the accountant's E&O insurance will protect her. The most common E&O policies are $1 million umbrella policies. Premiums cost a few hundred to several thousand dollars a year, depending on the client's record and his or her profession. A lawyer with a clean record might pay $2,500 a year for such a policy.

OFFICE GENERAL LIABILITY INSURANCE

Most entrepreneurs and professionals also get a business owner's policy, which provides comprehensive general liability and theft insurance in one inexpensive package because it bundles all coverages: fire, flood, vandalism, tornado, and more.

Comparison-shop for insurance. No one has a monopoly on
good ideas. However, because it looks bad to have several
different brokers going to the same companies, get the names
of the companies from the brokers before they contact them
to make sure there's no duplication.

It is difficult to set up hard-and-fast guidelines about insurance coverage—especially disability insurance coverage. There
are too many variables: riskiness of work, riskiness of life-style,
extent of medical insurance coverage, living expenses, escalat-
ing medical costs, etc. This is an area that really needs individual treatment and frequent examination and revision. However, as a general rule, it may make sense to arrange for
generous—if not maximum—coverage. What little extra the
corporation may pay for your being overinsured against possible disability is certainly worth the price in terms of peace of
mind. Besides, the premiums are paid out of pretax dollars, so
they're less expensive than they seem and may even pull your
corporation down from the 25 percent bracket into the 15 percent bracket.

11
MEDICAL
BENEFITS

First, the bad news. Prior to the Tax Reform Act of 1976, employees of corporations (but not individual proprietors) were able to take a sick-pay exclusion (and, in effect, receive tax-free income) when they were absent from work due to illness or injury. The Tax Reform Act has virtually put an end to these benefits for corporate employees, except in the case of permanent and total disability.

There's more bad news. Employees of S corporations are not entitled to the medical benefits in this chapter.* These perks are only for employees of C corporations.

Now, the good news. Employees of C corporations can still enjoy "free" medical insurance and payment of medical expenses and drugs for themselves and their families. They are "free" in that the corporation can write off the payments as a business expense, but they are not held by the IRS to be income to the individuals receiving them.

Although the IRS calls them "medical reimbursement plans," your corporation can actually pay your medical bills for you and your family directly, rather than reimbursing you for your medical expenses. While legally this plan can be informal and unwritten (especially if you are the sole employee and stockholder) and

*S corporations are entitled to deduct 100 percent of medical insurance premiums, but employees who own more than 2 percent of the stock must declare 70 percent (down from 75 percent in 1994) of those premiums as income and pay income, Social Security, and Medicare payroll taxes on the amount.

135

can consist of the understanding that the corporation will pay all medical bills, in actual practice, where the IRS is concerned, a formal written corporate resolution of the type shown later in this chapter carriers much more weight.

In a one-person corporation, that one officer/stockholder/ employee unquestionably provides significant services as an employee and can be covered, along with his or her family. In larger corporations, it has been held that medical reimbursement plans must benefit employees, rather than stockholders as such. The basis of the plan must be the employer-employee relationship, not the stockholder relationship. Of course, covered employees can also be stockholders, and, in fact, many closely held corporations limit participation in their medical reimbursement plans to officers who are also stockholders. If these officers contribute substantial services as employees, the medical reimbursement plan will resist challenge.

In a one-person reimbursement plan, the corporation can— and should—arrange to reimburse 100 percent of medical expenses because they're all yours. In a larger corporation, thought must be given to the total medical expenses among the plan's participants; it may be wise to set a limit on the amount of reimbursement per eligible employee. If your company has employees, your reimbursement is limited to 65 percent of the total reimbursement for all employees. It may also be advisable to set up a medical care reimbursement plan for stockholder/employees and to provide a more limited plan—or just Blue Cross/Blue Shield—for ordinary employees.

You may exclude the following employees from your corporate medical reimbursement plan:
- **Employees who have not completed 3 years of service**
- **Employees who have not attained age 25**
- **Part-time or seasonal employees**
- **Employees covered by a collective-bargaining agreement which includes accident and health benefits**

Following is a sample medical care reimbursement plan and minutes of a meeting of the board of directors approving the plan. As in other areas of corporate life, remember that your plan can be amended as situations change: as the corporation covers an increasing number of employees, it may be wise to lower the reimbursement limit per employee.

(NAME OF YOUR CORPORATION) MEDICAL REIMBURSEMENT PLAN

Article I   Benefits

The Corporation shall reimburse all eligible employees for expenses incurred by themselves and their dependents, as defined in IRC §152, as amended, for medical care, as defined in IRC §213(d), as amended, subject to the conditions and limitations as hereinafter set forth. It is the intention of the Corporation that the benefits payable to eligible employees hereunder shall be excluded from their gross income pursuant to IRC §105, as amended.

Article II   Eligibility

All corporate officers employed on a full-time basis at the date of inception of this Plan, including those who may be absent due to illness or injury on said date, are eligible employees under the Plan. A corporate officer shall be considered employed on a full-time basis if said officer customarily works at least seven months in each year and twenty hours in each week. Any person hereafter becoming an officer of the Corporation employed on a full-time basis shall be eligible under this Plan.

Article III   Limitations

(a) The Corporation shall reimburse any eligible employee (without limitation) (no more than $_____) in any fiscal year for medical care expenses.

(b) Reimbursement or payment provided under this Plan shall be made by the Corporation only in the event and to the extent that such reimbursement or payment is not provided under any insurance policy(ies), whether owned by the Corporation or the employee, or under any other health and accident or wage-continuation plan. In the event that there is such an insurance policy or plan in effect providing for reimbursement in whole or in part, then to the extent of the coverage under such policy or plan, the Corporation shall be relieved of any and all liability hereunder.

Article IV   Submission of Proof

Any eligible employee applying for reimbursement under this Plan shall submit to the Corporation, at least quarterly, all bills for medical care, including premium notices for accident or health insurance, for verification by the Corporation prior to payment. Failure to comply herewith may, at the discretion of the Corporation, terminate such eligible employee's right to said reimbursement.

Article V   Discontinuation

This Plan shall be subject to termination at any time by vote of the board of directors of the Corporation; provided, however, that medical care expenses incurred prior to such termination shall be reimbursed or paid in accordance with the terms of this Plan.

Article VI   Determination

The president shall determine all questions arising from the administration and interpretation of the Plan except where reimbursement is claimed by the president. In such case, determination shall be made by the board of directors.

MINUTES OF SPECIAL MEETING OF DIRECTORS
OF
(NAME OF YOUR CORPORATION)

A special meeting of the board of directors of (name of your corporation) was held on (date) at (time) at (address where meeting was held).

All of the directors being present, the meeting was called to order by the chairman. The chairman advised that the meeting was called to approve and adopt a medical care expense reimbursement plan. A copy of the plan was presented to those present and upon motion duly made, seconded, and unanimously carried, it was

RESOLVED, that the "Medical Care Reimbursement Plan" presented to the meeting is hereby approved and adopted, that a copy of the Plan shall be appended to these minutes, and that the proper officers of the corporation are hereby authorized to take whatever action is necessary to implement the Plan, and it is further

RESOLVED, that the signing of these minutes by the directors shall constitute full ratification thereof and waiver of notice of the meeting by the signatories.

There being no further business to come before the meeting, upon motion duly made, seconded, and unanimously carried, the meeting was adjourned.

_____
Secretary

_____   _____
Chairman   Director

_____   _____
Director   Director

The advantages of your corporation's paying all your medical bills are enormous. If you were to pay your medical bills yourself, as a sole proprietor (or if your corporation hadn't adopted the medical reimbursement plan), the totals would be reduced by

7.5 percent of your adjusted gross income, as shown in the example that follows. The dollar amount of these reductions can be quite sizable and in many cases can completely wipe out your medical deductions. Even the $150 you could always deduct in earlier years has been done away with.

However, a corporation is not subject to the 7.5 percent reductions; every penny of medical expense counts.

Let's look at some simple Schedule A returns. We'll assume that Entrepreneur's adjusted gross income is $20,000 and Worldly Wise's adjusted gross income is $40,000. We'll give them identical medical expenses:

Medicine and drugs	$1,500.00
Doctors, dentists, etc.	900.00
Other (eyeglasses)	300.00
Transportation to doctors	300.00
	$3,000.00

Entrepreneur's medical deductions have been slashed by 50 percent: from $3,000 to $1,500. If he is in the 15 percent tax bracket, his medical deductions are now worth only $225 in tax dollars. If his medical insurance cost $1,000, the adjustment would be worth only $38 in tax dollars. (It would rise to $45 in 1995.)

Poor Worldly Wise has fared even worse. His medical deductions have dwindled to zero. If his medical insurance cost $1,000, the adjustment would be worth only $76 in tax dollars. (It would rise to $84 in 1995.)

But your corporation is not subject to that 7.5 percent reduction. The total medical expenditures remain at $3,000, and consequently their value in tax dollars is much greater:

Corporate Income	Tax Bracket as Percentage	Dollar Value of $3,000 Deduction
$0–$50,000	15%	$ 450
$50,000–$75,000	25	750
$75,000–$100,000	34	1,020

Amazing, isn't it?

SCHEDULES A&B
(Form 1040)

Department of the Treasury
Internal Revenue Service   (O)

Schedule A—Itemized Deductions

(Schedule B is on back)

▶ Attach to Form 1040. ▶ See Instructions for Schedules A and B (Form 1040).

OMB No. 1545-0074

19**94**

Attachment
Sequence No. **07**

Name(s) shown on Form 1040

ENTREPRENEUR

Your social security number

000 : 00 : 0000

Medical and Dental Expenses		Caution: *Do not include expenses reimbursed or paid by others.*				
	1	Medical and dental expenses (see page A-1)	1	3,000 —		
	2	Enter amount from Form 1040, line 32. ⌊ 2 ⌋ 20,000 —				
	3	Multiply line 2 above by 7.5% (.075)	3	1,500 —		
	4	Subtract line 3 from line 1. If line 3 is more than line 1, enter -0-			4	1,500 —

SCHEDULES A&B
(Form 1040)

Department of the Treasury
Internal Revenue Service   (O)

Schedule A—Itemized Deductions

(Schedule B is on back)

▶ Attach to Form 1040. ▶ See Instructions for Schedules A and B (Form 1040).

OMB No. 1545-0074

19**94**

Attachment
Sequence No. **07**

Name(s) shown on Form 1040

WORLDLY WISE

Your social security number

000 : 00 : 0000

Medical and Dental Expenses		Caution: *Do not include expenses reimbursed or paid by others.*				
	1	Medical and dental expenses (see page A-1)	1	3,000 —		
	2	Enter amount from Form 1040, line 32. ⌊ 2 ⌋ 40,000 —				
	3	Multiply line 2 above by 7.5% (.075)	3	3,000 —		
	4	Subtract line 3 from line 1. If line 3 is more than line 1, enter -0-			4	0

12

ALL ABOUT ERISA:

Tax-Sheltered Pension and Profit-Sharing Plans

ERISA—the Employees' Retirement Income Security Act—is one of the most complicated and confusing pieces of legislation ever to be enacted. Even lawyers and accountants have trouble interpreting it, so if you find this chapter difficult to understand, you're not alone. There is a lot of paperwork to file with the IRS and the Labor Department (in some cases, the Labor Department will be satisfied with the IRS form), but the results are worth it. Your corporation will be able to put away for you, its (sole) employee, up to 25 percent of your annual compensation, even including bonuses, if you like—up to $30,000. Furthermore, *you* can add up to 10 percent of your annual compensation to this retirement fund as what is called a Voluntary Contribution, as long as you don't exceed the 25 percent/$30,000 limitations. And if you choose a defined-benefit plan, you can contribute even more.

The simplest, cheapest, and easiest-to-adopt plans are the money-purchase and profit-sharing plans, both of which are classified as defined-contribution plans.

DEFINED-CONTRIBUTION PLANS

Defined-contribution plans are just what they sound like: a set contribution that is made every year. The contribution is defined as a percentage of the employee's annual compensation.

MONEY-PURCHASE PLAN

A money-purchase plan is a defined-contribution plan with a specific contribution formula. Unlike a profit-sharing plan, which is also a defined-contribution plan, contributions to a money-purchase plan must be made *each year, whether or not the employer has a profit.* The annual contribution is based on a stated percentage of the employee's compensation. The contribution can range from less than 1 percent to 25 percent of compensation if the money-purchase plan is used alone. The money-purchase plan can also be combined with a profit-sharing plan or a defined-benefit plan, as explained later in this chapter.

Example: Your corporation agrees to contribute 10 percent of each employee's compensation each year. The contributions and earnings thereon are accumulated until the employee retires or leaves the employer. The benefit that the employee will receive depends on the amount to his or her credit and whether or not the terminated participant has a vested interest. An employee is always fully vested at normal retirement age, and usually at death or retirement because of disability. The rate of vesting depends on provisions in the plan. (A more thorough discussion of vesting is found in Chapter 9, "Your Employees.")

If you, your spouse, and family members are expected to be your corporation's only employees, opt for 100 percent vesting immediately. If you plan on having outside employees, use the vesting-plan strategy shown on pp. 125–126.

PROFIT-SHARING PLAN

As its name implies, a profit-sharing plan is a defined-contribution plan in which contributions are made only in years in which your corporation shows a profit. Contributions can range from less than 1 percent to 15 percent of compensation. Furthermore, there are unwritten IRS assumptions (which come to light if your corporation's tax return is audited) that contributions not only be a percentage of the employee's compensation but also not exceed a certain percentage of the corporation's profit. Thus, even though your corporation has a profit for the year, contributions to an employee profit-sharing plan probably should not exceed 60 percent of corporate profits. After all, the IRS doesn't want 80 or 90 percent of your corporation's profits being eaten up by retirement-plan contributions; it wants some profits left over so your corporation can pay income tax on them. Thus, in choosing a Trust Agreement and an Adoption Agreement (sample shown in Appendix C), to be discussed later in this chapter, your corporation should construct limits on profit-sharing contributions first on the basis of its profits and second on the basis of the desired contribution as a percentage of compensation.

Example: Your corporate Adoption Agreement could say: "So long as retirement-plan contributions are less than 60 percent of net profits, contributions to employee profit-sharing plans shall be made on the basis of 15 percent of compensation. If retirement-plan contributions are in excess of 60 percent of net profits, contributions to employee profit-sharing plans shall be reduced to 10 percent of compensation," or words to that effect. The simplest wording, with the greatest flexibility, is: "The employer shall contribute such amount to the profit-sharing plan as annually determined by its board of directors."

If your corporation provides both a money-purchase plan and a profit-sharing plan, the maximum annual additions to an individual account cannot exceed the lesser of 25 percent of compensation or $30,000. Since the profit-sharing contribution maximum is 15 percent, most employers choose a combination of a 15 percent (remember: this is a flexible maximum, meaning 0 to 15 percent) profit-sharing plan and a 10 percent money-purchase plan.

If you are thinking of choosing defined-contribution plans, it pays to investigate the pros and cons of money-purchase and profit-sharing plans. If you choose the money-purchase plan for a maximum contribution of 25 percent, your corporation doesn't have to show a profit in order to be entitled to make that 25 percent contribution. In the first few years of a new corporation's existence, this may be an important advantage, since under a money-purchase plan it could make contributions that it could not make if it were bound by profit-sharing-plan regulations. The corporation would have to borrow the money to make the initial contributions, but both it and the employee would have the benefit of those contributions.

On the other hand, the set-percentage contribution (not a set amount because raises in employee salaries automatically increase the contributions) feature of the money-purchase plan is also a liability: as long as it remains in effect, your corporation is locked into a fixed liability. It must make contributions every year. There are no options under the money-purchase plan, and this plan's lack of flexibility can be quite detrimental to many corporations when you realize that a fixed liability of what may run into thousands of dollars a year for many years has been created.

Profit-sharing plans offer the flexibility of determining contributions that money-purchase plans lack, but are limited to a maximum of 15 percent, compared to the money-purchase plan's maximum of 25 percent. Many corporate employers try to optimize the benefits of both plans by adopting profit-sharing plans that permit them to contribute 15 percent and 10 percent money-purchase plans for the total of 25 percent. In this way they can effectively choose contributions from a mandatory 10 percent to the full permitted 25 percent each year. And, of course, many corporations choose only the 15 percent profit-sharing plan option, rather than the combined 25 percent.

Generally speaking, the 25 percent money-purchase plan can be compared to the forced-saving element of Christmas Club bank accounts; the combined 10 percent money-purchase plan and 15 percent profit-sharing plan can be compared to an ordinary savings account, where the amount of money saved depends entirely on the saver, with no element of coercion or penalty for not saving. If you feel that you are psychologically oriented to saving by yourself, the combined 10 percent money-purchase plan and 15 percent profit-sharing plan will offer you greater flexibility. If, however, you need a spur to put away retirement funds every year, the 25 percent money-purchase plan is probably better for you; otherwise, you might find that your corporation is putting away only the mandatory 10 percent in the money-purchase plan.

	1995	*1996*	*1997*
Estimated compensation:			
Mine	$ _____	$ _____	$ _____
Other employees	_____	_____	_____
Total	$ _____	$ _____	$ _____
X money-purchase percentage			
(less than 1 to 25 percent if used alone)	X _____ %	X _____ %	X _____ %
	$ _____	$ _____	$ _____
X profit-sharing percentage			
(0 to 15 percent; total money-purchase and profit-sharing contributions cannot exceed 25 percent of compensation or $30,000)	X _____ %	X _____ %	X _____ %
	$ _____	$ _____	$ _____
Estimated defined-contribution payment	$ _____	$ _____	$ _____

These numbers may help you decide whether you and your new corporation will be more comfortable with a flat 25 percent money-purchase percentage, a 10 percent money-purchase percentage plus a 0 to 15 percent profit-sharing contribution, or another form of defined contribution.

Adopting a money-purchase or profit-sharing plan—especially for one-person or husband-and-wife corporations—has become easier in past years. That is the reason I have deleted the

Model Profit-Sharing Plan and Trust Agreement present in earlier editions of *Inc. Yourself.* The simplest method is to open an account with a brokerage house, mutual fund, or bank which has a prototype plan document and trust agreement that already has been approved by the IRS and to adopt that plan, which allows your corporation a number of options. If your corporation has other employees, consider using a bank or institution as trustee to limit your fiduciary liability. Since the prototype plan is automatically amended and updated whenever the laws change, your pension plan is always in compliance with the law. This automatic updating saves your corporation the necessity of hiring an attorney to redraft your pension plan, a savings of hundreds of dollars.

The cost for this administrative service is surprisingly reasonable: anywhere from $0 for the first and sometimes subsequent years to about $100 a year if your corporate pension plan covers a number of employees.

You do not need to retain an attorney to review the model plan as long as you know that it already has been given IRS approval. You just have to adopt the plan, review the adoption agreement, and keep a copy of the adoption agreement in your files.

Furthermore, once you make one investment-contribution with the institution whose plan you have adopted, you may invest with any other institution—for example, you may make a core purchase from a no-load mutual fund, then buy individual stocks or securities from a brokerage house or bank. In this case, you will have to keep good records.

Solely for your information, the Model Profit-Sharing Plan sets the rules and regulations that bind your corporation; the Trust Agreement goes further in discussing the areas your corporation is empowered to invest in and the means by which investments will be made and funds administered; the Adoption

Agreement, while usually used by mutual funds, can be used effectively by your corporation to nail down exactly which employees are covered, how contributions are calculated, how vesting is accomplished, and many other important details.

INTEGRATED DEFINED-CONTRIBUTION PLAN

There is one refinement on the defined-contribution plan that was discussed in Chapter 9, "Your Employees": the defined-contribution plan that is integrated with Social Security contributions and is thus called the integrated defined-contribution plan.

If you have a one-owner or family employee corporation, do not choose this plan. There are more generous defined-contribution plans you can adopt.

ESOPS

In the late 1970s and early 1980s, when the first editions of *Inc. Yourself* were published, ESOPs (Employee Stock Ownership Plans) were far more popular than they are now. Although this form of profit-sharing plan, created by California attorney Louis Kelso, was used most frequently by large corporations whose stock is traded publicly and therefore has actual determined value, back then many major accounting firms recommended ESOPs for one-person general business and professional corporations.

These tax professionals emphasized the beauty of the ESOP: that your corporation would generate tax deductions at the corporate level *without its having to contribute any money to the plan,* so-called "cashless deductions." But then, obviously, an ESOP would not provide any *direct* retirement benefits. Those would be funded by all the cumulative tax savings of having the cashless deduction.

But eventually most people realized that ESOPs simply created another layer of work and expense and generated problems in valuing the stock of small nonpublic corporations.

As a result, ESOPs make sense now primarily when your company is mature, when you are planning to retire, and when you wish to sell your corporation to your employees.

401(K) PLANS

> **If you are a one-person corporation, a 401(k) plan is not a good choice. You can defer more of your compensation with a deferred-compensation agreement.**

Most savvy employees want a 401(k) plan. They know that it provides immediate savings on federal income taxes and often on state and city income taxes.

A 401(k) plan, also known as a "cash or deferred arrangement" (CODA), is a nonforfeitable, immediately vesting deferred-compensation plan set up as a qualified profit-sharing or stock-bonus plan. Under the 401(k) plan, participating employees elect to defer both the receipt and *taxation* of a portion of their compensation by having their employer pay it into a trust set up under the plan. The corporation can also match the employees' contributions.

These elective deferrals are subject to limitations. The maximum amount an employee can contribute to the plan in a tax year is increased yearly by a cost-of-living adjustment. (The maximum contribution for 1995 is $9,240, unchanged from 1994.) Be aware that this amount is included in the $30,000 defined-contribution limitations; if you choose to contribute $9,240 to a 401(k) plan, your corporation will be limited to a maximum defined contribution of $20,760.

Distributions from a 401(k) plan are generally prohibited until age 59½, although hardship withdrawals may be permitted in specified situations. Loans from the plan are permitted.

Antidiscrimination rules regarding participation by high-compensation employees compared to low-compensation employees are stringent, but if your corporation cannot meet the antidiscrimination requirements, it may make additional matching contributions to bring your company's 401(k) plan into compliance.

Administration of a 401(k) plan can be complicated. If your corporation has fewer than 25 employees, consider the Salary Reduction SEP (Simplified Employee Pension Plan), which eliminates most administrative and recordkeeping requirements of a 401(k) plan.

A 401(k) plan has a number of contribution limitations, depending on the number of high-compensation versus low-compensation employees in the plan. Assuming that the limitations have not been violated, here's an example of how a 401(k) plan works. You plan to pay yourself a salary of $37,000 this year but would like to defer $7,000. This deferral is permitted because it is less than 25 percent of your compensation *after deferral* ($37,000 − $7,000 = $30,000 × 25% = $7,500).

While your corporation is permitted to deduct $7,000 from your salary, it can deduct only $2,250 for your pension-fund contribution because your $7,000 401(k) contribution is counted as part of the $9,250 25 percent contribution your corporation could make. You will be paid a salary of $30,000 and will pay federal and local income taxes on that amount. (You do have to pay Social Security tax on the entire $37,000.) If you are a single New York City taxpayer, your deferral of $7,000 would save you a total of almost *$3,000* in federal, state, and city income taxes in just one year.

Essentially, it's a trade-off. Without the 401(k) plan, you'd receive and pay income taxes on a salary of $37,000. However, your corporation would be able to take a deduction of $37,000 for your salary and $9,250 for your defined-contribution pension fund, for a total of $46,250. With the 401(k) plan, you'd receive and pay income taxes on a salary of $30,000, but your corporation would be permitted to take a deduction of only $39,250: $37,000 for your salary and $2,250 for your pension plan. Based on individual and corporate state and city income taxes, a 401(k) plan may be more or less attractive to you in terms of the tax savings it offers. Play with some spread sheets, then consult your tax adviser to determine whether a 401(k) plan would be profitable for you.

DEFINED-BENEFIT PLANS

The benefits in these plans are usually stated as an annual amount. The amount could be (a) a percentage of compensation, (b) a fixed dollar amount, (c) a dollar amount per month times the number of years of service, or (d) an annual percentage of compensation multiplied by years of service.

When the benefit is a percentage of compensation, compensation is usually defined as the average of the highest 3 or 5 *consecutive* years of compensation multiplied by years of service.

Examples of types of defined-benefit plans:

• Percentage of compensation. If the highest average compensation during years of participation is $50,000, the annual benefit at normal retirement age (normally age 65) would be $15,000 per year if the percentage was 30 percent.

• Fixed dollar amount. $1,000 per month.

• Dollar amount per month times number of years of service. If the monthly figure is $10 per year of service, someone with 20 years of service would receive $200 per month; someone with 10 years of service would receive $100 per month.

• Annual percentage of compensation times years of service. If the plan provides 1 percent of compensation each year times years of service, for a participant who worked for 25 years at an average compensation of $50,000, his benefit would be 25 percent (1 percent × 25) of $50,000, for an annual benefit of $12,500.

The benefit in a defined-benefit plan is limited to the lesser of $120,000 in 1995 ($118,800 in 1994), increased annually by a cost-of-living adjustment, or 100 percent of compensation based on a straight-life annuity.* This limit is decreased for a benefit that is payable to an individual with less than 10 years of participation at normal retirement age. A minimum benefit of $10,000 can be provided; it, too, is reduced for less than 10 years of participation.

An employer can provide both a defined-benefit plan and a defined-contribution plan covering the same employees. In addition to the statutory limits of each plan, the prior combined limit of 1.4 (140 percent) has been reduced by the Tax Equity and Fiscal Responsibility Act (TEFRA) to 1.0 (100 percent). However, the mechanical application of this reduction is tricky, and under certain circumstances, the effective rate may range up to 1.25 (125 percent). If you are interested in a defined-benefit plan, get more information from your accountant or tax lawyer.

Unlike the defined-contribution plans, where determining the contribution is as simple as calculating a percentage, the defined-benefit plans require the work of an actuary, since they are based on such individual factors as the participants' ages, the number of years to work before normal retirement age, and the retirement benefits desired. If your corporation chooses a defined-benefit plan through a bank or insurance company—usually in the form of an annuity—these institutions will prepare all the actuarial work and all the filing with the IRS. They usually have a master plan that has already been approved by the IRS and that your corporation can adopt simply by your signing your name as president of the corporation.

---

*Cost-of-living adjustments are rising more slowly, and will rise even more slowly in the future because the method for calculating them has changed. Compare these increases to 1991–92, when the benefit rose from $108,963 to $112,221.

(Incidentally, in all these plans, if you are a one-person corporation, you can be plan administrator, trustee, and fiduciary. You needn't have any other person acting in any capacity in supervising the plan.)

HOW AND WHAT TO INVEST IN

While most corporations wait until the end of the year or the following April to make contributions to their retirement funds, it's often better to make periodic contributions during the year to take advantage of more months of tax-preferred accumulation.

If you are a one-person or husband-and-wife corporation, your universe of investment choices is nearly boundless. Although the Tax Equity and Fiscal Responsibility Act has removed antiques, works of art, gemstones, jewelry, rare books, stamps, and coins from the list of permitted investments, your corporation can invest in stocks, bonds, mutual funds, and real estate—in fact, any investment that "a prudent man might reasonably make." Legally, this concept, which is called the prudent-man rule, governs most investments that are made on behalf of other people or institutions.

If your corporation includes outsiders, it would be wisest to stick to securities—stocks, bonds, and mutual funds. When retirement or other benefits have to be paid, it's much easier to sell shares of stock, bonds, or mutual funds than it is to figure out who owns what part of the real estate and to sell it quickly but profitably; or to try to divide a shopping center or to sell it, pay out the benefits, and reinvest the remainder in another shopping center.

Regardless of what investment vehicles are purchased, make sure that they are registered in the name of the corporation's retirement funds, as follows:

John Smith & Co., Inc. Retirement Fund—Profit-Sharing Plan

Jane Smith & Co., Inc. Retirement Fund—Money-Purchase
   Plan
Smith & Associates, Inc. Retirement Fund—Defined-Benefits
   Plan

If stocks and bonds are purchased, your corporation will
probably have to furnish the brokerage house where it has an
account with corporate resolutions appointing the brokerage
house as its broker and with copies of whichever retirement
plans are being used.

If a mutual fund is chosen, your corporation will have to
furnish it with whatever documents it requires: usually copies of
the retirement plan being used (usually its own plan approved by
the IRS), a Trust Agreement, and an Adoption Agreement, a
sample of which is shown in Appendix C.

Do not feel that your corporation must stick to only one type
of investment. If your Trust Agreement permits, your corporation can invest in a combination of stocks, bonds, mutual funds,
and real estate, choosing according to market conditions—or
according to whim, for that matter.

WHAT IF THE RETIREMENT PLANS HAVE PROFITS OR LOSSES?

In a defined-contribution plan, the gains and losses are divided
among all the participants, based on the account balance of each
participant as a ratio to the total of all participants' balances.
Simply put, profits and losses are prorated according to the size
of each participant's account.

In a defined-benefit plan, the situation is a little more complicated. As explained earlier, your corporation's annual contribution is based on actuarial calculations and includes an assumption that the fund will earn a stated percentage each year. If the
fund does not earn the stated percentage, your corporation's
contribution will be greater the following year to bring it up to
the required balance. Conversely, if the fund earns more than the

stated percentage, your corporation's next annual contribution will be lower. This will assure that when an employee is ready to retire, there is enough in the fund to provide his or her benefits. To ensure that your corporation will make its annual contribution, ERISA provides an excise tax penalty of 5 percent each year if the minimum funding standard is not met.

Before choosing any ERISA plan, discuss all the options with your lawyer and your accountant. These plans are very tricky, and an entire book could easily be written about any of the plans. This chapter is merely an overview. Get more information before you decide. But remember: if you decide to change your plan, you can. You don't have to be saddled with a bad choice. All you have to do is choose and adopt another retirement plan.

13

BUT I ALREADY HAVE A KEOGH PLAN!

If you have a Keogh plan at the time that you incorporate, you have three major choices: you can roll it over to an ERISA qualified retirement plan at the same institution (bank, insurance company, mutual fund); you can discontinue it and invest your ERISA funds elsewhere, in which case the Keogh plan is frozen until you retire, when you will collect from both the Keogh plan and your corporate retirement fund; or, under certain circumstances, you can transfer it to another institution.

If you choose the first option—a transfer to an ERISA account at the same institution—your paperwork will be minimal. Just write to the bank, insurance company, or mutual fund, notifying them of your incorporation and your desire to continue the investment program, but using the more generous contribution allowances permitted to corporations. Give the institution your new Employer Identification Number. You will be sent some forms to fill out to effect the transfer, and you will be told what to do. Most institutions have a prototype plan that your corporation can adopt as its pension plan.

If you choose the second option—freezing the Keogh and investing your ERISA funds elsewhere—just keep on collecting and filing the material you are sent by the Keogh plan institution every year. You will need it to calculate your tax liability on your pension when you retire. You would set up your corporate pension and profit-sharing plans as shown in Chapter 12, "All

156

About ERISA," just as though you had never had a Keogh plan.

The last option—merging your Keogh plan into your new corporate pension fund—is the most complicated, but by no means impossible. The Internal Revenue Code permits you to roll over an existing Keogh plan to a corporate pension and profit-sharing plan.

> **If you have chosen a defined-benefit plan and have enough money to fund it, you will get bigger tax deductions and retire with more money if you freeze your old Keogh plan and start from zero with your new corporate defined-benefit plan, rather than rolling over your Keogh plan.**

If you are transferring from one mutual fund to another, there are a number of steps to take involving the old Keogh plan mutual fund and the new ERISA mutual fund. First, you will want to get credit for your final contribution to the Keogh plan in your last year as sole proprietor. Accordingly, when you file your income tax return, you would send your Keogh contribution to the custodian bank and deduct the contribution on IRS Form 5500-K.*

Then, at some point during your first corporate year, but as soon as possible, you would apply to the new mutual fund you had chosen, either directly or through its custodian bank, and file the necessary forms to set up an ERISA plan with the fund. You would probably send a token check of $100 or $500 just to start the plan; the balance, of course, would be contributed in April of the following year or whenever the corporation's tax returns were filed. Having established an ERISA plan with a new mutual fund, you could then write to the Keogh custodian bank and the ERISA custodian bank to effect the transfer, using the following letters or similar wording:

*You do not have to file a 5500-K if your retirement-fund assets are worth less than $100,000.

ABC Bank as Custodian for
   DEF Mutual Fund
Address

To whom it may concern:
   Please transfer the funds in my DEF mutual fund Keogh plan account *directly* to GHI Bank as custodian for my ERISA account with the JKL mutual fund. My ERISA account number is _____ .

                                    Very truly yours,

cc: GHI Bank as Custodian
   for JKL Mutual Fund

GHI Bank as Custodian for
   JKL Mutual Fund
Address
To whom it may concern:
   Please accept, as custodian of the JKL mutual fund, the funds being transferred from ABC Bank as custodian of my Keogh plan account with the DEF mutual fund and use the funds to immediately purchase shares of the JKL mutual fund for my ERISA account number

_____ .

                                    Very truly yours,

cc: ABC Bank as Custodian
   for DEF Mutual Fund

In this way, when your Keogh custodian bank liquidates your mutual fund, rather than sending you a check for the proceeds that you would then send to the ERISA custodian bank to purchase new shares for your ERISA account, it sends a check directly to your new custodian bank.

These details may sound very picky, but they're extremely important. At all costs, you must avoid what the IRS calls "constructive use" of the funds, which would invalidate your Keogh plan and subject you to taxes and penalties. In fact, if you should receive the liquidating check from the Keogh custodian bank by mistake, *do not endorse it.* This would be constructive use. Don't even think of endorsing it and sending the new ERISA custodian bank your own corporate check. The safest procedure is to return the check to the Keogh custodian bank with another letter explaining what happened and what you want the bank to do.

Let's take a slightly more complicated case: transferring your Keogh plan funds to a brokerage house so that you can buy your own securities for your corporate retirement fund. First, of course, you would need a trust agreement that had been approved by the IRS; one designed to permit all prudent-man investments (such as stocks, bonds, mutual funds, or real estate) might be suitable. Most brokerage firms have a prototype plan that you can adopt.

With the IRS approval, you would open a brokerage account for your corporate retirement fund; this would be a completely separate account from your corporate account, if any. Then you would write to the Keogh custodian bank and to your brokerage house to effect the transfer of your Keogh funds, using the following letters or similar wording:

ABC Bank as Custodian for
  DEF Mutual Fund
Address

To whom it may concern:
    Please transfer the funds in my DEF mutual fund Keogh plan account *directly* to GHI brokerage house to be deposited to the (name of your corporation) Retirement Fund. The account number is_____ .

                          Very truly yours,

cc: GHI Brokerage House

GHI Brokerage House
Address

To whom it may concern:

Please accept the funds being transferred from ABC Bank as custodian of my Keogh plan account and deposit them in the (name of your corporation) Retirement Fund. The account number is _____ .

Very truly yours,

cc: ABC Bank as Custodian
for DEF Mutual Fund

Again, as in the previous case, under no circumstances should the liquidating check from the Keogh custodian bank come to you; if it should, return it. It's easier than trying to explain to the IRS that even though the check was sent to you, you didn't really have constructive use of the funds.

14

INVESTING YOUR CORPORATE SURPLUS

Let's hope you're running a successful business or you're a successful professional. After contributing to corporate pension and profit-sharing plans and paying taxes, your corporation still has a surplus. The great stock-market meltdown of October 1987 and the aftershock of October 1989 have receded in investors' minds, thanks to the runaway Dow Jones Industrial Average of early 1995, which tore through the terra incognita of 3900, 4000, 4100, 4200, 4300, 4400, 4500, 4600, and 4700. You, too, should be able to invest your corporate surplus profitably. Investing in common and preferred stocks, whose dividends paid to your corporation are 70 percent tax-free,* is a major benefit of forming a general business (C) corporation.

For the most part, investing your corporate surplus (after-tax profits) depends on the following variables:

1. How aggressive an investor you are
2. The length of time before your retirement
3. Whether these funds are only a part of your total investment portfolio
4. How much money you can invest each year

*The dividends—but not the capital gains—paid to your corporation by mutual funds are also 70 percent tax-free. In fact, there are some mutual funds geared specifically to the corporate market; their investment goals are high dividends, not capital gains.

The first two variables are closely interrelated; if you are 30 years old and plan to retire in 35 years, you can afford to assume more risks than if you are 50 and plan to retire in 10 years.

But this is the classic textbook approach to investment planning. In real life there are supercautious 23-year-olds and crap-shooting 53-year-olds. While bearing the classic investment strategies in mind, always take only the amount of risk you feel comfortable with.

> **If you have a personal portfolio as well as funds to invest to create a corporate portfolio, you should concentrate on using your corporate funds to generate tax-free dividend income that will compound year after year. Invest your corporate pension funds in growth stocks and growth-oriented mutual funds to maximize long-term growth and capital gains, and invest your personal funds in any combination of growth and income securities that seems appropriate to your investment goals and market conditions. *But invest your corporate funds solely for tax-free income.* Investment professionals call this strategy "asset allocation"; it's just taking advantage of the tax laws to maximize long-term growth and income and minimize your taxes.**

Perhaps the most important variable—in terms of its limiting your choices—is the last one: how much money you can invest every year. This amount will determine what kind of professional investment management help you can expect. After all, if you can invest $10,000 a year, your choices are much wider than if you can invest $1,000 a year.

Up until the time that your corporate portfolio reaches $25,000 to $50,000, it's virtually impossible to get any kind of professional management for your investments. About the best you can do is buy a mutual fund (preferably a no-load utility stock fund with a good track record); choose a good broker with excellent research capabilities; or subscribe to one or more investment services, do your own research, and have your orders executed by a discount broker so that you save on commissions.

> **As a hands-on entrepreneur, I recommend the last strategy. Your research will pay off not only in investing your corporate surplus, but also in investing your personal and pension funds.**

At $25,000 to $50,000, some banks will manage your portfolio on a pooled-trust basis, combining your portfolio with those of other investors with the same investment goals and creating, in effect, a mini-mutual fund. The fees for this service vary, but generally run about 1 to 2 percent per year—tax deductible, of course. When your portfolio reaches anywhere from $100,000 to $200,000, many banks will manage your portfolio as a separate entity.

When your corporation does get big enough for a bank to handle its investment, there is one major advantage—apart from professional investment advice—that a bank can offer. As an institution (as banks are known in the investment community), a bank has access to the negotiated commission market because its trading volume is so much greater than any individual's. These commissions can range from about 20 percent to about 50 percent of individual commissions, or a discount of from 50 percent to 80 percent. If your corporation invests or trades heavily, this may be an important consideration for you.

In order to get the best executions of orders for its clients, a bank will often use different brokers for different orders or will use what is called the "fourth market" (trading between the institutions themselves, as opposed to trading on the stock exchanges). This "shopping around" is aimed at getting both the best prices and the smallest commissions.

Banks do offer economies of size. The question you must answer for yourself is: are the bank's fees worth the savings in executions and commissions?

Without exception, all the professional investment analysts and money managers I interviewed emphasized the necessity of common stocks in a corporate portfolio. Not only are their dividends 70 percent tax-free at the corporate level, but also they are one of the most powerful hedges against long-term inflationary pressures. Even at the present low inflationary levels of economic recovery, the rate of inflation is still higher than the interest rate of AA-rated bonds, after taxes; and no one can predict long-term trends, except that inflation at one level or another is certain to be with us. Common stocks can help protect the investor against that inflation and erosion of his or her purchasing power. Over a period of years, common stocks have outperformed bonds and other money-market instruments (e.g., commercial paper) and preferred stocks. *And dividends on stocks owned by your corporation are 70 percent tax-free, whereas interest on bonds is fully taxed. For this reason, bonds really have no place in your corporate portfolio—although they may have, from time to time, a place in your personal portfolio or pension fund.*

Another advantage of common stocks over bonds is less obvious, but by no means less real. The stock market is far more liquid than the bond market: stocks are traded more frequently and in smaller quantities than bonds, so a buy order for 100 shares—or even less—is less likely to raise the price you pay, and a sell order for 100 shares or less is less likely to lower the price you receive. In contrast, the bond market deals with much greater numbers and dollar amounts: an "average" order is usually for 25 or 50 bonds ($25,000 or $50,000 face value). Orders from smaller investors for 1, 5, or 10 bonds are penalized at both ends: they pay more for the bonds when they buy them and receive less for the bonds when they sell them. Small orders tend to have a disproportionately large effect on bond prices, both up and down, but always to the disadvantage of the small investor.

Preferred stocks are a hybrid between bonds and common

stocks. Like bonds, preferred stocks pay their owners a fixed income. (In contrast, dividends on many common stocks are increased periodically.) Like bonds, most preferred stocks have a call date and call price, when the company can redeem the preferred stockholders' shares at a predetermined price. The call price becomes a ceiling past which the preferred stock price will not rise; no one would risk buying stock for $110 a share knowing it could be called away for $106. (In contrast, common stock prices can rise very substantially. Even the decided non-high-flier IBM more than doubled in 1994–95, rising from a low of 51 ⅜ to a high—so far—of 108 ⅝.)

Preferred stocks are also more like bonds than like common stocks in their limited liquidity and their lack of protection against inflation. All they do offer, like common stocks, is the valuable 70 percent dividend exclusion.

Stock-market sophisticates who are willing to trade off some tax-free income for growth may wish to consider a hybrid of the hybrid: the convertible preferred stock. This type of preferred stock can be converted into shares of common stock at a predetermined price, at the stockholder's option. (Sometimes this price—called the "conversion price"—rises slightly over time.) Convertible preferreds pay higher dividends and offer higher yields than their common stock and, since their price is tied to the price of the underlying common stock, their price has no ceiling, as straight preferreds' do. If the price of the common stock rises, so does the price of the convertible preferred, at approximately the same rate. But if the price of the common stock falls, the price of the convertible preferred does not fall as far because its dividend acts like a cushion: the convertible then behaves as if it were a straight preferred stock, and its price rises or falls primarily with changes in interest rates.

When the issuing company calls its convertible preferred, shareholders can sell their holdings in the open market, convert them into common stock, and either hold or sell the common shares. Because convertible preferreds are an arcane corner of the market, potential investors should either find a knowledgeable broker or take the time to learn about this area themselves.

(Value Line provides an excellent weekly service that deals with convertible bonds and preferred stocks.)

The stocks shown in the portfolio that follows are not to be construed as being recommendations; they are merely high-quality, high-yielding stocks suitable for corporate investment. The preferred stocks are at least BBB − -rated by Standard & Poor's Corporation; the common stocks are characterized by low P/E (price/earnings) ratio and good to high yield, combined with moderate growth.

REPRESENTATIVE CORPORATE PORTFOLIO

Standard & Poor's Rating	No. Shares	Preferred Stocks	Price 7/20/95	Dividend	Yield	Income
BBB+	400	Chase Manh. pfd. G	28⅜	$2.63	9.27%	$1,052
A−	300	Household Ind.	26½	2.38	8.98	· 714
BBB−	300	Salomon pfd. C	25	2.37	9.48	711
						$2,477
		Common Stocks				
A−	300	PP&L Resources*	19⅛	1.67	8.73	501
B+	100	Texas Utilities	33¾	3.08	9.23	308
						809
						$3,286

*Formerly Pennsylvania Power & Light.

The purpose of such a high-yield portfolio is the compounding of dividends, 70 percent of which are totally excluded from taxes, and 30 percent of which are taxed at 15 percent if net corporate income is less than $50,000, 25 percent if net corporate income is between $50,000 and $75,000, and 34 percent if net corporate income is between $75,000 and $100,000.

The following table shows the actual percentage that is taxed and the percentage of dividend income that your corporation retains:

Net Corporate Income	Tax Bracket	Percentage of Dividend Taxed	Effective Tax Rate	Percentage of Dividend Retained
Under $50,000	15%	30%	4.5%	95.5%
$50,000–$75,000	25	30	7.5	92.5
$75,000–$100,000	34	30	10.2	89.8

Even at the highest corporate tax brackets shown here, dividends received by your corporation are more than 89 percent tax-free!

To illustrate this point, let's assume the portfolio in the example I've just given. The annual income from the portfolio would be $3,286.

If the owner of the portfolio was a sole proprietor in the 31 percent bracket, he would have to pay $1,019 in taxes on his dividend income and could keep only $2,267.

Dividend income	$3,286
Tax rate	× .31
Tax	$1,019
Net dividend income	$2,267

However, if his corporation owned the portfolio, the taxes are *eleven times* lower if his corporation is in the 15 percent bracket and *more than six times lower* if his corporation is in the 25 percent bracket.

	Assuming 15 Percent Bracket Net Corp. Taxable Income Under $50M	Assuming 25 Percent Bracket Net Corp. Taxable Income $50M–$75M
Dividend Income	$ 3,286	$ 3,286
Less 70 percent exclusion	− 2,300	− 2,300
	$ 986	$ 986
Tax rate	× .15	× .25
Tax	$ 148	$ 247
Net dividend income	$ 3,138	$ 3,039

	Assuming *15 Percent Bracket* *Net Corp.* *Taxable Income* *Under $50M*	*Assuming* *25 Percent Bracket* *Net Corp.* *Taxable Income* *$50M–$75M*
Amount saved from individual tax	$ 871	$ 772
Percent saved from individual tax	85%*	76%*

*These percentages are especially impressive because they are compared with individual tax rates that have been reduced several times in the past ten years.

Furthermore, if we project this unchanged portfolio for five or ten years, it is easy to see how the more than $750 saved each year on the corporate stock portfolio alone can compound itself to more than $5,000 or $10,000. And if we go further and conceive of this portfolio as a unit, with an additional unit purchased each year, the savings are truly staggering.

The only thing we would have to worry about is that the portfolio income would not exceed 60 percent of total corporate income in any year, so that the corporation would not be construed by the IRS as a personal holding corporation, as discussed more fully in Chapter 1 and Chapter 8.

HOW AND WHEN YOUR CORPORATION DECLARES DIVIDENDS

So far we've talked about your corporation's *receiving* dividends from other corporations: dividends that are 70 percent tax-free. But what about your corporation's *paying* dividends to its stockholder(s)? In general, of course, you want to keep dividend income from common and preferred stocks in the corporation;

if you draw the dividends out for your own use, you will be taxed on them. Furthermore, they won't be able to accumulate at minimal tax rates.

You may be much better off taking the money as a raise in salary or as a special year-end bonus. The raise or bonus may enable your corporation to contribute more to your pension fund, and the amount of the raise or bonus will be taxed only once (to you) rather than twice (to your corporation and to you), as dividends are taxed.

Raise in salary	$_____
or	
Year-end bonus	$_____
Increase in pension-fund contribution	$_____
Decrease in corporate income tax(es)	$_____
Increase in personal income tax(es)	$_____

However, there are always times or special occasions that may warrant taking money out of the corporation, and this necessitates the corporation's declaring a dividend to the stockholders. A meeting of the board of directors of the corporation is called, and someone proposes that a dividend of X dollars per share be paid on a certain date to all stockholders who owned stock on a certain earlier date. The proposal is turned into a motion and voted on. When it is approved, as it is certain to be, it is recorded as Minutes of a Special Meeting of the Board of Directors and entered into the corporation's minute book. Then, on the payment date, the corporation gives or sends the dividend checks to its stockholders. Dividends do not have to be paid on a regular basis; it is thus wiser to declare each dividend as a special dividend.

TREATMENT OF CAPITAL GAINS

Up to now, I've emphasized dividends because dividend payments to corporations are 70 percent tax-free. Bond interest is taxed as though it were ordinary income: at 15 percent (to $50,000), 25 percent ($50,000–$75,000), or up to 34 percent ($75,000–$100,000), depending on your corporation's tax bracket. Capital gains on the sale of securities your corporation owns are taxed at the same rates as ordinary income as of mid–1995. However, in April 1995, the House passed legislation to restore favorable treatment for long-term capital gains, and the Senate is likely to pass similar legislation by the fall of 1995.

OTHER CORPORATE INVESTMENTS

Your corporation can make other investments besides stocks, bonds, mutual funds, and other securities. It can invest in real estate, antiques, art, gemstones or jewelry, or, in fact, anything of value that is tangible and not likely to depreciate in value. Your investment universe consists of anything and everything that would be selected by "a prudent man." (A company car would be a corporate possession, but would not be considered a prudent corporate investment because of its depreciability. A 1936 Rolls-Royce, however, would certainly qualify as an investment.)

If you are more comfortable with English furniture or Ming porcelain, nineteenth-century photographs or Old Master drawings, Lalique or Fabergé jewelry or just plain old diamonds or emeralds, set or unset, feel free to invest in them. Just make sure that you are paying for them with a corporate check and that they are insured in the name of the corporation. Antiques and art that are owned by the corporation must stay clearly on corporate territory: they may be displayed in your office, but not in your home. However, if your office is in your home, you do have more leeway about where to place them.

SUMMING UP

This chapter, like the rest of this book, has been written primarily for the one-person or husband-and-wife corporation. If you are part of a larger, nonfamily corporation, think carefully about investing in the more unusual corporate investments. They will be harder to liquidate, and this may generate problems. They will certainly be less divisible than stocks, bonds, or mutual fund shares, and they will surely be more difficult to value.

15

PUTTING IT ALL TOGETHER

It's often said that one picture is worth a thousand words. Let's look, then, at three pictures. Following are tax returns for three businesses at three different income levels, both as corporations and as sole proprietorships. To simplify matters, the individuals are assumed to be single and will take what amounts to the standard deduction, now included in the tax tables. Otherwise, at their income levels, they would lose most or all of their medical deduction.

First, there is George Gordon, a real estate broker whose earnings are $45,000 a year, with dividend income of $6,000 and medical expenses of $2,000. George prefers to retain as much corporate income as possible, so his corporation pays him a salary of $16,000 a year. His corporate return and his employee tax return, followed by his tax return as a sole proprietor, are shown on pages 175–183.

By accepting the low salary, George saves over 43 percent in taxes: $11,350 as a sole proprietor versus a total of $6,488; $3,798 in corporate taxes and $2,690 (including real cost of Social Security tax) in employee income taxes.

Geoffrey Fourmyle, a technical writer, has chosen a higher salary of $26,000, although his gross income is also $45,000 and his dividends are also $6,000. His medical expenses are $4,000. By taking the higher salary, however, he cuts his tax saving to 31 percent: $10,396 as a sole proprietor versus a total of $7,131; $2,176 in corporate taxes and $4,955 in employee income taxes. He is sheltering less of his income at the preferential corporate

rate; thus, his tax savings are smaller. See pages 184–192 for his tax returns.

Last, there is Tiffany Field, a successful designer who earned $100,000 last year and had dividend income of $10,000 and medical expenses of $6,000. By taking a salary of $40,000, she cuts her total tax bill from a maximum tax of $27,823 as a sole proprietor to $16,502, for a saving of $11,321 in just one year. If Tiffany took a higher salary, her corporate contribution would continue to rise; at $50,000, her corporation could contribute $12,500. However, she would be sheltering less income at low corporate rates. In this return, take special notice of the $10,000 dividend income. Tiffany's corporation was able to shelter $7,000 of it (see line 25(b) page 193), and was taxed on $3,000, for a tax liability of only $450. If Tiffany owned the stock herself, she would be taxed on the full $10,000, for a tax liability of approximately $3,100, nearly seven times greater than the corporate tax. For her tax returns, see pages 193–201.

Let's summarize the tax savings of incorporation shown on the sample returns this way:

Name	Corporate Income Taxes*	Employee Income Taxes	Employee SS Taxes	Total	Sole Proprietor Tax	Amount Saved	Percent Saved
Gordon	$3,798	$1,466	$1,224	$6,488	$11,350	$4,862	41%
Fourmyle	2,176	2,966	1,989	7,131	10,396	3,265	31
Field	6,942	6,500	3,060	16,502	27,823	11,321	41

*Includes real cost to corporation of Social Security tax.

In fact, the tax savings on dividend income are so enormous that they deserve their own tables:

AS INDIVIDUAL

Name	Dividends	Other Net Income	Total	Marginal Tax Bracket for Dividends	Tax on Dividends
Gordon	$6,000	$35,809	$41,809	28%	$1,680
Fourmyle	6,000	33,421	39,421	28	1,680
Field	10,000	74,800	84,800	31	3,100

AS CORPORATION

Name	Dividends	Less Exclusion	Net Dividends	Marginal Tax Bracket for Dividends	Tax on Dividends
Gordon	$6,000	$4,200	$1,800	15%	$225
Fourmyle	6,000	4,200	1,800	15	225
Field	10,000	7,000	3,000	15	450

SUMMARY

	Gordon & Fourmyle		Field	
	As Individual	As Corporation	As Individual	As Corporation
Dividends escaping tax	$ 0	$4,200	$ 0	$7,000
Dividends taxed	6,000	1,800	10,000	3,000
Tax rate	28%	15%	31%	15%
Tax on dividends	1,680	270	3,100	450
Amount saved		1,410		2,650
Percent saved		84%		85%

Just for fun, why don't you pull out last year's tax return and pencil your numbers in on one of the sample returns? If your figures show savings of several thousand dollars a year, it might be a good idea for you to incorporate.

Form **1120-A**	**U.S. Corporation Short-Form Income Tax Return**	OMB No. 1545-0890

Department of the Treasury
Internal Revenue Service

See separate instructions to make sure the corporation qualifies to file Form 1120-A.

For calendar year 1994 or tax year beginning ...., 1994, ending............., 19....   **1994**

	Use IRS label. Otherwise, please print or type.	Name GEORGE GORDON + Co., INC.	B Employer identification number 13:2000000

Check this box if the corp. is a personal service corp. (as defined in Temporary Regs. section 1.441-4T—see instructions) ▶ ☐

Number, street, and room or suite no. (If a P.O. box, see page 6 of instructions.) 350 FIFTH AVENUE

C Date incorporated 1/2/82

City or town, state, and ZIP code NEW YORK, NY 10118

D Total assets (see Specific Instructions) $ 94,581 —

Check applicable boxes: (1) ☐ Initial return   (2) ☐ Change of address
Check method of accounting: (1) ☑ Cash   (2) ☐ Accrual   (3) ☐ Other (specify) · · ▶

Income	1a Gross receipts or sales	b Less returns and allowances	c Balance ▶ 1c	45,000 —
	2 Cost of goods sold (see instructions)		2	
	3 Gross profit. Subtract line 2 from line 1c		3	
	4 Domestic corporation dividends subject to the 70% deduction		4	6,000 —
	5 Interest		5	
	6 Gross rents		6	
	7 Gross royalties		7	
	8 Capital gain net income (attach Schedule D (Form 1120))		8	
	9 Net gain or (loss) from Form 4797, Part II, line 20 (attach Form 4797)		9	
	10 Other income (see instructions)		10	
	11 **Total income.** Add lines 3 through 10 · · · · · · · · · · ▶		11	51,000 —
Deductions (limitations on deductions)	12 Compensation of officers (see instructions)		12	16,000 —
	13 Salaries and wages (less employment credits)		13	
	14 Repairs and maintenance		14	
	15 Bad debts		15	
	16 Rents		16	3,000 —
	17 Taxes and licenses SOC. SEC.		17	1,224 —
	18 Interest EMPLOYEE MEDICAL		18	2,000 —
	19 Charitable contributions (see instructions for 10% limitation)		19	
	20 Depreciation (attach Form 4562) 20 1,000 —			
	21 Less depreciation claimed elsewhere on return 21a 0		21b	1,000 —
	22 Other deductions (attach schedule) PENSION PLAN 4,000, PHONES + POSTAGE 1,191		22	5,191 —
	23 **Total deductions.** Add lines 12 through 22 · · · · · · · · · ▶		23	28,415 —
	24 Taxable income before net operating loss deduction and special deductions. Subtract line 23 from line 11		24	22,585 —
	25 **Less: a** Net operating loss deduction (see instructions) 25a 0			
	b Special deductions (see instructions). 70% DIVIDENDS 25b 4,200 —		25c	4,200 —
	26 **Taxable income.** Subtract line 25c from line 24		26	18,385 —
	27 **Total tax** (from page 2, Part I, line 7)		27	2,758 —
Tax and Payments	28 **Payments:**			
	a 1993 overpayment credited to 1994 28a			
	b 1994 estimated tax payments 28b 2,500 —			
	c Less 1994 refund applied for on Form 4466 28c ( ) Bal ▶ 28d		28d	
	e Tax deposited with Form 7004 28e		28e	
	f Credit from regulated investment companies (attach Form 2439) 28f		28f	
	g Credit for Federal tax on fuels (attach Form 4136). See instructions 28g		28g	
	h **Total payments.** Add lines 28d through 28g · · · · · · · ·		28h	2,500 —
	29 Estimated tax penalty (see instructions). Check if Form 2220 is attached · · · · · ▶ ☐		29	0
	30 **Tax due.** If line 28h is smaller than the total of lines 27 and 29, enter amount owed · · ·		30	258 —
	31 **Overpayment.** If line 28h is larger than the total of lines 27 and 29, enter amount overpaid · · ·		31	
	32 Enter amount of line 31 you want: **Credited to 1995 estimated tax** ▶	Refunded ▶	32	

Please Sign Here

Under penalties of perjury, I declare that I have examined this return, including accompanying schedules and statements, and to the best of my knowledge and belief, it is true, correct, and complete. Declaration of preparer (other than taxpayer) is based on all information of which preparer has any knowledge.

▶ _____ 3/15/95 ▶ PRESIDENT
Signature of officer   Date   Title

Paid Preparer's Use Only

Preparer's signature ▶	Date	Check if self-employed ▶ ☐	Preparer's social security number
Firm's name (or yours if self-employed) and address		E.I. No. ▶ ZIP code ▶	

For Paperwork Reduction Act Notice, see page 1 of the instructions.   Cat. No. 11456E   Form **1120-A** (1994)

Form 1120-A (1994)   Page

Part I   Tax Computation (See instructions.)

1 Income tax. If the corporation is a qualified personal service corporation (see page 14), check here ▶ ☐	1	2,758 —
2a General business credit. Check if from: ☐ Form 3800 ☐ Form 3468 ☐ Form 5884 ☐ Form 6478 ☐ Form 6765 ☐ Form 8586 ☐ Form 8830 ☐ Form 8826 ☐ Form 8835 ☐ Form 8844 ☐ Form 8845 ☐ Form 8846 ☐ Form 8847 2a		
b Credit for prior year minimum tax (attach Form 8827) 2b		
3 Total credits. Add lines 2a and 2b	3	0
4 Subtract line 3 from line 1	4	2,758 —
5 Recapture taxes. Check if from: ☐ Form 4255 ☐ Form 8611	5	0
6 Alternative minimum tax (attach Form 4626)	6	0
7 Total tax. Add lines 4 through 6. Enter here and on line 27, page 1	7	2,758 —

Part II   Other Information (See instructions.)

1 Refer to page 19 of the instructions and state the principal:
  a Business activity code no. ▶ 5520
  b Business activity ▶
  c Product or service ▶ REAL ESTATE BROKERAGE

2 Did any individual, partnership, estate, or trust at the end of the tax year own, directly or indirectly, 50% or more of the corporation's voting stock? (For rules of attribution, see section 267(c).) . . . . ☑ Yes ☐ No
GEORGE GORDON, 350 FIFTH AVENUE, NY NY 10118, SS 000-00-0000
If "Yes," attach a schedule showing name and identifying number.

3 Enter the amount of tax-exempt interest received or accrued during the tax year ▶ |$ 0 |

4 Enter amount of cash distributions and the book value of property (other than cash) distributions made in this tax year . . . . ▶ |$ 0 |

5a If an amount is entered on line 2, page 1, see the worksheet page 12 for amounts to enter below:
  (1) Purchases
  (2) Additional sec. 263A costs (see instructions—attach schedule) .
  (3) Other costs (attach schedule)
  b Do the rules of section 263A (for property produced or acquired f resale) apply to the corporation? . . . . . . ☐ Yes ☑ N

6 At any time during the 1994 calendar year, did the corporation hav an interest in or a signature or other authority over a financial accou in a foreign country (such as a bank account, securities account, other financial account)? If "Yes," the corporation may have to f Form TD F 90-22.1 . . . . ☐ Yes ☑ N
If "Yes," enter the name of the foreign country ▶

Part III   Balance Sheets

		(a) Beginning of tax year	(b) End of tax year
Assets	1 Cash	5,383 —	14,581 —
	2a Trade notes and accounts receivable		
	b Less allowance for bad debts	( ) (	) (
	3 Inventories		
	4 U.S. government obligations		
	5 Tax-exempt securities (see instructions)		
	6 Other current assets (attach schedule)		
	7 Loans to stockholders	4,000 —	0
	8 Mortgage and real estate loans		
	9a Depreciable, depletable, and intangible assets		
	b Less accumulated depreciation, depletion, and amortization	( ) (	) (
	10 Land (net of any amortization)		
	11 Other assets (attach schedule)	62,250 —	80,000 —
	12 Total assets	71,583 —	94,581 —
Liabilities and Stockholders' Equity	13 Accounts payable	8,250 —	8,000 —
	14 Other current liabilities (attach schedule)		
	15 Loans from stockholders		
	16 Mortgages, notes, bonds payable		
	17 Other liabilities (attach schedule)	3,333 —	6,754 —
	18 Capital stock (preferred and common stock)	10,000 —	10,000 —
	19 Paid-in or capital surplus		
	20 Retained earnings	50,000 —	69,827 —
	21 Less cost of treasury stock	( ) (	) (
	22 Total liabilities and stockholders' equity	71,583 —	94,581 —

Part IV   Reconciliation of Income (Loss) per Books With Income per Return (You are not required to complete Part IV if the total assets on line 12, column (b), Part III are less than $25,000.)

1 Net income (loss) per books	19,827 —	6 Income recorded on books this year not included on this return (itemize)		0
2 Federal income tax	2,758 —			
3 Excess of capital losses over capital gains	0	7 Deductions on this return not charged against book income this year (itemize)		0
4 Income subject to tax not recorded on books this year (itemize)	0			
5 Expenses recorded on books this year not deducted on this return (itemize)	0	8 Income (line 24, page 1). Enter the sum of lines 1 through 5 less the sum of lines 6 and 7		22,585 —

♻ Printed on recycled paper   ☆ U.S. GPO: 1994-375-292

Form **1040**

Department of the Treasury—Internal Revenue Service
U.S. Individual Income Tax Return (O) **1994**

IRS Use Only—Do not write or staple in this space.

For the year Jan. 1–Dec. 31, 1994, or other tax year beginning _____ , 1994, ending _____ , 19 _____ | OMB No. 1545-0074

Label
(See instructions on page 12.)

Use the IRS label. Otherwise, please print or type.

L A B E L   H E R E

Your first name and initial: GEORGE
Last name: GORDON
Your social security number: 000 00 0000

If a joint return, spouse's first name and initial / Last name
Spouse's social security number

Home address (number and street). If you have a P.O. box, see page 12.
350 FIFTH AVENUE
Apt. no. PH

City, town or post office, state, and ZIP code. If you have a foreign address, see page 12.
NEW YORK, NY 10118

For Privacy Act and Paperwork Reduction Act Notice, see page 4.

Presidential Election Campaign
(See page 12.)

Do you want $3 to go to this fund? . . . . | Yes | No ✓
If a joint return, does your spouse want $3 to go to this fund? . . . .

Note: Checking "Yes" will not change your tax or reduce your refund.

Filing Status
(See page 12.)

Check only one box.

1 ✓ Single
2 ☐ Married filing joint return (even if only one had income)
3 ☐ Married filing separate return. Enter spouse's social security no. above and full name here. ▶ _____
4 ☐ Head of household (with qualifying person). (See page 13.) If the qualifying person is a child but not your dependent, enter this child's name here. ▶ _____
5 ☐ Qualifying widow(er) with dependent child (year spouse died ▶ 19___). (See page 13.)

Exemptions
(See page 13.)

If more than six dependents, see page 14.

6a ✓ **Yourself.** If your parent (or someone else) can claim you as a dependent on his or her tax return, **do not** check box 6a. But be sure to check the box on line 33b on page 2
b ☐ Spouse . . . .

c Dependents: (1) Name (first, initial, and last name)	(2) Check if under age 1	(3) If age 1 or older, dependent's social security number	(4) Dependent's relationship to you	(5) No. of months lived in your home in 1994

No. of boxes checked on 6a and 6b: 1
No. of your children on 6c who:
• lived with you: 0
• didn't live with you due to divorce or separation (see page 14): 0
Dependents on 6c not entered above: 0

d If your child didn't live with you but is claimed as your dependent under a pre-1985 agreement, check here ▶ ☐
e Total number of exemptions claimed

Add numbers entered on lines above ▶ 1

Income

Attach Copy B of your Forms W-2, W-2G, and 1099-R here.

If you did not get a W-2, see page 15.

Enclose, but do not attach, any payment with your return.

7 Wages, salaries, tips, etc. Attach Form(s) W-2 . . . . | 7 | 16,000 –
8a Taxable interest income (see page 15). Attach Schedule B if over $400 . . . . . | 8a |
b Tax-exempt interest (see page 16). DON'T include on line 8a | 8b |
9 Dividend income. Attach Schedule B if over $400 . . . . . | 9 |
10 Taxable refunds, credits, or offsets of state and local income taxes (see page 16) . . | 10 |
11 Alimony received . . . . | 11 |
12 Business income or (loss). Attach Schedule C or C-EZ . . . | 12 |
13 Capital gain or (loss). If required, attach Schedule D (see page 16) . . . | 13 |
14 Other gains or (losses). Attach Form 4797 . . . . . . | 14 |
15a Total IRA distributions . . | 15a | b Taxable amount (see page 17) | 15b |
16a Total pensions and annuities | 16a | b Taxable amount (see page 17) | 16b |
17 Rental real estate, royalties, partnerships, S corporations, trusts, etc. Attach Schedule E | 17 |
18 Farm income or (loss). Attach Schedule F . . . . . . | 18 |
19 Unemployment compensation (see page 18) . . . . . . | 19 |
20a Social security benefits | 20a | b Taxable amount (see page 18) | 20b |
21 Other income. List type and amount—see page 18 . . . . | 21 |
22 Add the amounts in the far right column for lines 7 through 21. This is your **total income** ▶ | 22 | 16,000 –

Adjustments to Income

Caution: See instructions . . ▶

23a Your IRA deduction (see page 19) . . . . . | 23a |
b Spouse's IRA deduction (see page 19) . . . . . | 23b |
24 Moving expenses. Attach Form 3903 or 3903-F . . . | 24 |
25 One-half of self-employment tax . . . . | 25 |
26 Self-employed health insurance deduction (see page 21) . | 26 |
27 Keogh retirement plan and self-employed SEP deduction | 27 |
28 Penalty on early withdrawal of savings . . . . . | 28 |
29 Alimony paid. Recipient's SSN ▶ | 29 |
30 Add lines 23a through 29. These are your **total adjustments** . . . . ▶ | 30 | 0

Adjusted Gross Income

31 Subtract line 30 from line 22. This is your **adjusted gross income**. If less than $25,296 and a child lived with you (less than $9,000 if a child didn't live with you), see "Earned Income Credit" on page 27 ▶ | 31 | 16,000 –

Cat. No. 11320B

Form **1040** (1994)

Form 1040 (1994)   Page **2**

Tax Compu- tation (See page 23.)	32	Amount from line 31 (adjusted gross income)	32	16,000 —
	33a	Check if: ☐ **You** were 65 or older, ☐ Blind; ☐ **Spouse** was 65 or older, ☐ Blind. Add the number of boxes checked above and enter the total here . . . . ▶ 33a ☐		
	b	If your parent (or someone else) can claim you as a dependent, check here . ▶ 33b ☐		
	c	If you are married filing separately and your spouse itemizes deductions or you are a dual-status alien, see page 23 and check here . . . . ▶ 33c ☐		
	34	Enter the **larger** of your: **Itemized deductions** from Schedule A, line 29, **OR** **Standard deduction** shown below for your filing status. **But if you checked any box on line 33a or b,** go to page 23 to find your standard deduction. If you checked **box 33c,** your standard deduction is zero. • Single—$3,800 • Head of household—$5,600 • Married filing jointly or Qualifying widow(er)—$6,350 • Married filing separately—$3,175	34	3,800 —
	35	Subtract line 34 from line 32	35	12,200 —
	36	If line 32 is $83,850 or less, multiply $2,450 by the total number of exemptions claimed on line 6e. If line 32 is over $83,850, see the worksheet on page 24 for the amount to enter .	36	2,450 —
If you want the IRS to figure your tax, see page 24.	37	**Taxable income.** Subtract line 36 from line 35. If line 36 is more than line 35, enter -0-	37	9,750 —
	38	Tax. Check if from a ☑ Tax Table, b ☐ Tax Rate Schedules, c ☐ Capital Gain Tax Work- sheet, or d ☐ Form 8615 (see page 24). Amount from Form(s) 8814 ▶ _____	38	1,466 —
	39	Additional taxes. Check if from a ☐ Form 4970 b ☐ Form 4972	39	0
	40	Add lines 38 and 39 . . . . ▶	40	1,466 —

Credits (See page 24.)	41	Credit for child and dependent care expenses. Attach Form 2441	41		
	42	Credit for the elderly or the disabled. Attach Schedule R .	42		
	43	Foreign tax credit. Attach Form 1116	43		
	44	Other credits (see page 25). Check if from a ☐ Form 3800 b ☐ Form 8396 c ☐ Form 8801 d ☐ Form (specify) _____	44		
	45	Add lines 41 through 44		45	0
	46	Subtract line 45 from line 40. If line 45 is more than line 40, enter -0- . . . . . ▶		46	1,466 —

Other Taxes (See page 25.)	47	Self-employment tax. Attach Schedule SE	47	
	48	Alternative minimum tax. Attach Form 6251	48	
	49	Recapture taxes. Check if from a ☐ Form 4255 b ☐ Form 8611 c ☐ Form 8828	49	
	50	Social security and Medicare tax on tip income not reported to employer. Attach Form 4137	50	
	51	Tax on qualified retirement plans, including IRAs. If required, attach Form 5329 . .	51	
	52	Advance earned income credit payments from Form W-2	52	
	53	Add lines 46 through 52. This is your **total tax** . . . . ▶	53	1,466 —

Payments Attach Forms W-2, W-2G, and 1099-R on the front.	54	Federal income tax withheld. If any is from Form(s) 1099, check ▶ ☐	54	1,500 —	
	55	1994 estimated tax payments and amount applied from 1993 return .	55		
	56	**Earned income credit.** If required, attach Schedule EIC (see page 27). Nontaxable earned income: amount ▶ _____ and type ▶	56		
	57	Amount paid with Form 4868 (extension request)	57		
	58	Excess social security and RRTA tax withheld (see page 32) .	58		
	59	Other payments. Check if from a ☐ Form 2439 b ☐ Form 4136	59		
	60	Add lines 54 through 59. These are your **total payments** . . . . ▶		60	1,500 —

Refund or Amount You Owe	61	If line 60 is more than line 53, subtract line 53 from line 60. This is the amount you **OVERPAID.** ▶	61	34 —
	62	Amount of line 61 you want **REFUNDED TO YOU.** . . . . ▶	62	34 —
	63	Amount of line 61 you want **APPLIED TO YOUR 1995 ESTIMATED TAX** ▶	63	
	64	If line 53 is more than line 60, subtract line 60 from line 53. This is the **AMOUNT YOU OWE.** For details on how to pay, including what to write on your payment, see page 32 . . . ▶	64	
	65	Estimated tax penalty (see page 33). Also include on line 64	65	

Sign Here Keep a copy of this return for your records.	Under penalties of perjury, I declare that I have examined this return and accompanying schedules and statements, and to the best of my knowledge and belief, they are true, correct, and complete. Declaration of preparer (other than taxpayer) is based on all information of which preparer has any knowledge.		
	Your signature ▶	Date 4/15/95	Your occupation REAL ESTATE BROKER
	Spouse's signature. If a joint return, BOTH must sign.	Date	Spouse's occupation

Paid Preparer's Use Only	Preparer's signature ▶	Date	Check if self-employed ☐	Preparer's social security no.
	Firm's name (or yours if self-employed) and address ▶		E.I. No.	
			ZIP code	

♻ *Printed on recycled paper*   *U.S. Government Printing Office: 1994 — 375-188

Form 1040 Department of the Treasury—Internal Revenue Service
U.S. Individual Income Tax Return (O) **1994**

For the year Jan. 1–Dec. 31, 1994, or other tax year beginning _____ , 1994, ending _____ , 19 ___   OMB No. 1545-0074

IRS Use Only—Do not write or staple in this space.

Label (See instructions on page 12.)
Use the IRS label. Otherwise, please print or type.

Your first name and initial: **GEORGE**   Last name: **GORDON**
Your social security number: **000 00 0000**

If a joint return, spouse's first name and initial _____ Last name _____
Spouse's social security number _____

Home address (number and street). If you have a P.O. box, see page 12.: **350 FIFTH AVENUE**   Apt. no. **PH**

City, town or post office, state, and ZIP code. If you have a foreign address, see page 12.: **NEW YORK, NY 10118**

For Privacy Act and Paperwork Reduction Act Notice, see page 4.

Presidential Election Campaign (See page 12.)
Do you want $3 to go to this fund? — Yes ___ No ✓
If a joint return, does your spouse want $3 to go to this fund? — Yes ___ No ___

Note: Checking "Yes" will not change your tax or reduce your refund.

Filing Status (See page 12.) Check only one box.

1. ✓ Single
2. ☐ Married filing joint return (even if only one had income)
3. ☐ Married filing separate return. Enter spouse's social security no. above and full name here. ▶ _____
4. ☐ Head of household (with qualifying person). (See page 13.) If the qualifying person is a child but not your dependent, enter this child's name here. ▶ _____
5. ☐ Qualifying widow(er) with dependent child (year spouse died ▶ 19___). (See page 13.)

Exemptions (See page 13.)

If more than six dependents, see page 14.

6a ☑ **Yourself.** If your parent (or someone else) can claim you as a dependent on his or her tax return, **do not** check box 6a. But be sure to check the box on line 33b on page 2.

b ☐ **Spouse**

c **Dependents:**

(1) Name (first, initial, and last name)	(2) Check if under age 1	(3) If age 1 or older, dependent's social security number	(4) Dependent's relationship to you	(5) No. of months lived in your home in 1994

No. of boxes checked on 6a and 6b: **1**

No. of your children on 6c who:
• lived with you: **0**
• didn't live with you due to divorce or separation (see page 14): **0**

Dependents on 6c not entered above: **0**

d If your child didn't live with you but is claimed as your dependent under a pre-1985 agreement, check here ▶ ☐
e Total number of exemptions claimed

Add numbers entered on lines above ▶ **1**

Income

Attach Copy B of your Forms W-2, W-2G, and 1099-R here.

If you did not get a W-2, see page 15.

Enclose, but do not attach, any payment with your return.

7	Wages, salaries, tips, etc. Attach Form(s) W-2	7	
8a	**Taxable** interest income (see page 15). Attach Schedule B if over $400	8a	
b	Tax-exempt interest (see page 16). DON'T include on line 8a [8b]		
9	Dividend income. Attach Schedule B if over $400	9	6,000 —
10	Taxable refunds, credits, or offsets of state and local income taxes (see page 16)	10	
11	Alimony received	11	
12	Business income or (loss). Attach Schedule C or C-EZ	12	35,809 —
13	Capital gain or (loss). If required, attach Schedule D (see page 16)	13	
14	Other gains or (losses). Attach Form 4797	14	
15a	Total IRA distributions [15a] — b Taxable amount (see page 17)	15b	
16a	Total pensions and annuities [16a] — b Taxable amount (see page 17)	16b	
17	Rental real estate, royalties, partnerships, S corporations, trusts, etc. Attach Schedule E	17	
18	Farm income or (loss). Attach Schedule F	18	
19	Unemployment compensation (see page 18)	19	
20a	Social security benefits [20a] — b Taxable amount (see page 18)	20b	
21	Other income. List type and amount—see page 18	21	
22	Add the amounts in the far right column for lines 7 through 21. This is your **total income** ▶	22	41,809 —

Adjustments to Income

Caution: See instructions . . ▶

23a	Your IRA deduction (see page 19) [23a]		
b	Spouse's IRA deduction (see page 19) [23b]		
24	Moving expenses. Attach Form 3903 or 3903-F [24]		
25	One-half of self-employment tax [25] 2,530 —		
26	Self-employed health insurance deduction (see page 21) [26]		
27	Keogh retirement plan and self-employed SEP deduction [27]		
28	Penalty on early withdrawal of savings [28]		
29	Alimony paid. Recipient's SSN ▶ [29]		
30	Add lines 23a through 29. These are your **total adjustments** ▶	30	2,530 —

Adjusted Gross Income

31 Subtract line 30 from line 22. This is your **adjusted gross income.** If less than $25,296 and a child lived with you (less than $9,000 if a child didn't live with you), see "Earned Income Credit" on page 27 ▶ | 31 | 39,279 — |

Cat. No. 11320B   Form **1040** (1994)

Form 1040 (1994)   Page **2**

Tax Computation (See page 23.)	32	Amount from line 31 (adjusted gross income)		**32**	39,279 —

33a Check if: ☐ **You** were 65 or older, ☐ Blind; ☐ **Spouse** was 65 or older, ☐ Blind. Add the number of boxes checked above and enter the total here . . . . ▶ **33a**

b If your parent (or someone else) can claim you as a dependent, check here . ▶ **33b** ☐

c If you are married filing separately and your spouse itemizes deductions or you are a dual-status alien, see page 23 and check here. . . . . ▶ **33c** ☐

34 Enter the **larger** of your:
- **Itemized deductions** from Schedule A, line 29, **OR**
- **Standard deduction** shown below for your filing status. **But if you checked any box on line 33a or b,** go to page 23 to find your standard deduction. If you checked **box 33c,** your standard deduction is zero.
  - Single—$3,800   • Head of household—$5,600
  - Married filing jointly or Qualifying widow(er)—$6,350
  - Married filing separately—$3,175

34	3,800 —

35 Subtract line 34 from line 32 . . . .   **35** 35,479 —

36 If line 32 is $83,850 or less, multiply $2,450 by the total number of exemptions claimed on line 6e. If line 32 is over $83,850, see the worksheet on page 24 for the amount to enter .   **36** 2,450 —

If you want the IRS to figure your tax, see page 24.

37 **Taxable income.** Subtract line 36 from line 35. If line 36 is more than line 35, enter -0- .   **37** 33,029 —

38 Tax. Check if from a ☑ Tax Table, b ☐ Tax Rate Schedules, c ☐ Capital Gain Worksheet, or d ☐ Form 8615 (see page 24). Amount from Form(s) 8814 ▶ e _____   **38** 6,290 —

39 Additional taxes. Check if from a ☐ Form 4970 b ☐ Form 4972 . . . . .   **39** 0

40 Add lines 38 and 39 . . . . ▶   **40** 6,290 —

Credits (See page 24.)

41	Credit for child and dependent care expenses. Attach Form 2441	**41**	
42	Credit for the elderly or the disabled. Attach Schedule R .	**42**	
43	Foreign tax credit. Attach Form 1116	**43**	
44	Other credits (see page 25). Check if from a ☐ Form 3800 b ☐ Form 8396 c ☐ Form 8801 d ☐ Form (specify) _____	**44**	

45 Add lines 41 through 44 . . . .   **45** 0

46 Subtract line 45 from line 40. If line 45 is more than line 40, enter -0- . . . . ▶   **46** 6,290 —

Other Taxes (See page 25.)

47 Self-employment tax. Attach Schedule SE . . . .   **47** 5,060 —

48 Alternative minimum tax. Attach Form 6251 . . . .   **48**

49 Recapture taxes. Check if from a ☐ Form 4255 b ☐ Form 8611 c ☐ Form 8828 .   **49**

50 Social security and Medicare tax on tip income not reported to employer. Attach Form 4137 .   **50**

51 Tax on qualified retirement plans, including IRAs. If required, attach Form 5329 . .   **51**

52 Advance earned income credit payments from Form W-2 . . . .   **52**

53 Add lines 46 through 52. This is your **total tax** . . . . ▶   **53** 11,350 —

Payments

Attach Forms W-2, W-2G, and 1099-R on the front.

54	Federal income tax withheld. If any is from Form(s) 1099, check ▶ ☐	**54**	
55	1994 estimated tax payments and amount applied from 1993 return .	**55**	11,500 —
56	**Earned income credit.** If required, attach Schedule EIC (see page 27). Nontaxable earned income: amount ▶ _____ and type ▶	**56**	
57	Amount paid with Form 4868 (extension request)	**57**	
58	Excess social security and RRTA tax withheld (see page 32) .	**58**	
59	Other payments. Check if from a ☐ Form 2439 b ☐ Form 4136	**59**	

60 Add lines 54 through 59. These are your **total payments** . . . . ▶   **60** 11,500 —

Refund or Amount You Owe

61 If line 60 is more than line 53, subtract line 53 from line 60. This is the amount you **OVERPAID**. . ▶   **61** 150 —

62 Amount of line 61 you want **REFUNDED TO YOU.** . . . . ▶   **62** 150 —

63 Amount of line 61 you want **APPLIED TO YOUR 1995 ESTIMATED TAX** ▶ | **63** |

64 If line 53 is more than line 60, subtract line 60 from line 53. This is the **AMOUNT YOU OWE.** For details on how to pay, including what to write on your payment, see page 32 . . .   **64**

65 Estimated tax penalty (see page 33). Also include on line 64 | **65** |

Sign Here

Keep a copy of this return for your records.

Under penalties of perjury, I declare that I have examined this return and accompanying schedules and statements, and to the best of my knowledge and belief, they are true, correct, and complete. Declaration of preparer (other than taxpayer) is based on all information of which preparer has any knowledge.

Your signature	Date	Your occupation
	4/15/95	REAL ESTATE BROKER
Spouse's signature. If a joint return, BOTH must sign.	Date	Spouse's occupation

Paid Preparer's Use Only

Preparer's signature ▶	Date	Check if self-employed ☐	Preparer's social security no.
Firm's name (or yours if self-employed) and address ▶		E.I. No.	
		ZIP code	

♻ *Printed on recycled paper*   *U.S. Government Printing Office: 1994 — 375-188*

SCHEDULE C (Form 1040)	Profit or Loss From Business	OMB No. 1545-0074

(Sole Proprietorship)

▶ Partnerships, joint ventures, etc., must file Form 1065.

Department of the Treasury, Internal Revenue Service   (O)   ▶ **Attach to Form 1040 or Form 1041.**   ▶ **See Instructions for Schedule C (Form 1040).**

Attachment Sequence No. **09**

1994

Name of proprietor: GEORGE GORDON

Social security number (SSN): 000 00 0000

A Principal business or profession, including product or service (see page C-1): REAL ESTATE BROKER

B Enter principal business code (see page C-6) ▶ 5 5 2 0

C Business name. If no separate business name, leave blank.: GEORGE GORDON REALTY

D Employer ID number (EIN), if any

E Business address (including suite or room no.) ▶ 350 FIFTH AVENUE, PH, New York, NY 10118
City, town or post office, state, and ZIP code

F Accounting method: (1) ☑ Cash (2) ☐ Accrual (3) ☐ Other (specify) ▶ ....

G Method(s) used to value closing inventory: (1) ☐ Cost (2) ☐ Lower of cost or market (3) ☐ Other (attach explanation) (4) ☑ Does not apply (if checked, skip line H)

	Yes	No

H Was there any change in determining quantities, costs, or valuations between opening and closing inventory? If "Yes," attach explanation

I Did you "materially participate" in the operation of this business during 1994? If "No," see page C-2 for limit on losses. . . | ✓ |

J If you started or acquired this business during 1994, check here . . . . ▶ ☐

Part I Income

1	Gross receipts or sales. **Caution:** If this income was reported to you on Form W-2 and the "Statutory employee" box on that form was checked, see page C-2 and check here ▶ ☐	1	
2	Returns and allowances	2	
3	Subtract line 2 from line 1	3	
4	Cost of goods sold (from line 40 on page 2)	4	
5	**Gross profit.** Subtract line 4 from line 3	5	45,000 —
6	Other income, including Federal and state gasoline or fuel tax credit or refund (see page C-2)	6	
7	**Gross income.** Add lines 5 and 6 ▶	7	45,000 —

Part II Expenses. Enter expenses for business use of your home **only** on line 30.

8	Advertising	8		19	Pension and profit-sharing plans	19	4,000 —
9	Bad debts from sales or services (see page C-3)	9		20	Rent or lease (see page C-4):		
10	Car and truck expenses (see page C-3)	10		a	Vehicles, machinery, and equipment	20a	
11	Commissions and fees	11		b	Other business property	20b	3,000 —
12	Depletion	12		21	Repairs and maintenance	21	
13	Depreciation and section 179 expense deduction (not included in Part III) (see page C-3)	13	1,000 —	22	Supplies (not included in Part III)	22	
				23	Taxes and licenses	23	
				24	Travel, meals, and entertainment:		
14	Employee benefit programs (other than on line 19)	14		a	Travel	24a	450 —
15	Insurance (other than health)	15		b	Meals and entertainment		
16	Interest:			c	Enter 50% of line 24b subject to limitations (see page C-4)		
a	Mortgage (paid to banks, etc.)	16a					
b	Other	16b		d	Subtract line 24c from line 24b	24d	
17	Legal and professional services	17		25	Utilities + TELEPHONE	25	491 —
				26	Wages (less employment credits)	26	
18	Office expense	18	100 —	27	Other expenses (from line 46 on page 2) POSTAGE	27	150 —
28	**Total expenses** before expenses for business use of home. Add lines 8 through 27 in columns ▶					28	9,191 —
29	Tentative profit (loss). Subtract line 28 from line 7					29	
30	Expenses for business use of your home. Attach **Form 8829**					30	
31	**Net profit or (loss).** Subtract line 30 from line 29.					31	35,809 —

* If a profit, enter on **Form 1040, line 12,** and ALSO on **Schedule SE, line 2** (statutory employees, see page C-5). Estates and trusts, enter on Form 1041, line 3.

* If a loss, you MUST go on to line 32.

32 If you have a loss, check the box that describes your investment in this activity (see page C-5).

* If you checked 32a, enter the loss on **Form 1040, line 12,** and ALSO on **Schedule SE, line 2** (statutory employees, see page C-5). Estates and trusts, enter on Form 1041, line 3.

* If you checked 32b, you MUST attach **Form 6198.**

32a ☐ All investment is at risk.
32b ☐ Some investment is not at risk.

For Paperwork Reduction Act Notice, see Form 1040 instructions.   Cat. No. 11334P   Schedule C (Form 1040) 1994

SCHEDULE SE	**Self-Employment Tax**	OMB No. 1545-0074
(Form 1040)	▶ See Instructions for Schedule SE (Form 1040).	19**94**
Department of the Treasury Internal Revenue Service (O)	▶ Attach to Form 1040.	Attachment Sequence No. **17**

Name of person with **self-employment** income (as shown on Form 1040) GEORGE GORDON	Social security number of person with **self-employment** income ▶	000 00 0000

Who Must File Schedule SE

You must file Schedule SE if:

- You had net earnings from self-employment from other than church employee income (line 4 of Short Schedule SE or line 4c o Long Schedule SE) of $400 or more, **OR**
- You had church employee income of $108.28 or more. Income from services you performed as a minister or a member of religious order **is not** church employee income. See page SE-1.

Note: *Even if you have a loss or a small amount of income from self-employment, it may be to your benefit to file Schedule SE an use either "optional method" in Part II of Long Schedule SE. See page SE-2.*

Exception. If your only self-employment income was from earnings as a minister, member of a religious order, or Christian Scienc practitioner, **and** you filed Form 4361 and received IRS approval not to be taxed on those earnings, **do not** file Schedule SE Instead, write "Exempt–Form 4361" on Form 1040, line 47.

May I Use Short Schedule SE or MUST I Use Long Schedule SE?

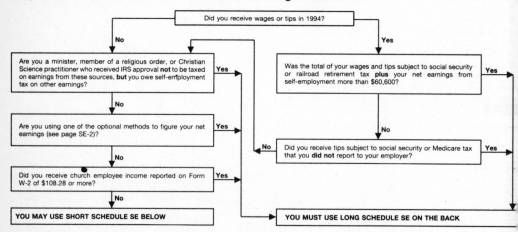

YOU MAY USE SHORT SCHEDULE SE BELOW	YOU MUST USE LONG SCHEDULE SE ON THE BACK

Section A—Short Schedule SE. Caution: *Read above to see if you can use Short Schedule SE.*

1	Net farm profit or (loss) from Schedule F, line 36, and farm partnerships, Schedule K-1 (Form 1065), line 15a	**1**	0
2	Net profit or (loss) from Schedule C, line 31; Schedule C-EZ, line 3; and Schedule K-1 (Form 1065), line 15a (other than farming). Ministers and members of religious orders see page SE-1 for amounts to report on this line. See page SE-2 for other income to report	**2**	35,809
3	Combine lines 1 and 2	**3**	35,809
4	**Net earnings from self-employment.** Multiply line 3 by 92.35% (.9235). If less than $400, **do not** file this schedule; you do not owe self-employment tax . . . . ▶	**4**	33,070

5	**Self-employment tax.** If the amount on line 4 is:
	   • $60,600 or less, multiply line 4 by 15.3% (.153). Enter the result here and on **Form 1040, line 47.**
	   • More than $60,600, multiply line 4 by 2.9% (.029). Then, add $7,514.40 to the result. Enter the total here and on **Form 1040, line 47.**
		5	5,060

6	**Deduction for one-half of self-employment tax.** Multiply line 5 by 50% (.5). Enter the result here and on **Form 1040, line 25**	**6**	2,530

For Paperwork Reduction Act Notice, see Form 1040 instructions.   Cat. No. 11358Z   **Schedule SE (Form 1040) 199**

Form **4562**	**Depreciation and Amortization**	OMB No. 1545-0172
	(Including Information on Listed Property)	**1994**
Department of the Treasury Internal Revenue Service (O)	▶ See separate instructions. ▶ Attach this form to your return.	Attachment Sequence No. **67**

Name(s) shown on return: GEORGE GORDON

Identifying number: 000-00-0000

Business or activity to which this form relates: REAL ESTATE BROKERAGE

Part I   Election To Expense Certain Tangible Property (Section 179) (Note: *If you have any "Listed Property," complete Part V before you complete Part I.*)

1	Maximum dollar limitation (If an enterprise zone business, see instructions.)	1	$17,500
2	Total cost of section 179 property placed in service during the tax year (see instructions)	2	
3	Threshold cost of section 179 property before reduction in limitation	3	$200,000
4	Reduction in limitation. Subtract line 3 from line 2. If zero or less, enter -0-	4	
5	Dollar limitation for tax year. Subtract line 4 from line 1. If zero or less, enter -0-. (If married filing separately, see instructions.)	5	

(a) Description of property	(b) Cost	(c) Elected cost
6		

7	Listed property. Enter amount from line 26.	7	
8	Total elected cost of section 179 property. Add amounts in column (c), lines 6 and 7	8	
9	Tentative deduction. Enter the smaller of line 5 or line 8	9	
10	Carryover of disallowed deduction from 1993 (see instructions)	10	
11	Taxable income limitation. Enter the smaller of taxable income (not less than zero) or line 5 (see instructions)	11	
12	Section 179 expense deduction. Add lines 9 and 10, but do not enter more than line 11	12	
13	Carryover of disallowed deduction to 1995. Add lines 9 and 10, less line 12 ▶ 13		

Note: *Do not use Part II or Part III below for listed property (automobiles, certain other vehicles, cellular telephones, certain computers, or property used for entertainment, recreation, or amusement). Instead, use Part V for listed property.*

Part II   MACRS Depreciation For Assets Placed in Service ONLY During Your 1994 Tax Year (Do Not Include Listed Property)

(a) Classification of property	(b) Month and year placed in service	(c) Basis for depreciation (business/investment use only—see instructions)	(d) Recovery period	(e) Convention	(f) Method	(g) Depreciation deduction
Section A—General Depreciation System (GDS) (see instructions)						
14a 3-year property						
b 5-year property						
c 7-year property						
d 10-year property						
e 15-year property						
f 20-year property						
g Residential rental property			27.5 yrs.	MM	S/L	
			27.5 yrs.	MM	S/L	
h Nonresidential real property			39 yrs.	MM	S/L	
				MM	S/L	
Section B—Alternative Depreciation System (ADS) (see instructions)						
15a Class life					S/L	
b 12-year			12 yrs.		S/L	
c 40-year			40 yrs.	MM	S/L	

Part III   Other Depreciation (Do Not Include Listed Property)

16	GDS and ADS deductions for assets placed in service in tax years beginning before 1994 (see instructions)	16	
17	Property subject to section 168(f)(1) election (see instructions)	17	
18	ACRS and other depreciation (see instructions)	18	1,000 —

Part IV   Summary

19	Listed property. Enter amount from line 25.	19	
20	**Total.** Add deductions on line 12, lines 14 and 15 in column (g), and lines 16 through 19. Enter here and on the appropriate lines of your return. (Partnerships and S corporations—see instructions)	20	1,000 —
21	For assets shown above and placed in service during the current year, enter the portion of the basis attributable to section 263A costs (see instructions)	21	

For Paperwork Reduction Act Notice, see page 1 of the separate instructions.   Cat. No. 12906N   Form **4562** (1994)

Form 1120-A
Department of the Treasury
Internal Revenue Service

U.S. Corporation Short-Form Income Tax Return

See separate instructions to make sure the corporation qualifies to file Form 1120-A.
For calendar year 1994 or tax year beginning ...., 1994, ending.............., 19.....

OMB No. 1545-0890

1994

A Check this box if the corp. is a personal service corp. (as defined in Temporary Regs. section 1.441-4T—see instructions) ▶ ☐

Use IRS label. Otherwise, please print or type.

Name
GEOFFREY FOURMYLE & Co. INC.
Number, street, and room or suite no. (If a P.O. box, see page 6 of instructions.)
5217 CERES BOULEVARD
City or town, state, and ZIP code
SAN FRANCISCO, CA 94701

B Employer identification number
00 0000000

C Date incorporated
1/2/94

D Total assets (see Specific Instructions)
$ **67,148 —**

E Check applicable boxes: (1) ☑ Initial return (2) ☐ Change of address
F Check method of accounting: (1) ☑ Cash (2) ☐ Accrual (3) ☐ Other (specify) . . ▶

Income

1a	Gross receipts or sales	**b** Less returns and allowances	**c** Balance ▶ 1c **45,000 —**
2	Cost of goods sold (see instructions)		2
3	Gross profit. Subtract line 2 from line 1c		3
4	Domestic corporation dividends subject to the 70% deduction		4 **6,000 —**
5	Interest		5
6	Gross rents		6
7	Gross royalties		7
8	Capital gain net income (attach Schedule D (Form 1120))		8
9	Net gain or (loss) from Form 4797, Part II, line 20 (attach Form 4797)		9
10	Other income (see instructions) . . . . ▶		10
11	**Total income.** Add lines 3 through 10 . . . . ▶		11 **51,000 —**

Deductions

(See instructions for limitations on deductions.)

12	Compensation of officers (see instructions)		12 **26,000 —**
13	Salaries and wages (less employment credits)		13
14	Repairs and maintenance		14
15	Bad debts		15
16	Rents		16 **3,000 —**
17	Taxes and licenses Soc. Sec.		17 **1,989 —**
18	~~Interest~~ EMPLOYEE MEDICAL		18 **4,000 —**
19	Charitable contributions (see instructions for 10% limitation) . .		19
20	Depreciation (attach Form 4562)	20 **1,000 —**	20
21	Less depreciation claimed elsewhere on return .	21a **0**	21b **1,000 —**
22	Other deductions (attach schedule) PENSION 6,500, UTILITIES + PHONE 729, TRAVEL 250, PUB. 100		22 **7,579 —**
23	**Total deductions.** Add lines 12 through 22 . . . . . ▶		23 **43,568 —**
24	Taxable income before net operating loss deduction and special deductions. Subtract line 23 from line 11		24 **7,432 —**
25	**Less: a** Net operating loss deduction (see instructions)	25a **0**	
	b Special deductions (see instructions) 70% DIVIDEND .	25b **4,200 —**	25c **4,200 —**
26	**Taxable income.** Subtract line 25c from line 24		26 **3,232 —**
27	**Total tax** (from page 2, Part I, line 7)		27 **485 —**

Tax and Payments

28	**Payments:**		
a	1993 overpayment credited to 1994	28a	
b	1994 estimated tax payments .	28b **450 —**	
c	Less 1994 refund applied for on Form 4466	28c ( ) Bal ▶	28d **450 —**
e	Tax deposited with Form 7004		28e
f	Credit from regulated investment companies (attach Form 2439) .		28f
g	Credit for Federal tax on fuels (attach Form 4136). See instructions		28g
h	**Total payments.** Add lines 28d through 28g		28h **450 —**
29	Estimated tax penalty (see instructions). Check if Form 2220 is attached . . . . . ▶ ☐		29
30	**Tax due.** If line 28h is smaller than the total of lines 27 and 29, enter amount owed . .		30 **35 —**
31	**Overpayment.** If line 28h is larger than the total of lines 27 and 29, enter amount overpaid . .		31
32	Enter amount of line 31 you want: **Credited to 1995 estimated tax** ▶	Refunded ▶	32

Please Sign Here

Under penalties of perjury, I declare that I have examined this return, including accompanying schedules and statements, and to the best of my knowledge and belief, it is true, correct, and complete. Declaration of preparer (other than taxpayer) is based on all information of which preparer has any knowledge.

▶ _(signature)_   Signature of officer   **3/15/95** Date   ▶ **PRESIDENT** Title

Paid Preparer's Use Only

Preparer's signature ▶		Date	Check if self-employed ▶ ☐	Preparer's social security number
Firm's name (or yours if self-employed) and address ▶			E.I. No. ▶	
			ZIP code ▶	

For Paperwork Reduction Act Notice, see page 1 of the instructions.   Cat. No. 11456E   Form **1120-A** (1994)

Form 1120-A (1994)   Page **2**

Part I — Tax Computation (See instructions.)

1	Income tax. If the corporation is a qualified personal service corporation (see page 14), check here ▶ ☐	**1** 485 —
2a	General business credit. Check if from: ☐ Form 3800 ☐ Form 3468 ☐ Form 5884 ☐ Form 6478 ☐ Form 6765 ☐ Form 8586 ☐ Form 8830 ☐ Form 8826 ☐ Form 8835 ☐ Form 8844 ☐ Form 8845 ☐ Form 8846 ☐ Form 8847 . . . . **2a**	
b	Credit for prior year minimum tax (attach Form 8827) **2b**	
3	**Total credits.** Add lines 2a and 2b	**3** 0
4	Subtract line 3 from line 1	**4** 485 —
5	Recapture taxes. Check if from: ☐ Form 4255 ☐ Form 8611	**5** 0
6	Alternative minimum tax (attach Form 4626)	**6** 0
7	**Total tax.** Add lines 4 through 6. Enter here and on line 27, page 1	**7** 485 —

Part II — Other Information (See instructions.)

1 Refer to page 19 of the instructions and state the principal:

  a   Business activity code no. ▶ 7.88.0 ....

  b   Business activity ▶ TECHNICAL WRITING ....

  c   Product or service ▶ REPORTS ....

2 Did any individual, partnership, estate, or trust at the end of the tax year own, directly or indirectly, 50% or more of the corporation's voting stock? (For rules of attribution, see section 267(c).) . . . . ☑ Yes   ☐ No

↪ GEOFFREY FOURMYLE .5217 CERES BLVD, SAN FRANCISCO CA 94701,
If "Yes," attach a schedule showing name and identifying number 55000-00-0000

3 Enter the amount of tax-exempt interest received or accrued during the tax year . . . . . ▶ $ 0

4 Enter amount of cash distributions and the book value of property (other than cash) distributions made in this tax year . . . . ▶ $ 0

5a If an amount is entered on line 2, page 1, see the worksheet on page 12 for amounts to enter below:

  (1) Purchases . . . . . .

  (2) Additional sec. 263A costs (see instructions—attach schedule) .

  (3) Other costs (attach schedule) .

  b Do the rules of section 263A (for property produced or acquired for resale) apply to the corporation? . . . . . . ☐ Yes ☑ No

6 At any time during the 1994 calendar year, did the corporation have an interest in or a signature or other authority over a financial account in a foreign country (such as a bank account, securities account, or other financial account)? If "Yes," the corporation may have to file Form TD F 90-22.1 . . . . ☐ Yes ☑ No

If "Yes," enter the name of the foreign country ▶ ....

Part III — Balance Sheets

		(a) Beginning of tax year		(b) End of tax year	
	Assets				
1	Cash			1,481	—
2a	Trade notes and accounts receivable				
b	Less allowance for bad debts . . .	(	)	(	)
3	Inventories				
4	U.S. government obligations				
5	Tax-exempt securities (see instructions) . .	INCORPORATED			
6	Other current assets (attach schedule) . . .	1/2/94			
7	Loans to stockholders				
8	Mortgage and real estate loans	INITIAL			
9a	Depreciable, depletable, and intangible assets . . .	RETURN		6,667	—
b	Less accumulated depreciation, depletion, and amortization	(	)	(1,000	)
10	Land (net of any amortization)				
11	Other assets (attach schedule)			60,000	
12	Total assets			67,148	—
	Liabilities and Stockholders' Equity				
13	Accounts payable				
14	Other current liabilities (attach schedule) . .				
15	Loans from stockholders				
16	Mortgages, notes, bonds payable . . .				
17	Other liabilities (attach schedule) . . .				
18	Capital stock (preferred and common stock)			10,000	—
19	Paid-in or capital surplus			50,000	—
20	Retained earnings			7,148	—
21	Less cost of treasury stock	(	)	(	)
22	Total liabilities and stockholders' equity . .			67,148	—

Part IV — Reconciliation of Income (Loss) per Books With Income per Return (You are not required to complete Part IV if the total assets on line 12, column (b), Part III are less than $25,000.)

1	Net income (loss) per books	6,947 —	6	Income recorded on books this year not included on this return (itemize)	0
2	Federal income tax	485 —	7	Deductions on this return not charged against book income this year (itemize)	0
3	Excess of capital losses over capital gains . .	0			
4	Income subject to tax not recorded on books this year (itemize)	0	8	Income (line 24, page 1). Enter the sum of lines 1 through 5 less the sum of lines 6 and 7 . . .	7,432 —
5	Expenses recorded on books this year not deducted on this return (itemize)	0			

♻ *Printed on recycled paper*   ☆ U.S. GPO:1994-375-292

Form **1040**	Department of the Treasury—Internal Revenue Service **U.S. Individual Income Tax Return** (O) **1994**		IRS Use Only—Do not write or staple in this space.

For the year Jan. 1–Dec. 31, 1994, or other tax year beginning   , 1994, ending   , 19   OMB No. 1545-0074

Label
(See instructions on page 12.)

Use the IRS label. Otherwise, please print or type.

L A B E L   H E R E

Your first name and initial: **GEOFFREY**   Last name: **FOURMYLE**

Your social security number: **000 00 0000**

If a joint return, spouse's first name and initial   Last name

Spouse's social security number

Home address (number and street). If you have a P.O. box, see page 12. **5217 CERES BOULEVARD**   Apt. no.

City, town or post office, state, and ZIP code. If you have a foreign address, see page 12. **SAN FRANCISCO, CA 94701**

For Privacy Act and Paperwork Reduction Act Notice, see page 4.

Presidential Election Campaign (See page 12.)

Do you want $3 to go to this fund? . . . .

If a joint return, does your spouse want $3 to go to this fund? . . . . .

Yes | No   **Note:** *Checking "Yes" will not change your tax or reduce your refund.*
(No checked for first)

Filing Status
(See page 12.)

Check only one box.

1 ✓ Single
2   Married filing joint return (even if only one had income)
3   Married filing separate return. Enter spouse's social security no. above and full name here. ▶ _____
4   Head of household (with qualifying person). (See page 13.) If the qualifying person is a child but not your dependent, enter this child's name here. ▶ _____
5   Qualifying widow(er) with dependent child (year spouse died ▶ 19 ____). (See page 13.)

Exemptions
(See page 13.)

6a ✓ **Yourself.** If your parent (or someone else) can claim you as a dependent on his or her tax return, **do not** check box 6a. But be sure to check the box on line 33b on page 2 ⟩

No. of boxes checked on 6a and 6b: **1**

b ☐ Spouse . . . .

c Dependents:
(1) Name (first, initial, and last name)

	(2) Check if under age 1	(3) If age 1 or older, dependent's social security number	(4) Dependent's relationship to you	(5) No. of months lived in your home in 1994

If more than six dependents, see page 14.

No. of your children on 6c who:
• lived with you: **0**
• didn't live with you due to divorce or separation (see page 14): **0**

Dependents on 6c not entered above: **0**

d If your child didn't live with you but is claimed as your dependent under a pre-1985 agreement, check here ▶ ☐

e Total number of exemptions claimed . . . .

Add numbers entered on lines above ▶ **1**

Income

Attach Copy B of your Forms W-2, W-2G, and 1099-R here.

If you did not get a W-2, see page 15.

Enclose, but do not attach, any payment with your return.

7	Wages, salaries, tips, etc. Attach Form(s) W-2	7 26,000 —
8a	Taxable interest income (see page 15). Attach Schedule B if over $400	8a
b	Tax-exempt interest (see page 16). DON'T include on line 8a 8b	
9	Dividend income. Attach Schedule B if over $400	9
10	Taxable refunds, credits, or offsets of state and local income taxes (see page 16) . .	10
11	Alimony received	11
12	Business income or (loss). Attach Schedule C or C-EZ . . .	12
13	Capital gain or (loss). If required, attach Schedule D (see page 16) .	13
14	Other gains or (losses). Attach Form 4797	14
15a	Total IRA distributions . 15a b Taxable amount (see page 17)	15b
16a	Total pensions and annuities 16a b Taxable amount (see page 17)	16b
17	Rental real estate, royalties, partnerships, S corporations, trusts, etc. Attach Schedule E	17
18	Farm income or (loss). Attach Schedule F	18
19	Unemployment compensation (see page 18)	19
20a	Social security benefits 20a b Taxable amount (see page 18)	20b
21	Other income. List type and amount—see page 18	21
22	Add the amounts in the far right column for lines 7 through 21. This is your **total income** ▶	22 26,000 —

Adjustments to Income

Caution: See instructions . . ▶

23a	Your IRA deduction (see page 19)	23a
b	Spouse's IRA deduction (see page 19)	23b
24	Moving expenses. Attach Form 3903 or 3903-F . . .	24
25	One-half of self-employment tax	25
26	Self-employed health insurance deduction (see page 21)	26
27	Keogh retirement plan and self-employed SEP deduction	27
28	Penalty on early withdrawal of savings	28
29	Alimony paid. Recipient's SSN ▶	29
30	Add lines 23a through 29. These are your **total adjustments** . . . . . . ▶	30 0

Adjusted Gross Income

31 Subtract line 30 from line 22. This is your **adjusted gross income**. If less than $25,296 and a child lived with you (less than $9,000 if a child didn't live with you), see "Earned Income Credit" on page 27 ▶ | 31   26,000 —

Cat. No. 11320B   Form **1040** (1994)

Form 1040 (1994)   Page **2**

Tax Computation (See page 23.)	**32** Amount from line 31 (adjusted gross income)	**32** 26,000
	33a Check if: ☐ **You** were 65 or older, ☐ Blind; ☐ **Spouse** was 65 or older, ☐ Blind. Add the number of boxes checked above and enter the total here . . . . ▶ **33a**	
	b If your parent (or someone else) can claim you as a dependent, check here . ▶ **33b** ☐	
	c If you are married filing separately and your spouse itemizes deductions or you are a dual-status alien, see page 23 and check here . . . . ▶ **33c** ☐	
	34 Enter the larger of your: **Itemized deductions** from Schedule A, line 29, **OR** **Standard deduction** shown below for your filing status. **But if you checked any box on line 33a or b**, go to page 23 to find your standard deduction. If you checked **box 33c**, your standard deduction is zero. • Single—$3,800 • Head of household—$5,600 • Married filing jointly or Qualifying widow(er)—$6,350 • Married filing separately—$3,175	**34** 3,800
	35 Subtract line 34 from line 32	**35** 22,200
	36 If line 32 is $83,850 or less, multiply $2,450 by the total number of exemptions claimed on line 6e. If line 32 is over $83,850, see the worksheet on page 24 for the amount to enter .	**36** 2,450
If you want the IRS to figure your tax, see page 24.	**37** **Taxable income.** Subtract line 36 from line 35. If line 36 is more than line 35, enter -0-	**37** 19,750
	38 Tax. Check if from **a** ☑ Tax Table, **b** ☐ Tax Rate Schedules, **c** ☐ Capital Gain Tax Worksheet, or **d** ☐ Form 8615 (see page 24). Amount from Form(s) 8814 ▶ **e** _____	**38** 2,966
	39 Additional taxes. Check if from **a** ☐ Form 4970 **b** ☐ Form 4972	**39** 0
	40 Add lines 38 and 39 . . . . ▶	**40** 2,966
Credits (See page 24.)	**41** Credit for child and dependent care expenses. Attach Form 2441 **41**	
	42 Credit for the elderly or the disabled. Attach Schedule R . **42**	
	43 Foreign tax credit. Attach Form 1116 . . . . . **43**	
	44 Other credits (see page 25). Check if from **a** ☐ Form 3800 **b** ☐ Form 8396 **c** ☐ Form 8801 **d** ☐ Form (specify)_____ **44**	
	45 Add lines 41 through 44	**45** 0
	46 Subtract line 45 from line 40. If line 45 is more than line 40, enter -0- . . . . . . ▶	**46** 2,966
Other Taxes (See page 25.)	**47** Self-employment tax. Attach Schedule SE	**47**
	48 Alternative minimum tax. Attach Form 6251	**48**
	49 Recapture taxes. Check if from **a** ☐ Form 4255 **b** ☐ Form 8611 **c** ☐ Form 8828 . .	**49**
	50 Social security and Medicare tax on tip income not reported to employer. Attach Form 4137	**50**
	51 Tax on qualified retirement plans, including IRAs. If required, attach Form 5329 . . .	**51**
	52 Advance earned income credit payments from Form W-2	**52**
	53 Add lines 46 through 52. This is your **total tax** . . . . ▶	**53** 2,966
Payments Attach Forms W-2, W-2G, and 1099-R on the front.	**54** Federal income tax withheld. If any is from Form(s) 1099, check ▶ ☐ **54** 3,000	
	55 1994 estimated tax payments and amount applied from 1993 return . **55**	
	56 **Earned income credit.** If required, attach Schedule EIC (see page 27). Nontaxable earned income: amount ▶ _____ and type ▶ **56**	
	57 Amount paid with Form 4868 (extension request) **57**	
	58 Excess social security and RRTA tax withheld (see page 32) **58**	
	59 Other payments. Check if from **a** ☐ Form 2439 **b** ☐ Form 4136 **59**	
	60 Add lines 54 through 59. These are your **total payments** . . . . ▶	**60** 3,000
Refund or Amount You Owe	**61** If line 60 is more than line 53, subtract line 53 from line 60. This is the amount you **OVERPAID**. ▶	**61** 34
	62 Amount of line 61 you want **REFUNDED TO YOU**. . . . . ▶	**62** 34
	63 Amount of line 61 you want **APPLIED TO YOUR 1995 ESTIMATED TAX** ▶ **63**	
	64 If line 53 is more than line 60, subtract line 60 from line 53. This is the **AMOUNT YOU OWE**. For details on how to pay, including what to write on your payment, see page 32 . . .	**64**
	65 Estimated tax penalty (see page 33). Also include on line 64 **65**	

Sign Here
Keep a copy of this return for your records.

Under penalties of perjury, I declare that I have examined this return and accompanying schedules and statements, and to the best of my knowledge and belief, they are true, correct, and complete. Declaration of preparer (other than taxpayer) is based on all information of which preparer has any knowledge.

Your signature	Date 4/15/95	Your occupation TECHNICAL WRITER
Spouse's signature. If a joint return, BOTH must sign.	Date	Spouse's occupation

Paid Preparer's Use Only

Preparer's signature ▶	Date	Check if self-employed ☐	Preparer's social security no.
Firm's name (or yours if self-employed) and address ▶		E.I. No.	
		ZIP code	

♻ Printed on recycled paper   *U.S. Government Printing Office: 1994 — 375-188

Form **1040**

Department of the Treasury—Internal Revenue Service
U.S. Individual Income Tax Return (O) **1994**

For the year Jan. 1–Dec. 31, 1994, or other tax year beginning , 1994, ending , 19 OMB No. 1545-0074

IRS Use Only—Do not write or staple in this space.

Label
(See instructions on page 12.)

Use the IRS label. Otherwise, please print or type.

L A B E L H E R E

Your first name and initial: **GEOFFREY** Last name: **FOURMYLE**
Your social security number: **000 00 0000**

If a joint return, spouse's first name and initial Last name
Spouse's social security number:

Home address (number and street). If you have a P.O. box, see page 12.: **5217 CERES BOULEVARD** Apt. no.

City, town or post office, state, and ZIP code. If you have a foreign address, see page 12.: **SAN FRANCISCO CA 94701**

For Privacy Act and Paperwork Reduction Act Notice, see page 4.

Presidential Election Campaign (See page 12.)

Do you want $3 to go to this fund? . . . .   Yes   No ✓

If a joint return, does your spouse want $3 to go to this fund? . . . .

Note: Checking "Yes" will not change your tax or reduce your refund.

Filing Status
(See page 12.)

Check only one box.

1 ✓ Single
2   Married filing joint return (even if only one had income)
3   Married filing separate return. Enter spouse's social security no. above and full name here. ▶
4   Head of household (with qualifying person). (See page 13.) If the qualifying person is a child but not your dependent, enter this child's name here. ▶
5   Qualifying widow(er) with dependent child (year spouse died ▶ 19). (See page 13.)

Exemptions
(See page 13.)

6a ✓ **Yourself.** If your parent (or someone else) can claim you as a dependent on his or her tax return, **do not** check box 6a. But be sure to check the box on line 33b on page 2

b   Spouse . . . .

No. of boxes checked on 6a and 6b: **1**

c **Dependents:**

(1) Name (first, initial, and last name)	(2) Check if under age 1	(3) If age 1 or older, dependent's social security number	(4) Dependent's relationship to you	(5) No. of months lived in your home in 1994

If more than six dependents, see page 14.

No. of your children on 6c who:
• lived with you: **0**
• didn't live with you due to divorce or separation (see page 14): **0**

Dependents on 6c not entered above: **0**

d If your child didn't live with you but is claimed as your dependent under a pre-1985 agreement, check here ▶ ☐

e Total number of exemptions claimed

Add numbers entered on lines above ▶ **1**

Income

Attach Copy B of your Forms W-2, W-2G, and 1099-R here.

If you did not get a W-2, see page 15.

Enclose, but do not attach, any payment with your return.

7 Wages, salaries, tips, etc. Attach Form(s) W-2 **7**
8a **Taxable** interest income (see page 15). Attach Schedule B if over $400 . . . . **8a**
b **Tax-exempt** interest (see page 16). DON'T include on line 8a **8b**
9 Dividend income. Attach Schedule B if over $400 **9**   **6,000 –**
10 Taxable refunds, credits, or offsets of state and local income taxes (see page 16) . . **10**
11 Alimony received **11**
12 Business income or (loss). Attach Schedule C or C-EZ **12**   **33,421 –**
13 Capital gain or (loss). If required, attach Schedule D (see page 16) **13**
14 Other gains or (losses). Attach Form 4797 . . . . **14**
15a Total IRA distributions . **15a** b Taxable amount (see page 17) **15b**
16a Total pensions and annuities **16a** b Taxable amount (see page 17) **16b**
17 Rental real estate, royalties, partnerships, S corporations, trusts, etc. Attach Schedule E **17**
18 Farm income or (loss). Attach Schedule F **18**
19 Unemployment compensation (see page 18) **19**
20a Social security benefits **20a** b Taxable amount (see page 18) **20b**
21 Other income. List type and amount—see page 18 . . . . **21**
22 Add the amounts in the far right column for lines 7 through 21. This is your **total income** ▶ **22**   **39,421 –**

Adjustments to Income

Caution: See instructions . . ▶

23a Your IRA deduction (see page 19) **23a**
b Spouse's IRA deduction (see page 19) . . . **23b**
24 Moving expenses. Attach Form 3903 or 3903-F . . . **24**
25 One-half of self-employment tax . . . . . . **25** **2,361 –**
26 Self-employed health insurance deduction (see page 21) **26**
27 Keogh retirement plan and self-employed SEP deduction **27**
28 Penalty on early withdrawal of savings **28**
29 Alimony paid. Recipient's SSN ▶ **29**
30 Add lines 23a through 29. These are your **total adjustments** . . . . ▶ **30**   **2,361 –**

Adjusted Gross Income

31 Subtract line 30 from line 22. This is your **adjusted gross income.** If less than $25,296 and a child lived with you (less than $9,000 if a child didn't live with you), see "Earned Income Credit" on page 27 ▶ **31**   **37,060 –**

Cat. No. 11320B   Form **1040** (1994)

Form 1040 (1994)
Page **2**

Tax Compu-ation (See page 3.)	32	Amount from line 31 (adjusted gross income)	32	37,060 —
	33a	Check if: ☐ **You** were 65 or older, ☐ Blind; ☐ **Spouse** was 65 or older, ☐ Blind. Add the number of boxes checked above and enter the total here . . . . ▶ **33a**		
	b	If your parent (or someone else) can claim you as a dependent, check here . ▶ **33b** ☐		
	c	If you are married filing separately and your spouse itemizes deductions or you are a dual-status alien, see page 23 and check here . . . . ▶ **33c** ☐		
	34	Enter the **larger** of your: { **Itemized deductions** from Schedule A, line 29, **OR Standard deduction** shown below for your filing status. **But if you checked any box on line 33a or b,** go to page 23 to find your standard deduction. If you checked box 33c, your standard deduction is zero. • Single—$3,800 • Head of household—$5,600 • Married filing jointly or Qualifying widow(er)—$6,350 • Married filing separately—$3,175 }	34	3,800 —
	35	Subtract line 34 from line 32	35	33,260 —
	36	If line 32 is $83,850 or less, multiply $2,450 by the total number of exemptions claimed on line 6e. If line 32 is over $83,850, see the worksheet on page 24 for the amount to enter .	36	2,450 —
(If you want the IRS to figure your tax, see page 24.)	37	**Taxable income.** Subtract line 36 from line 35. If line 36 is more than line 35, enter -0-	37	30,810 —
	38	Tax. Check if from a ☑ Tax Table, b ☐ Tax Rate Schedules, c ☐ Capital Gain Tax Work-sheet, or d ☐ Form 8615 (see page 24). Amount from Form(s) 8814 ▶ e _____	38	5,674 —
	39	Additional taxes. Check if from a ☐ Form 4970 b ☐ Form 4972	39	0
	40	Add lines 38 and 39 . . . . ▶	40	5,674 —
Credits (See page 24.)	41	Credit for child and dependent care expenses. Attach Form 2441	41	
	42	Credit for the elderly or the disabled. Attach Schedule R . .	42	
	43	Foreign tax credit. Attach Form 1116	43	
	44	Other credits (see page 25). Check if from a ☐ Form 3800 b ☐ Form 8396 c ☐ Form 8801 d ☐ Form (specify) _____	44	
	45	Add lines 41 through 44	45	0
	46	Subtract line 45 from line 40. If line 45 is more than line 40, enter -0-. . . . . ▶	46	5,674 —
Other Taxes (See page 25.)	47	Self-employment tax. Attach Schedule SE	47	4,722 —
	48	Alternative minimum tax. Attach Form 6251	48	
	49	Recapture taxes. Check if from a ☐ Form 4255 b ☐ Form 8611 c ☐ Form 8828	49	
	50	Social security and Medicare tax on tip income not reported to employer. Attach Form 4137	50	
	51	Tax on qualified retirement plans, including IRAs. If required, attach Form 5329 . .	51	
	52	Advance earned income credit payments from Form W-2 . . .	52	
	53	Add lines 46 through 52. This is your **total tax** . . . . ▶	53	10,396 —
Payments Attach Forms W-2, W-2G, and 1099-R on the front.	54	Federal income tax withheld. If any is from Form(s) 1099, check ▶ ☐	54	
	55	1994 estimated tax payments and amount applied from 1993 return .	55	10,400 —
	56	**Earned income credit.** If required, attach Schedule EIC (see page 27). Nontaxable earned income: amount ▶ _____ and type ▶	56	
	57	Amount paid with Form 4868 (extension request)	57	
	58	Excess social security and RRTA tax withheld (see page 32) . .	58	
	59	Other payments. Check if from a ☐ Form 2439 b ☐ Form 4136	59	
	60	Add lines 54 through 59. These are your **total payments** . . . . ▶	60	10,400 —
Refund or Amount You Owe	61	If line 60 is more than line 53, subtract line 53 from line 60. This is the amount you **OVERPAID**. ▶	61	4 —
	62	Amount of line 61 you want **REFUNDED TO YOU.** . . . . ▶	62	4 —
	63	Amount of line 61 you want **APPLIED TO YOUR 1995 ESTIMATED TAX** ▶	63	
	64	If line 53 is more than line 60, subtract line 60 from line 53. This is the **AMOUNT YOU OWE.** For details on how to pay, including what to write on your payment, see page 32 . . .	64	
	65	Estimated tax penalty (see page 33). Also include on line 64	65	

Sign Here

Keep a copy of this return for your records.

Under penalties of perjury, I declare that I have examined this return and accompanying schedules and statements, and to the best of my knowledge and belief, they are true, correct, and complete. Declaration of preparer (other than taxpayer) is based on all information of which preparer has any knowledge.

▶ Your signature _~~~~_	Date 4/15/95	Your occupation TECHNICAL WRITER
▶ Spouse's signature. If a joint return, BOTH must sign.	Date	Spouse's occupation

Paid Preparer's Use Only

Preparer's signature ▶	Date	Check if self-employed ☐	Preparer's social security no.
Firm's name (or yours if self-employed) and address ▶		E.I. No.	
		ZIP code	

♲ *Printed on recycled paper*

*U.S. Government Printing Office: 1994 — 375-188

SCHEDULE C
(Form 1040)

Department of the Treasury
Internal Revenue Service (O)

Profit or Loss From Business

(Sole Proprietorship)

▶ **Partnerships, joint ventures, etc., must file Form 1065.**

▶ **Attach to Form 1040 or Form 1041.** ▶ **See Instructions for Schedule C (Form 1040).**

OMB No. 1545-0074

1994

Attachment
Sequence No. **09**

Name of proprietor	Social security number (SSN)
GEOFFREY FOURMYLE	000 00 0000

A Principal business or profession, including product or service (see page C-1)	B Enter principal business code
TECHNICAL WRITER	(see page C-6) ▶ 7 8 8 0

C Business name. If no separate business name, leave blank.	D Employer ID number (EIN), if any

E Business address (including suite or room no.) ▶ 5217 CERES BOULEVARD

City, town or post office, state, and ZIP code   SAN FRANCISCO, CA 94701

F Accounting method: (1) ☑ Cash   (2) ☐ Accrual   (3) ☐ Other (specify) ▶ ....

G Method(s) used to value closing inventory: (1) ☐ Cost   (2) ☐ Lower of cost or market   (3) ☐ Other (attach explanation)   (4) ☑ Does not apply (if checked, skip line H)

	Yes	No
H Was there any change in determining quantities, costs, or valuations between opening and closing inventory? If "Yes," attach explanation		
I Did you "materially participate" in the operation of this business during 1994? If "No," see page C-2 for limit on losses. . . .	✓	
J If you started or acquired this business during 1994, check here . . . . ▶ ☑		

Part I Income

1	Gross receipts or sales. **Caution:** If this income was reported to you on Form W-2 and the "Statutory employee" box on that form was checked, see page C-2 and check here . . . . . . ▶ ☐	1	
2	Returns and allowances	2	
3	Subtract line 2 from line 1	3	
4	Cost of goods sold (from line 40 on page 2)	4	
5	**Gross profit.** Subtract line 4 from line 3	5	45,000
6	Other income, including Federal and state gasoline or fuel tax credit or refund (see page C-2) .	6	
7	**Gross income.** Add lines 5 and 6 . . . . ▶	7	45,000

Part II Expenses. Enter expenses for business use of your home **only** on line 30.

8	Advertising	8		19 Pension and profit-sharing plans	19	6,500
9	Bad debts from sales or services (see page C-3) . .	9		20 Rent or lease (see page C-4):		
				a Vehicles, machinery, and equipment .	20a	
10	Car and truck expenses (see page C-3)	10		b Other business property . .	20b	3,000
11	Commissions and fees. . .	11		21 Repairs and maintenance . .	21	
12	Depletion.	12		22 Supplies (not included in Part III) .	22	
13	Depreciation and section 179 expense deduction (not included in Part III) (see page C-3) .	13	1,000	23 Taxes and licenses	23	
				24 Travel, meals, and entertainment:		
				a Travel	24a	250
14	Employee benefit programs (other than on line 19) . .	14		b Meals and entertainment .		
15	Insurance (other than health) .	15		c Enter 50% of line 24b subject to limitations (see page C-4) .		
16	Interest:					
a	Mortgage (paid to banks, etc.) .	16a		d Subtract line 24c from line 24b	24d	
b	Other	16b		25 Utilities + TELEPHONE . .	25	729
17	Legal and professional services	17		26 Wages (less employment credits) .	26	
				27 Other expenses (from line 46 on page 2) DUES + PUBLICATIONS	27	100
18	Office expense	18				

28	**Total expenses** before expenses for business use of home. Add lines 8 through 27 in columns . ▶	28	11,579
29	Tentative profit (loss). Subtract line 28 from line 7	29	
30	Expenses for business use of your home. Attach **Form 8829**	30	
31	**Net profit or (loss).** Subtract line 30 from line 29.		
	• If a profit, enter on **Form 1040, line 12,** and ALSO on **Schedule SE, line 2** (statutory employees, see page C-5). Estates and trusts, enter on Form 1041, line 3.	31	33,421
	• If a loss, you MUST go on to line 32.		

32 If you have a loss, check the box that describes your investment in this activity (see page C-5).

• If you checked 32a, enter the loss on **Form 1040, line 12,** and ALSO on **Schedule SE, line 2** (statutory employees, see page C-5). Estates and trusts, enter on Form 1041, line 3.

• If you checked 32b, you MUST attach **Form 6198.**

32a ☑ All investment is at risk.
32b ☐ Some investment is not at risk.

For Paperwork Reduction Act Notice, see Form 1040 instructions.   Cat. No. 11334P   **Schedule C (Form 1040) 1994**

SCHEDULE SE			
(Form 1040)	**Self-Employment Tax**		OMB No. 1545-0074
Department of the Treasury Internal Revenue Service (O)	▶ See Instructions for Schedule SE (Form 1040). ▶ Attach to Form 1040.		19**94** Attachment Sequence No. **17**

Name of person with **self-employment** income (as shown on Form 1040) GEOFFREY FOURMYLE	Social security number of person with **self-employment** income ▶ 000 00 0000

Who Must File Schedule SE

You must file Schedule SE if:

● You had net earnings from self-employment from other than church employee income (line 4 of Short Schedule SE or line 4c of Long Schedule SE) of $400 or more, **OR**

● You had church employee income of $108.28 or more. Income from services you performed as a minister or a member of a religious order **is not** church employee income. See page SE-1.

Note: *Even if you have a loss or a small amount of income from self-employment, it may be to your benefit to file Schedule SE and use either "optional method" in Part II of Long Schedule SE. See page SE-2.*

Exception. If your only self-employment income was from earnings as a minister, member of a religious order, or Christian Science practitioner, **and** you filed Form 4361 and received IRS approval not to be taxed on those earnings, **do not** file Schedule SE. Instead, write "Exempt–Form 4361" on Form 1040, line 47.

May I Use Short Schedule SE or MUST I Use Long Schedule SE?

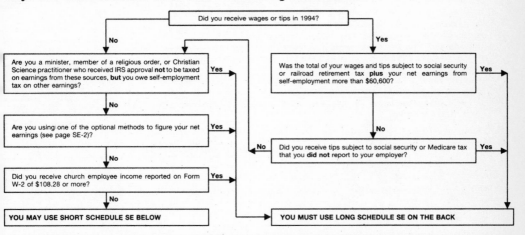

Section A—Short Schedule SE. Caution: *Read above to see if you can use Short Schedule SE.*

1	Net farm profit or (loss) from Schedule F, line 36, and farm partnerships, Schedule K-1 (Form 1065), line 15a	**1**	0
2	Net profit or (loss) from Schedule C, line 31; Schedule C-EZ, line 3; and Schedule K-1 (Form 1065), line 15a (other than farming). Ministers and members of religious orders see page SE-1 for amounts to report on this line. See page SE-2 for other income to report	**2**	33,421 —
3	Combine lines 1 and 2	**3**	33,421 —
4	**Net earnings from self-employment.** Multiply line 3 by 92.35% (.9235). If less than $400, **do not** file this schedule; you do not owe self-employment tax . . . . ▶	**4**	30,864 —
5	**Self-employment tax.** If the amount on line 4 is:		
	● $60,600 or less, multiply line 4 by 15.3% (.153). Enter the result here and on **Form 1040, line 47.**	**5**	4,722 —
	● More than $60,600, multiply line 4 by 2.9% (.029). Then, add $7,514.40 to the result. Enter the total here and on **Form 1040, line 47.**		
6	**Deduction for one-half of self-employment tax.** Multiply line 5 by 50% (.5). Enter the result here and on **Form 1040, line 25**	**6** 2,361 —	

For Paperwork Reduction Act Notice, see Form 1040 instructions.   Cat. No. 11358Z   **Schedule SE (Form 1040) 1994**

Form **4562**	**Depreciation and Amortization**	OMB No. 1545-0172
Department of the Treasury Internal Revenue Service (O)	**(Including Information on Listed Property)** ▶ See separate instructions. ▶ Attach this form to your return.	**1994** Attachment Sequence No. **67**

Name(s) shown on return	Identifying number
GEOFFREY FOURMYLE	000-00-0000

Business or activity to which this form relates

Part I   **Election To Expense Certain Tangible Property (Section 179)** (Note: *If you have any "Listed Property," complete Part V before you complete Part I.*)

1	Maximum dollar limitation (If an enterprise zone business, see instructions.)	1	$17,500
2	Total cost of section 179 property placed in service during the tax year (see instructions)	2	
3	Threshold cost of section 179 property before reduction in limitation	3	$200,000
4	Reduction in limitation. Subtract line 3 from line 2. If zero or less, enter -0-	4	
5	Dollar limitation for tax year. Subtract line 4 from line 1. If zero or less, enter -0-. (If married filing separately, see instructions.)	5	

(a) Description of property	(b) Cost	(c) Elected cost	
6			

7	Listed property. Enter amount from line 26.	7		
8	Total elected cost of section 179 property. Add amounts in column (c), lines 6 and 7	8	
9	Tentative deduction. Enter the smaller of line 5 or line 8	9	
10	Carryover of disallowed deduction from 1993 (see instructions)	10	
11	Taxable income limitation. Enter the smaller of taxable income (not less than zero) or line 5 (see instructions)	11	
12	Section 179 expense deduction. Add lines 9 and 10, but do not enter more than line 11	12	
13	Carryover of disallowed deduction to 1995. Add lines 9 and 10, less line 12 ▶	13	

Note: *Do not use Part II or Part III below for listed property (automobiles, certain other vehicles, cellular telephones, certain computers, or property used for entertainment, recreation, or amusement). Instead, use Part V for listed property.*

Part II   **MACRS Depreciation For Assets Placed in Service ONLY During Your 1994 Tax Year (Do Not Include Listed Property)**

(a) Classification of property	(b) Month and year placed in service	(c) Basis for depreciation (business/investment use only—see instructions)	(d) Recovery period	(e) Convention	(f) Method	(g) Depreciation deduction
Section A—General Depreciation System (GDS) (see instructions)						
14a 3-year property						
b 5-year property						
c 7-year property						
d 10-year property						
e 15-year property						
f 20-year property						
g Residential rental property			27.5 yrs.	MM	S/L	
			27.5 yrs.	MM	S/L	
h Nonresidential real property			39 yrs.	MM	S/L	
				MM	S/L	
Section B—Alternative Depreciation System (ADS) (see instructions)						
15a Class life					S/L	
b 12-year			12 yrs.		S/L	
c 40-year			40 yrs.	MM	S/L	

Part III   **Other Depreciation (Do Not Include Listed Property)**

16	GDS and ADS deductions for assets placed in service in tax years beginning before 1994 (see instructions)	16	
17	Property subject to section 168(f)(1) election (see instructions)	17	
18	ACRS and other depreciation (see instructions)	18	1,000 —

Part IV   **Summary**

19	Listed property. Enter amount from line 25.	19	
20	**Total.** Add deductions on line 12, lines 14 and 15 in column (g), and lines 16 through 19. Enter here and on the appropriate lines of your return. (Partnerships and S corporations—see instructions.)	20	1,000 —
21	For assets shown above and placed in service during the current year, enter the portion of the basis attributable to section 263A costs (see instructions)	21	

For Paperwork Reduction Act Notice, see page 1 of the separate instructions.   Cat. No. 12906N   Form **4562** (1994)

Form 1120-A — U.S. Corporation Short-Form Income Tax Return

Department of the Treasury
Internal Revenue Service

See separate instructions to make sure the corporation qualifies to file Form 1120-A.
For calendar year 1994 or tax year beginning .... **, 1994, ending** .... **, 19** ....

OMB No. 1545-0890

1994

A Check this box if the corp. is a personal service corp. (as defined in Temporary Regs. section 1.441-4T—see instructions) ▶ ☐

Use IRS label. Other-wise, please print or type.

Name: TIFFANY FIELD
Number, street, and room or suite no. (If a P.O. box, see page 6 of instructions.): 795 FIFTH AVENUE
City or town, state, and ZIP code: NEW YORK, NY 10021

B Employer identification number: 13 : 0000000
C Date incorporated: 1/2/94
D Total assets (see Specific Instructions): $ 112,940 —

E Check applicable boxes: (1) ☑ Initial return   (2) ☐ Change of address
F Check method of accounting: (1) ☑ Cash   (2) ☐ Accrual   (3) ☐ Other (specify) · ▶

Income

1a	Gross receipts or sales	b Less returns and allowances	c Balance ▶ 1c	100,000 —
2	Cost of goods sold (see instructions)		2	
3	Gross profit. Subtract line 2 from line 1c		3	
4	Domestic corporation dividends subject to the 70% deduction		4	10,000 —
5	Interest		5	
6	Gross rents		6	
7	Gross royalties		7	
8	Capital gain net income (attach Schedule D (Form 1120))		8	
9	Net gain or (loss) from Form 4797, Part II, line 20 (attach Form 4797)		9	
10	Other income (see instructions)		10	
11	**Total income.** Add lines 3 through 10 ▶		11	110,000 —

Deductions

(See instructions for limitations on deductions.)

12	Compensation of officers (see instructions)		12	40,000 —
13	Salaries and wages (less employment credits)		13	
14	~~Repairs and maintenance~~ UTILITIES + PHONE		14	3,500 —
15	~~Bad debts~~ EMPLOYEE MEDICAL		15	6,000 —
16	Rents		16	6,000 —
17	Taxes and licenses SOC. SEC.		17	3,060 —
18	~~Interest~~ PENSION + PROFIT SHARING		18	10,000 —
19	Charitable contributions (see instructions for 10% limitation)		19	
20	Depreciation (attach Form 4562)	20	1,000 —	
21	Less depreciation claimed elsewhere on return	21a	0	21b	1,000 —
22	Other deductions (attach schedule)		22	4,500 —
23	**Total deductions.** Add lines 12 through 22 ▶		23	74,060 —
24	Taxable income before net operating loss deduction and special deductions. Subtract line 23 from line 11		24	35,940 —
25	**Less: a** Net operating loss deduction (see instructions)	25a	0	
	b Special deductions (see instructions). 70% DIVIDEND	25b	7,000 —	
	c		25c	7,000 —
26	**Taxable income.** Subtract line 25c from line 24		26	28,940 —
27	**Total tax** (from page 2, Part I, line 7)		27	4,341 —

Tax and Payments

28	**Payments:**		
a	1993 overpayment credited to 1994	28a	
b	1994 estimated tax payments	28b	4,000 —
c	Less 1994 refund applied for on Form 4466	28c (	) Bal ▶ 28d
e	Tax deposited with Form 7004	28e	
f	Credit from regulated investment companies (attach Form 2439)	28f	
g	Credit for Federal tax on fuels (attach Form 4136). See instructions	28g	
h	Total payments. Add lines 28d through 28g		28h	4,000 —
29	Estimated tax penalty (see instructions). Check if Form 2220 is attached ▶ ☐		29	
30	**Tax due.** If line 28h is smaller than the total of lines 27 and 29, enter amount owed		30	341 —
31	**Overpayment.** If line 28h is larger than the total of lines 27 and 29, enter amount overpaid		31	
32	Enter amount of line 31 you want: **Credited to 1995 estimated tax ▶**	Refunded ▶	32	

Please Sign Here

Under penalties of perjury, I declare that I have examined this return, including accompanying schedules and statements, and to the best of my knowledge and belief, it is true, correct, and complete. Declaration of preparer (other than taxpayer) is based on all information of which preparer has any knowledge.

Signature of officer ▶ _(signed)_   Date: 3/15/95   Title: PRESIDENT

Paid Preparer's Use Only

Preparer's signature ▶	Date	Check if self-employed ▶ ☐	Preparer's social security number
Firm's name (or yours if self-employed) and address ▶		E.I. No. ▶
		ZIP code ▶

For Paperwork Reduction Act Notice, see page 1 of the instructions.   Cat. No. 11456E   Form **1120-A** (1994)

Form 1120-A (1994)   Page

Part I   Tax Computation (See instructions.)

1	Income tax. If the corporation is a qualified personal service corporation (see page 14), check here ▶ ☐	1	4,341 —
2a	General business credit. Check if from: ☐ Form 3800 ☐ Form 3468 ☐ Form 5884		
	☐ Form 6478 ☐ Form 6765 ☐ Form 8586 ☐ Form 8830 ☐ Form 8826 ☐ Form 8835		
	☐ Form 8844 ☐ Form 8845 ☐ Form 8846 ☐ Form 8847 . . . . . **2a**		
b	Credit for prior year minimum tax (attach Form 8827) **2b**		
3	**Total credits.** Add lines 2a and 2b	3	
4	Subtract line 3 from line 1	4	4,341 —
5	Recapture taxes. Check if from: ☐ Form 4255 ☐ Form 8611	5	0
6	Alternative minimum tax (attach Form 4626)	6	0
7	**Total tax.** Add lines 4 through 6. Enter here and on line 27, page 1 . . .	7	4,341 —

Part II   Other Information (See instructions.)

1 Refer to page 19 of the instructions and state the principal:
   a Business activity code no. ▶ 7880
   b Business activity ▶
   c Product or service ▶ DESIGNING JEWELRY
2 Did any individual, partnership, estate, or trust at the end of the tax year own, directly or indirectly, 50% or more of the corporation's voting stock? (For rules of attribution, see section 267(c).) . . . . ☑ Yes ☐ No
   ↪ TIFFANY FIELD, 795 FIFTH AVENUE, NY NY 10021, 5000-00 –
   If "Yes," attach a schedule showing name and identifying number. 0000
3 Enter the amount of tax-exempt interest received or accrued during the tax year . . . . . ▶ $ 0
4 Enter amount of cash distributions and the book value of property (other than cash) distributions made in this tax year . . . . ▶ $ 0

5a If an amount is entered on line 2, page 1, see the worksheet page 12 for amounts to enter below:

(1)	Purchases	
(2)	Additional sec. 263A costs (see instructions—attach schedule) .	
(3)	Other costs (attach schedule) .	

b Do the rules of section 263A (for property produced or acquired resale) apply to the corporation? . . . . ☐ Yes ☑
6 At any time during the 1994 calendar year, did the corporation ha an interest in or a signature or other authority over a financial accou in a foreign country (such as a bank account, securities account, other financial account)? If "Yes," the corporation may have to Form TD F 90-22.1 . . . . ☐ Yes ☑
   If "Yes," enter the name of the foreign country ▶

Part III   Balance Sheets

		(a) Beginning of tax year	(b) End of tax year
1	Cash		30,607 —
2a	Trade notes and accounts receivable		
b	Less allowance for bad debts	( )	(
3	Inventories		
4	U.S. government obligations	INCORPORATED	
5	Tax-exempt securities (see instructions) . . .	1/2/94	
6	Other current assets (attach schedule)		
7	Loans to stockholders	INITIAL	
8	Mortgage and real estate loans	RETURN	
9a	Depreciable, depletable, and intangible assets . . .		3,333 —
b	Less accumulated depreciation, depletion, and amortization	( )	1,000
10	Land (net of any amortization) . . .		
11	Other assets (attach schedule) STOCKS		80,000 —
12	Total assets		112,940 —
13	Accounts payable		
14	Other current liabilities (attach schedule) GOLD DUST TWINS		2,000 —
15	Loans from stockholders		
16	Mortgages, notes, bonds payable . . .		
17	Other liabilities (attach schedule)		
18	Capital stock (preferred and common stock) . . .		10,000 —
19	Paid-in or capital surplus		65,000 —
20	Retained earnings		35,940 —
21	Less cost of treasury stock	( )	(
22	Total liabilities and stockholders' equity		112,940 —

Assets (rows 1–12)
Liabilities and Stockholders' Equity (rows 13–22)

Part IV   Reconciliation of Income (Loss) per Books With Income per Return (You are not required to complete Part IV if the total assets on line 12, column (b), Part III are less than $25,000.)

1	Net income (loss) per books	31,599 —	6	Income recorded on books this year not included on this return (itemize)	0
2	Federal income tax	4,341 —		
3	Excess of capital losses over capital gains . .	0	7	Deductions on this return not charged against book income this year (itemize)	0
4	Income subject to tax not recorded on books this year (itemize)	0		
5	Expenses recorded on books this year not deducted on this return (itemize)	0	8	Income (line 24, page 1). Enter the sum of lines 1 through 5 less the sum of lines 6 and 7 . .	35,940

♲ Printed on recycled paper   ☆ U.S. GPO: 1994-375-292

1040

Department of the Treasury—Internal Revenue Service

U.S. Individual Income Tax Return (O) 1994

For the year Jan. 1–Dec. 31, 1994, or other tax year beginning _____ , 1994, ending _____ , 19 __

IRS Use Only—Do not write or staple in this space.

OMB No. 1545-0074

Label		
(See instructions on page 12.)	**Your first name and initial** TIFFANY	**Last name** FIELD

Your social security number 000 00 0000

Use the IRS label. Otherwise, please print or type.

If a joint return, spouse's first name and initial ___ Last name ___

Spouse's social security number

Home address (number and street). If you have a P.O. box, see page 12. 795 FIFTH AVENUE   Apt. no. __

For Privacy Act and Paperwork Reduction Act Notice, see page 4.

City, town or post office, state, and ZIP code. If you have a foreign address, see page 12. NEW YORK, NY 10021

Presidential Election Campaign (See page 12.)

	Yes	No	
Do you want $3 to go to this fund?	✓		Note: *Checking "Yes" will not change your tax or reduce your refund.*
If a joint return, does your spouse want $3 to go to this fund?			

Filing Status

(See page 12.)

Check only one box.

1 ✓ Single
2 ☐ Married filing joint return (even if only one had income)
3 ☐ Married filing separate return. Enter spouse's social security no. above and full name here. ▶ _____
4 ☐ Head of household (with qualifying person). (See page 13.) If the qualifying person is a child but not your dependent, enter this child's name here. ▶ _____
5 ☐ Qualifying widow(er) with dependent child (year spouse died ▶ 19 __). (See page 13.)

Exemptions

(See page 13.)

If more than six dependents, see page 14.

6a ☑ **Yourself.** If your parent (or someone else) can claim you as a dependent on his or her tax return, **do not** check box 6a. But be sure to check the box on line 33b on page 2.
b ☐ **Spouse**

No. of boxes checked on 6a and 6b	1

c **Dependents:**

(1) Name (first, initial, and last name)	(2) Check if under age 1	(3) If age 1 or older, dependent's social security number	(4) Dependent's relationship to you	(5) No. of months lived in your home in 1994

No. of your children on 6c who:	
• lived with you	0
• didn't live with you due to divorce or separation (see page 14)	0
Dependents on 6c not entered above	0

d If your child didn't live with you but is claimed as your dependent under a pre-1985 agreement, check here ▶ ☐
e Total number of exemptions claimed

Add numbers entered on lines above ▶	1

Income

Attach Copy B of your Forms W-2, W-2G, and 1099-R here.

If you did not get a W-2, see page 15.

Enclose, but do not attach, any payment with your return.

7	Wages, salaries, tips, etc. Attach Form(s) W-2	7	40,000 —
8a	**Taxable** interest income (see page 15). Attach Schedule B if over $400	8a	
b	**Tax-exempt** interest (see page 16). DON'T include on line 8a 8b [ ]		
9	Dividend income. Attach Schedule B if over $400	9	
10	Taxable refunds, credits, or offsets of state and local income taxes (see page 16)	10	
11	Alimony received	11	
12	Business income or (loss). Attach Schedule C or C-EZ	12	
13	Capital gain or (loss). If required, attach Schedule D (see page 16)	13	
14	Other gains or (losses). Attach Form 4797	14	
15a	Total IRA distributions 15a [ ] b Taxable amount (see page 17)	15b	
16a	Total pensions and annuities 16a [ ] b Taxable amount (see page 17)	16b	
17	Rental real estate, royalties, partnerships, S corporations, trusts, etc. Attach Schedule E	17	
18	Farm income or (loss). Attach Schedule F	18	
19	Unemployment compensation (see page 18)	19	
20a	Social security benefits 20a [ ] b Taxable amount (see page 18)	20b	
21	Other income. List type and amount—see page 18	21	
22	Add the amounts in the far right column for lines 7 through 21. This is your **total income** ▶	22	40,000 —

Adjustments to Income

Caution: See instructions. ▶

23a	Your IRA deduction (see page 19) 23a [ ]		
b	Spouse's IRA deduction (see page 19) 23b [ ]		
24	Moving expenses. Attach Form 3903 or 3903-F 24 [ ]		
25	One-half of self-employment tax 25 [ ]		
26	Self-employed health insurance deduction (see page 21) 26 [ ]		
27	Keogh retirement plan and self-employed SEP deduction 27 [ ]		
28	Penalty on early withdrawal of savings 28 [ ]		
29	Alimony paid. Recipient's SSN ▶ 29 [ ]		
30	Add lines 23a through 29. These are your **total adjustments** ▶	30	0

Adjusted Gross Income

31	Subtract line 30 from line 22. This is your **adjusted gross income**. If less than $25,296 and a child lived with you (less than $9,000 if a child didn't live with you), see "Earned Income Credit" on page 27 ▶	31	40,000 —

Cat. No. 11320B   Form **1040** (1994)

Form 1040 (1994)   Page

Tax Computation (See page 23.)	32	Amount from line 31 (adjusted gross income)	32	40,000 —
	33a	Check if: ☐ **You** were 65 or older, ☐ Blind; ☐ **Spouse** was 65 or older, ☐ Blind. Add the number of boxes checked above and enter the total here . . . . ▶ 33a		
	b	If your parent (or someone else) can claim you as a dependent, check here . ▶ 33b ☐		
	c	If you are married filing separately and your spouse itemizes deductions or you are a dual-status alien, see page 23 and check here . . . . . ▶ 33c ☐		
	34	Enter the **larger** of your: **Itemized deductions** from Schedule A, line 29, **OR** **Standard deduction** shown below for your filing status. **But if you checked any box on line 33a or b,** go to page 23 to find your standard deduction. If you checked **box 33c,** your standard deduction is zero. • Single—$3,800 • Head of household—$5,600 • Married filing jointly or Qualifying widow(er)—$6,350 • Married filing separately—$3,175	34	3,800 —
If you want the IRS to figure your tax, see page 24.	35	Subtract line 34 from line 32	35	36,200 —
	36	If line 32 is $83,850 or less, multiply $2,450 by the total number of exemptions claimed on line 6e. If line 32 is over $83,850, see the worksheet on page 24 for the amount to enter .	36	2,450 —
	37	**Taxable income.** Subtract line 36 from line 35. If line 36 is more than line 35, enter -0-	37	33,750 —
	38	Tax. Check if from **a** ☑ Tax Table, **b** ☐ Tax Rate Schedules, **c** ☐ Capital Gain Tax Worksheet, or **d** ☐ Form 8615 (see page 24). Amount from Form(s) 8814 ▶ **e** _____	38	6,500 —
	39	Additional taxes. Check if from **a** ☐ Form 4970 **b** ☐ Form 4972 . . .	39	0
	40	Add lines 38 and 39 . . . . ▶	40	6,500 —
Credits (See page 24.)	41	Credit for child and dependent care expenses. Attach Form 2441	41	
	42	Credit for the elderly or the disabled. Attach Schedule R .	42	
	43	Foreign tax credit. Attach Form 1116	43	
	44	Other credits (see page 25). Check if from **a** ☐ Form 3800 **b** ☐ Form 8396 **c** ☐ Form 8801 **d** ☐ Form (specify) _____	44	
	45	Add lines 41 through 44	45	0
	46	Subtract line 45 from line 40. If line 45 is more than line 40, enter -0- . . . . ▶	46	6,500 —
Other Taxes (See page 25.)	47	Self-employment tax. Attach Schedule SE	47	
	48	Alternative minimum tax. Attach Form 6251	48	
	49	Recapture taxes. Check if from **a** ☐ Form 4255 **b** ☐ Form 8611 **c** ☐ Form 8828	49	
	50	Social security and Medicare tax on tip income not reported to employer. Attach Form 4137 .	50	
	51	Tax on qualified retirement plans, including IRAs. If required, attach Form 5329 .	51	
	52	Advance earned income credit payments from Form W-2	52	
	53	Add lines 46 through 52. This is your **total tax** . . . . ▶	53	6,500 —
Payments Attach Forms W-2, W-2G, and 1099-R on the front.	54	Federal income tax withheld. If any is from Form(s) 1099, check ▶ ☐ 54 7,000 —		
	55	1994 estimated tax payments and amount applied from 1993 return . 55		
	56	**Earned income credit.** If required, attach Schedule EIC (see page 27). Nontaxable earned income: amount ▶ _____ and type ▶ _____ 56		
	57	Amount paid with Form 4868 (extension request) 57		
	58	Excess social security and RRTA tax withheld (see page 32) . 58		
	59	Other payments. Check if from **a** ☐ Form 2439 **b** ☐ Form 4136 59		
	60	Add lines 54 through 59. These are your **total payments** . . . . ▶	60	7,000 —
Refund or Amount You Owe	61	If line 60 is more than line 53, subtract line 53 from line 60. This is the amount you **OVERPAID.** ▶	61	500 —
	62	Amount of line 61 you want **REFUNDED TO YOU.** . . . . ▶	62	500 —
	63	Amount of line 61 you want **APPLIED TO YOUR 1995 ESTIMATED TAX** ▶ 63		
	64	If line 53 is more than line 60, subtract line 60 from line 53. This is the **AMOUNT YOU OWE.** For details on how to pay, including what to write on your payment, see page 32 . .	64	
	65	Estimated tax penalty (see page 33). Also include on line 64 65		

Sign Here Keep a copy of this return for your records.	Under penalties of perjury, I declare that I have examined this return and accompanying schedules and statements, and to the best of my knowledge and belief, they are true, correct, and complete. Declaration of preparer (other than taxpayer) is based on all information of which preparer has any knowledge	
	Your signature ✗ _~T~ F~_	Date 4/15/95	Your occupation DESIGNER
	Spouse's signature. If a joint return, BOTH must sign.	Date	Spouse's occupation
Paid Preparer's Use Only	Preparer's signature ▶	Date	Check if self-employed ☐	Preparer's social security r
	Firm's name (or yours if self-employed) and address ▶		E.I. No.	
			ZIP code	

♻ *Printed on recycled paper*   *U.S. Government Printing Office: 1994 — 375-

FORM 1040

Department of the Treasury—Internal Revenue Service

U.S. Individual Income Tax Return (O) **1994**

IRS Use Only—Do not write or staple in this space.

For the year Jan. 1–Dec. 31, 1994, or other tax year beginning ____, 1994, ending ____, 19 __ | OMB No. 1545-0074

Label
(See instructions on page 12.)
Use the IRS label.
Otherwise, please print or type.

Your first name and initial: TIFFANY   Last name: FIELD

Your social security number: 000 00 0000

If a joint return, spouse's first name and initial ____ Last name ____

Spouse's social security number ____

Home address (number and street). If you have a P.O. box, see page 12.: 795 FIFTH AVENUE   Apt. no. ____

City, town or post office, state, and ZIP code. If you have a foreign address, see page 12.: NEW YORK, NY 10021

For Privacy Act and Paperwork Reduction Act Notice, see page 4.

Presidential Election Campaign (See page 12.)
Do you want $3 to go to this fund? .... Yes [✓] No [ ]
If a joint return, does your spouse want $3 to go to this fund? ......

Note: Checking "Yes" will not change your tax or reduce your refund.

Filing Status
(See page 12.)
Check only one box.

1 [✓] Single
2 [ ] Married filing joint return (even if only one had income)
3 [ ] Married filing separate return. Enter spouse's social security no. above and full name here. ▶ ____
4 [ ] Head of household (with qualifying person). (See page 13.) If the qualifying person is a child but not your dependent, enter this child's name here. ▶ ____
5 [ ] Qualifying widow(er) with dependent child (year spouse died ▶ 19 __). (See page 13.)

Exemptions
(See page 13.)

6a [✓] **Yourself.** If your parent (or someone else) can claim you as a dependent on his or her tax return, **do not** check box 6a. But be sure to check the box on line 33b on page 2 .
b [ ] Spouse

No. of boxes checked on 6a and 6b: 1

c **Dependents:**

(1) Name (first, initial, and last name)	(2) Check if under age 1	(3) If age 1 or older, dependent's social security number	(4) Dependent's relationship to you	(5) No. of months lived in your home in 1994

If more than six dependents, see page 14.

No. of your children on 6c who:
• lived with you: 0
• didn't live with you due to divorce or separation (see page 14): 0
Dependents on 6c not entered above: 0

d If your child didn't live with you but is claimed as your dependent under a pre-1985 agreement, check here ▶ [ ]
e Total number of exemptions claimed . . . .

Add numbers entered on lines above ▶ [1]

Income

Attach Copy B of your Forms W-2, W-2G, and 1099-R here.

If you did not get a W-2, see page 15.

Enclose, but do not attach, any payment with your return.

7	Wages, salaries, tips, etc. Attach Form(s) W-2	7	40,000 —
8a	**Taxable** interest income (see page 15). Attach Schedule B if over $400 . . .	8a	
b	**Tax-exempt** interest (see page 16). DON'T include on line 8a	8b	
9	Dividend income. Attach Schedule B if over $400	9	
10	Taxable refunds, credits, or offsets of state and local income taxes (see page 16) . .	10	
11	Alimony received	11	
12	Business income or (loss). Attach Schedule C or C-EZ	12	
13	Capital gain or (loss). If required, attach Schedule D (see page 16) . . .	13	
14	Other gains or (losses). Attach Form 4797	14	
15a	Total IRA distributions . 15a	b Taxable amount (see page 17)	15b	
16a	Total pensions and annuities 16a	b Taxable amount (see page 17)	16b	
17	Rental real estate, royalties, partnerships, S corporations, trusts, etc. Attach Schedule E	17	
18	Farm income or (loss). Attach Schedule F	18	
19	Unemployment compensation (see page 18)	19	
20a	Social security benefits 20a	b Taxable amount (see page 18)	20b	
21	Other income. List type and amount—see page 18	21	
22	Add the amounts in the far right column for lines 7 through 21. This is your **total income** ▶	22	40,000 —

Adjustments to Income

Caution: See instructions . . ▶

23a	Your IRA deduction (see page 19)	23a	
b	Spouse's IRA deduction (see page 19)	23b	
24	Moving expenses. Attach Form 3903 or 3903-F . .	24	
25	One-half of self-employment tax	25	
26	Self-employed health insurance deduction (see page 21)	26	
27	Keogh retirement plan and self-employed SEP deduction	27	
28	Penalty on early withdrawal of savings	28	
29	Alimony paid. Recipient's SSN ▶	29	
30	Add lines 23a through 29. These are your **total adjustments** . . . . . . ▶	30	0

Adjusted Gross Income

31 Subtract line 30 from line 22. This is your **adjusted gross income**. If less than $25,296 and a child lived with you (less than $9,000 if a child didn't live with you), see "Earned Income Credit" on page 27 ▶ | 31 | 40,000 —

Cat. No. 11320B

Form **1040** (1994)

Form 1040 (1994)   Page **2**

Tax Compu-tation	32	Amount from line 31 (adjusted gross income)	32	79,841 —
(See page 23.)	33a	Check if: ☐ **You** were 65 or older, ☐ Blind; ☐ **Spouse** was 65 or older, ☐ Blind. Add the number of boxes checked above and enter the total here . . . . ▶ 33a		
	b	If your parent (or someone else) can claim you as a dependent, check here . ▶ 33b ☐		
	c	If you are married filing separately and your spouse itemizes deductions or you are a dual-status alien, see page 23 and check here . . . . ▶ 33c ☐		
	34	Enter the larger of your: **Itemized deductions** from Schedule A, line 29, **OR** **Standard deduction** shown below for your filing status. **But if you checked any box on line 33a or b,** go to page 23 to find your standard deduction. If you checked **box 33c,** your standard deduction is zero. • Single—$3,800 • Head of household—$5,600 • Married filing jointly or Qualifying widow(er)—$6,350 • Married filing separately—$3,175	34	3,800 —
	35	Subtract line 34 from line 32	35	76,041 —
	36	If line 32 is $83,850 or less, multiply $2,450 by the total number of exemptions claimed on line 6e. If line 32 is over $83,850, see the worksheet on page 24 for the amount to enter .	36	2,450 —
If you want the IRS to figure your tax, see page 24.	37	**Taxable income.** Subtract line 36 from line 35. If line 36 is more than line 35, enter -0-	37	73,591 —
	38	Tax. Check if from a ☑ Tax Table, b ☐ Tax Rate Schedules, c ☐ Capital Gain Tax Worksheet, or d ☐ Form 8615 (see page 24). Amount from Form(s) 8814 ▶ e _____	38	18,306 —
	39	Additional taxes. Check if from a ☐ Form 4970 b ☐ Form 4972	39	0
	40	Add lines 38 and 39 . . . . ▶	40	18,306 —
Credits	41	Credit for child and dependent care expenses. Attach Form 2441	41	
(See page 24.)	42	Credit for the elderly or the disabled. Attach Schedule R . .	42	
	43	Foreign tax credit. Attach Form 1116	43	
	44	Other credits (see page 25). Check if from a ☐ Form 3800 b ☐ Form 8396 c ☐ Form 8801 d ☐ Form (specify) _____	44	
	45	Add lines 41 through 44	45	0
	46	Subtract line 45 from line 40. If line 45 is more than line 40, enter -0- . . . . . ▶	46	18,306 —
Other Taxes	47	Self-employment tax. Attach Schedule SE	47	9,517 —
(See page 25.)	48	Alternative minimum tax. Attach Form 6251	48	
	49	Recapture taxes. Check if from a ☐ Form 4255 b ☐ Form 8611 c ☐ Form 8828 .	49	
	50	Social security and Medicare tax on tip income not reported to employer. Attach Form 4137	50	
	51	Tax on qualified retirement plans, including IRAs. If required, attach Form 5329 . .	51	
	52	Advance earned income credit payments from Form W-2	52	
	53	Add lines 46 through 52. This is your **total tax** . . . . ▶	53	27,823 —
Payments	54	Federal income tax withheld. If any is from Form(s) 1099, check ▶ ☐	54	
	55	1994 estimated tax payments and amount applied from 1993 return .	55	28,000 —
Attach Forms W-2, W-2G, and 1099-R on the front.	56	**Earned income credit.** If required, attach Schedule EIC (see page 27). Nontaxable earned income: amount ▶ _____ and type ▶	56	
	57	Amount paid with Form 4868 (extension request) . . .	57	
	58	Excess social security and RRTA tax withheld (see page 32)	58	
	59	Other payments. Check if from a ☐ Form 2439 b ☐ Form 4136	59	
	60	Add lines 54 through 59. These are your **total payments** . . . . ▶	60	
Refund or Amount You Owe	61	If line 60 is more than line 53, subtract line 53 from line 60. This is the amount you **OVERPAID**. ▶	61	177 —
	62	Amount of line 61 you want **REFUNDED TO YOU**. . . . . ▶	62	177 —
	63	Amount of line 61 you want **APPLIED TO YOUR 1995 ESTIMATED TAX** ▶ 63		
	64	If line 53 is more than line 60, subtract line 60 from line 53. This is the **AMOUNT YOU OWE.** For details on how to pay, including what to write on your payment, see page 32 . . .	64	
	65	Estimated tax penalty (see page 33). Also include on line 64 65		

Sign Here Keep a copy of this return for your records.	Under penalties of perjury, I declare that I have examined this return and accompanying schedules and statements, and to the best of my knowledge and belief, they are true, correct, and complete. Declaration of preparer (other than taxpayer) is based on all information of which preparer has any knowledge.

Your signature ▶ *T~ F~*   Date 4/15/95   Your occupation JEWELRY DESIGNER

Spouse's signature. If a joint return, BOTH must sign. ▶   Date   Spouse's occupation

Paid Preparer's Use Only	Preparer's signature ▶ Date Check if self-employed ☐ Preparer's social security no.
	Firm's name (or yours if self-employed) and address ▶ E.I. No. ZIP code

✹ *Printed on recycled paper*   *U.S. Government Printing Office: 1994 — 375-188*

SCHEDULE C (Form 1040)	**Profit or Loss From Business** (Sole Proprietorship)	OMB No. 1545-0074 **1994**
Department of the Treasury Internal Revenue Service (O)	▶ Partnerships, joint ventures, etc., must file Form 1065. ▶ Attach to Form 1040 or Form 1041. ▶ See Instructions for Schedule C (Form 1040).	Attachment Sequence No. **09**

Name of proprietor	Social security number (SSN)
TIFFANY FIELD	000 00 0000

A Principal business or profession, including product or service (see page C-1)
JEWELRY DESIGNER

B Enter principal business code (see page C-6) ▶ 7 8 8 0

C Business name. If no separate business name, leave blank.
TIFFANY FIELDS DESIGNS

D Employer ID number (EIN), if any

E Business address (including suite or room no.) ▶ 795 FIFTH AVENUE, New York, N.Y. 10021
City, town or post office, state, and ZIP code

F Accounting method: (1) ☑ Cash (2) ☐ Accrual (3) ☐ Other (specify) ▶ ....

G Method(s) used to value closing inventory: (1) ☐ Cost (2) ☐ Lower of cost or market (3) ☐ Other (attach explanation) (4) ☑ Does not apply (if checked, skip line H)   Yes No

H Was there any change in determining quantities, costs, or valuations between opening and closing inventory? If "Yes," attach explanation

I Did you "materially participate" in the operation of this business during 1994? If "No," see page C-2 for limit on losses.

J If you started or acquired this business during 1994, check here . . . . ▶ ☑

Part I Income

1	Gross receipts or sales. **Caution:** If this income was reported to you on Form W-2 and the "Statutory employee" box on that form was checked, see page C-2 and check here . . . . . ▶ ☐	1	
2	Returns and allowances	2	
3	Subtract line 2 from line 1	3	
4	Cost of goods sold (from line 40 on page 2)	4	
5	**Gross profit.** Subtract line 4 from line 3	5	
6	Other income, including Federal and state gasoline or fuel tax credit or refund (see page C-2) . .	6	
7	**Gross income.** Add lines 5 and 6 . . . . ▶	7	100,000 —

Part II Expenses. Enter expenses for business use of your home **only** on line 30.

8	Advertising	8		19	Pension and profit-sharing plans	19	10,000 —
9	Bad debts from sales or services (see page C-3) .	9		20	Rent or lease (see page C-4):		
				a	Vehicles, machinery, and equipment .	20a	
10	Car and truck expenses (see page C-3)	10		b	Other business property .	20b	6,000 —
11	Commissions and fees. .	11		21	Repairs and maintenance .	21	
12	Depletion	12		22	Supplies (not included in Part III) .	22	
13	Depreciation and section 179 expense deduction (not included in Part III) (see page C-3) . .	13	1,000 —	23	Taxes and licenses . .	23	
				24	Travel, meals, and entertainment:		
				a	Travel	24a	1,000 —
14	Employee benefit programs (other than on line 19) . .	14	200 —	b	Meals and entertainment .		
15	Insurance (other than health) .	15		c	Enter 50% of line 24b subject to limitations (see page C-4) .		
16	Interest:						
a	Mortgage (paid to banks, etc.) .	16a		d	Subtract line 24c from line 24b	24d	
b	Other	16b		25	Utilities + TELEPHONE .	25	3,500 —
17	Legal and professional services	17		26	Wages (less employment credits) .	26	
18	Office expense	18	1,000 —	27	Other expenses (from line 46 on page 2) PUBLICATIONS 1,500 POSTAGE + XEROX 1,000	27	2,500 —

28	**Total expenses** before expenses for business use of home. Add lines 8 through 27 in columns . . ▶	28	25,200 —
29	Tentative profit (loss). Subtract line 28 from line 7	29	74,800 —
30	Expenses for business use of your home. Attach **Form 8829**	30	
31	**Net profit or (loss).** Subtract line 30 from line 29.		
	• If a profit, enter on Form 1040, line 12, and ALSO on **Schedule SE, line 2** (statutory employees, see page C-5). Estates and trusts, enter on Form 1041, line 3.	31	74,800 —
	• If a loss, you MUST go on to line 32.		
32	If you have a loss, check the box that describes your investment in this activity (see page C-5).		
	• If you checked 32a, enter the loss on **Form 1040, line 12,** and ALSO on **Schedule SE, line 2** (statutory employees, see page C-5). Estates and trusts, enter on Form 1041, line 3.	32a ☑ All investment is at risk. 32b ☐ Some investment is not	
	• If you checked 32b, you MUST attach **Form 6198.**	at risk.	

For Paperwork Reduction Act Notice, see Form 1040 instructions.   Cat. No. 11334P   Schedule C (Form 1040) 1994

Schedule SE (Form 1040) 1994   Attachment Sequence No. **17**   Page **2**

Name of person with **self-employment** income (as shown on Form 1040)	Social security number of person with **self-employment** income ▶	

Section B—Long Schedule SE

Part I　Self-Employment Tax

Note: *If your only income subject to self-employment tax is church employee income, skip lines 1 through 4b. Enter -0- on line 4c and go to line 5a. Income from services you performed as a minister or a member of a religious order is not church employee income. See page SE-1.*

A   If you are a minister, member of a religious order, or Christian Science practitioner **and** you filed Form 4361, but you had $400 or more of **other** net earnings from self-employment, check here and continue with Part I . . . . . . ▶ ☐

1	Net farm profit or (loss) from Schedule F, line 36, and farm partnerships, Schedule K-1 (Form 1065), line 15a. **Note:** *Skip this line if you use the farm optional method. See page SE-3* . .	**1**	o
2	Net profit or (loss) from Schedule C, line 31; Schedule C-EZ, line 3; and Schedule K-1 (Form 1065), line 15a (other than farming). Ministers and members of religious orders see page SE-1 for amounts to report on this line. See page SE-2 for other income to report. **Note:** *Skip this line if you use the nonfarm optional method. See page SE-3.*	**2**	74,800 —
3	Combine lines 1 and 2	**3**	74,800 —
4a	If line 3 is more than zero, multiply line 3 by 92.35% (.9235). Otherwise, enter amount from line 3	**4a**	69,078 —
b	If you elected one or both of the optional methods, enter the total of lines 15 and 17 here . .	**4b**	—
c	Combine lines 4a and 4b. If less than $400, **do not** file this schedule; you do not owe self-employment tax. **Exception.** If less than $400 and you had church employee income, enter -0- and continue . ▶	**4c**	69,078 —
5a	Enter your church employee income from Form W-2. **Caution:** *See page SE-1 for definition of church employee income*	**5a** o	
b	Multiply line 5a by 92.35% (.9235). If less than $100, enter -0-	**5b**	o
6	**Net earnings from self-employment.** Add lines 4c and 5b	**6**	69,078 —
7	Maximum amount of combined wages and self-employment earnings subject to social security tax or the 6.2% portion of the 7.65% railroad retirement (tier 1) tax for 1994	**7**	60,600 00
8a	Total social security wages and tips (total of boxes 3 and 7 on Form(s) W-2) and railroad retirement (tier 1) compensation	**8a** o	
b	Unreported tips subject to social security tax (from Form 4137, line 9)	**8b** o	
c	Add lines 8a and 8b	**8c**	o
9	Subtract line 8c from line 7. If zero or less, enter -0- here and on line 10 and go to line 11 . ▶	**9**	60,600 —
10	Multiply the **smaller** of line 6 or line 9 by 12.4% (.124)	**10**	7,514 —
11	Multiply line 6 by 2.9% (.029)	**11**	2,003 —
12	**Self-employment tax.** Add lines 10 and 11. Enter here and on **Form 1040, line 47** . . .	**12**	9,517 —
13	**Deduction for one-half of self-employment tax.** Multiply line 12 by 50% (.5). Enter the result here and on **Form 1040, line 25**	**13** 4,959 —	

Part II　Optional Methods To Figure Net Earnings (See page SE-2.)

Farm Optional Method. You may use this method **only** if:
- Your gross farm income[1] was not more than $2,400, **or**
- Your gross farm income[1] was more than $2,400 and your net farm profits[2] were less than $1,733.

14	Maximum income for optional methods	**14**	1,600 00
15	Enter the **smaller** of: two-thirds (⅔) of gross farm income[1] (not less than zero) **or** $1,600. Also, include this amount on line 4b above	**15**	

Nonfarm Optional Method. You may use this method **only** if:
- Your net nonfarm profits[3] were less than $1,733 and also less than 72.189% of your gross nonfarm income,[4] **and**
- You had net earnings from self-employment of at least $400 in 2 of the prior 3 years.

Caution: *You may use this method no more than five times.*

16	Subtract line 15 from line 14	**16**	
17	Enter the **smaller** of: two-thirds (⅔) of gross nonfarm income[4] (not less than zero) **or** the amount on line 16. Also, include this amount on line 4b above	**17**	

[1]From Schedule F, line 11, and Schedule K-1 (Form 1065), line 15b.   [3]From Schedule C, line 31; Schedule C-EZ, line 3; and Schedule K-1 (Form 1065), line 15a.
[2]From Schedule F, line 36, and Schedule K-1 (Form 1065), line 15a.   [4]From Schedule C, line 7; Schedule C-EZ, line 1; and Schedule K-1 (Form 1065), line 15c.

♻ **Printed on recycled paper**   *U.S. Government Printing Office: 1994 — 375-218

Form 4562

Department of the Treasury
Internal Revenue Service   (O)

Depreciation and Amortization
(Including Information on Listed Property)

▶ See separate instructions.   ▶ Attach this form to your return.

OMB No. 1545-0172

1994

Attachment
Sequence No. **67**

Name(s) shown on return

TIFFANY FIELD

Identifying number

000-00-0000

Business or activity to which this form relates

JEWELRY DESIGN

Part I **Election To Expense Certain Tangible Property (Section 179)** (Note: *If you have any "Listed Property," complete Part V before you complete Part I.*)

1	Maximum dollar limitation (If an enterprise zone business, see instructions.)	**1**	$17,500
2	Total cost of section 179 property placed in service during the tax year (see instructions)	**2**	
3	Threshold cost of section 179 property before reduction in limitation	**3**	$200,000
4	Reduction in limitation. Subtract line 3 from line 2. If zero or less, enter -0-	**4**	
5	Dollar limitation for tax year. Subtract line 4 from line 1. If zero or less, enter -0-. (If married filing separately, see instructions.)	**5**	

(a) Description of property	(b) Cost	(c) Elected cost

7	Listed property. Enter amount from line 26.	**7**	
8	Total elected cost of section 179 property. Add amounts in column (c), lines 6 and 7	**8**	
9	Tentative deduction. Enter the smaller of line 5 or line 8	**9**	
10	Carryover of disallowed deduction from 1993 (see instructions).	**10**	
11	Taxable income limitation. Enter the smaller of taxable income (not less than zero) or line 5 (see instructions)	**11**	
12	Section 179 expense deduction. Add lines 9 and 10, but do not enter more than line 11	**12**	
13	Carryover of disallowed deduction to 1995. Add lines 9 and 10, less line 12 ▶	**13**	

Note: *Do not use Part II or Part III below for listed property (automobiles, certain other vehicles, cellular telephones, certain computers, or property used for entertainment, recreation, or amusement). Instead, use Part V for listed property.*

Part II **MACRS Depreciation For Assets Placed in Service ONLY During Your 1994 Tax Year (Do Not Include Listed Property)**

(a) Classification of property	(b) Month and year placed in service	(c) Basis for depreciation (business/investment use only—see instructions)	(d) Recovery period	(e) Convention	(f) Method	(g) Depreciation deduction
Section A—General Depreciation System (GDS) (see instructions)						
14a 3-year property						
b 5-year property						
c 7-year property						
d 10-year property						
e 15-year property						
f 20-year property						
g Residential rental property			27.5 yrs.	MM	S/L	
			27.5 yrs.	MM	S/L	
h Nonresidential real property			39 yrs.	MM	S/L	
				MM	S/L	
Section B—Alternative Depreciation System (ADS) (see instructions)						
15a Class life					S/L	
b 12-year			12 yrs.		S/L	
c 40-year			40 yrs.	MM	S/L	

Part III **Other Depreciation (Do Not Include Listed Property)**

16	GDS and ADS deductions for assets placed in service in tax years beginning before 1994 (see instructions)	**16**	
17	Property subject to section 168(f)(1) election (see instructions)	**17**	
18	ACRS and other depreciation (see instructions)	**18**	1,000 —

Part IV **Summary**

19	Listed property. Enter amount from line 25.	**19**	
20	**Total.** Add deductions on line 12, lines 14 and 15 in column (g), and lines 16 through 19. Enter here and on the appropriate lines of your return. (Partnerships and S corporations—see instructions)	**20**	1,000 —
21	For assets shown above and placed in service during the current year, enter the portion of the basis attributable to section 263A costs (see instructions)	**21**	

For Paperwork Reduction Act Notice, see page 1 of the separate instructions.   Cat. No. 12906N   Form **4562** (1994)

16

RETIRE WITH THE BIGGEST TAX BREAK POSSIBLE

When you retire, you will be liquidating your corporation, which has served you well all these years, and distributing all the assets and liabilities to the stockholders in exchange for all the stock. The excess of the value of the assets over the liabilities and investment in the stock is treated as a capital gain. Although the Tax Reform Act of 1986 destroyed favorable capital-gains treatment by repealing the capital-gains deduction, the House voted to restore favorable capital-gains treatment in April 1995, and the Senate is expected to vote similarly by the fall of 1995. So now, to the extent to which you haven't declared corporate dividends, which would be taxed to you at ordinary income-tax rates, you may be able to turn those dividends into capital gains if you can wait until you liquidate your corporation.

You don't necessarily have to sell the stock in your corporate portfolio, either. You can distribute in cash or in kind: you give your stock back to the corporation, and the corporation gives you its assets—its stock portfolio and anything else it owns.

In this case, you'd have to send the corporation's stock to the transfer agent so that it can be reissued in your name alone.

You would also have to notify the IRS thirty days after adopting your plan of liquidation. You would have to have a meeting of the board of directors, which, as you know by now, can be just you, while you're watching *M*A*S*H* reruns.

Liquidation of your corporation is treated by the IRS as a sale because essentially it's a sale of your stock. Liquidation rules have changed with virtually every edition of *Inc. Yourself,* and they are likely to change again before you are ready to liquidate your corporation.

But first let's take a profitable little digression to talk about raising the basis of your corporate stock. Why do you want to increase the basis of your stock? You want to make your basis as high as possible so that when you liquidate the corporation, as much money as possible is considered a return of capital and exempt from taxes. Thus, if your stock had a basis of $10,000 and you liquidated a corporation with assets of $100,000, the $10,000 would be considered a return of capital; you would subtract it from the $100,000 and start your calculations with $90,000.

If your corporation deals in services, you can still contribute to the corporation during its life. Attractive contributions would be in areas where corporations get preferential treatment, as opposed to individuals: either cash, with which the corporation could buy stocks, or the stocks themselves, since as soon as the stocks were transferred to the corporation, their dividends would be 70 percent tax-free. But remember: once you give the cash or stock to the corporation, you cannot use the dividends yourself or take the money out of the corporation without declaring a distribution and being taxed on it.

You could also buy paintings and other works of art or antiques for your corporation to raise the basis of your stock, but you would have to use your own funds to do so. While you are increasing the basis of the stock, you are increasing the assets of your corporation at the same time; in a sense, you are adding the same quantity to both sides of a balance, so that there is actually no net change. It would be far more desirable to give the corporation money to purchase stocks or the stocks themselves, since corporations are able to shelter 70 percent of dividends from taxes and individuals are not, as explained above. If you do transfer stock to the corporation, remember that you must use your cost—not the current market price—as the basis.

In this connection, a sixty-year-old professional could incorporate and turn over his stock portfolio to his corporation, at which point his dividends would be 70 percent tax-exempt. As long as his earned income constituted 40 percent or more of his total annual income, he would not be held to be a personal holding corporation. He could then retire at sixty-five or seventy with lots of tax-free dividend accumulation and a fairly high basis on his stock, so that when his corporation was liquidated, a good part of the assets would be considered a return of capital and therefore be tax-free. At present, you can choose from two forms of liquidation: the lump-sum method (§331) or the installment method. To understand how these differ, let's take the same corporation through both liquidation options.

Example: The XYZ Corporation liquidates on June 30, 1996. It has fixed assets valued at $10,000, receivables of $30,000, and inventory of $10,000. The stockholder's basis in his stock is $20,000.

§331—LUMP-SUM METHOD

The lump-sum method is a complete liquidation. There is no time requirement. With this method, each asset takes a basis to its value at the date of liquidation:

Total assets	$ 50,000
Less basis in stock	− 20,000
Capital gain	$ 30,000

The stockholder pays tax on a capital gain of $30,000.

Whether the corporation pays taxes depends on *its* basis. For example, if its fixed assets had been depreciated to $5,000, it would have a basis of $45,000 and a taxable capital gain of $5,000—which would probably be taxed at half ordinary-income rates in 1996 and thereafter.

To elect the lump-sum method of liquidation, your corporation would file IRS Form 966.

INSTALLMENT METHOD

§453 liquidation, mentioned in earlier editions of *Inc. Yourself,* was killed by the Tax Equity and Fiscal Responsibility Act, but there is still a way to get installment treatment when you liquidate your corporation. This method is suitable only for sales of real estate, plant and equipment, or other major tangible assets worth at least $50,000.

Essentially, the corporation makes the sale at the corporate level at liquidation and passes the mortgage notes on to the shareholder, who is taxed as payment is received, as though he himself had made the installment sale.

Let's return to XYZ Corporation to see how the installment method works.

First, the gross profit percentage is calculated by dividing the gross profit (total assets less the stockholder's basis) by the contract price (total assets):

$$\$30,000 \div \$50,000 = 60\%$$

Thus, the gross profit percentage is 60 percent. Therefore, only 60 percent of each annual installment is taxed at capital-gains rates; the remaining 40 percent is treated as a return of capital and is therefore not taxed.

If our stockholder takes 30 percent in 1996—the year of the sale—as his first installment, the calculations look like this:

$ 15,000	Installment payment
− 6,000	Return of capital
$ 9,000	Gain—taxed at long-term capital-gains rates

In the remaining seven years—from 1997 through 2003—if 10 percent is paid out each year, the calculations for each year look like this:

$ 5,000   Installment payment
−2,000   Return of capital
$ 3,000   Gain—taxed at long-term
          capital-gains rates

This method of liquidation is complicated and requires professional tax advice.

> **In a qualified installment sale, you have the option of taking out as little as $0 in the first year. In fact, you may take out *any amount any year*. Plan carefully so that you'll pay the lowest taxes possible.**

Again, it's important to note that you must make sure that your corporation is in liquidation status during this entire time. Of course, you could close down the corporation and still work in semiretirement as a sole proprietor; many people do.

To elect the installment method of liquidation, your corporation would file IRS Form 966.

YOUR PENSION

Liquidating your corporation is only half the story; the other half is drawing your pension. Like corporate assets, retirement-fund assets can be either converted to cash or distributed in kind. Your lump-sum distribution (the entire balance of the retirement fund within one taxable year) may have favorable tax advantages if you have reached the age of 59½ at the time of distribution.

Workaholics will be delighted to know that there is no maximum age for retirement, although they will have to start receiving distributions at age 70½.

When you liquidate your pension plan, your gain is calculated as the value of its assets in excess of amounts already taxed—for example, the 10 percent Voluntary Contribution mentioned in Chapter 12, "All About ERISA." Similar to an installment method of liquidation, your pension gain is subject to a special 5-year averaging computation, so that taxes are minimized.*

In order to perform the calculation, reduce the gain by the minimum distribution allowance. The minimum distribution allowance is equal to the lesser of $10,000 or ½ the distribution − (⅕ the distributions in excess of $20,000.

Let's look at some examples:

If your pension is $25,000 and your contribution is $0, your gain is $25,000. The minimum distribution allowance is equal to

$$\$10,000 \ - \ ⅕ \ (\$25,000 \ - \ \$20,000)$$
$$\$10,000 \ - \ ⅕ \ (\$5,000)$$
$$\$10,000 \ - \ \$1,000 \ = \ \$9,000$$

Thus, your minimum distribution allowance is $9,000, and the net value of your pension is $16,000.

As you can see, the smaller the distribution is, the higher the minimum distribution allowance will be. On pensions smaller than $20,000, the minimum distribution allowance is the full $10,000; the benefits of the minimum distribution allowance are completely phased out when the distribution is $70,000 or more:

$$\$10,000 \ - \ ⅕ \ (\$70,000 \ - \ \$20,000)$$
$$\$10,000 \ - \ ⅕ \ (\$50,000)$$
$$\$10,000 \ - \ \$10,000 \ = \ \$0$$

Although the $25,000 in the first example (taxed as $16,000) or the $70,000 in the second example (taxed as $70,000) is received as a lump sum, the distribution is taxed as though it were received over a period of 5 years. The tax is paid all in one year,

*If you were born before January 1, 1936, a special ten-year averaging may apply to you even if you are not 59½ years old. Consult your tax professional.

but the tax rate is the low income-averaging rate. In a sense, this lump-sum pension distribution is analogous to the lump-sum liquidation of the corporation's assets under §331.

There is also a pension-distribution plan analogous to the installment-method liquidation of the corporation. In this case, the pension distribution is taken down as an annuity and would be taxed under the annuity rules, which are the same as the installment rules.

Thus, you are left with two choices: taking your pension as a lump sum or as an annuity. *This is a one-time choice, so make it carefully.* Since both the lump-sum and the annuity options are treated similarly by the IRS, which should you take? Essentially, it's a question of life-style. Some people are happier with a lump sum; some people need that lump sum; some people need to have their money doled out to them because they're spendthrifts. But since taxes in the aggregate are higher with the annuity option, it may be wisest for even the spendthrifts to take the lump sum, pay the taxes on it, and then buy a mutual fund that will send them a check every month or every quarter.

17

LONG-TERM PLANNING FOR YOURSELF AND YOUR HEIRS

In the daily running of your corporation, it's easy to overlook the big picture: where you want to be five, ten, or more years from now, and how to pass your corporation on to your heirs.

Let's start with you.

DEFERRED COMPENSATION

Incorporation offers a valuable feature which is not available to sole proprietors. Deferred compensation defers current income—*and income taxes*—and provides future benefits. It can fund your retirement, provide security for the future, and even designate your choice of beneficiary. The key difference between this form of deferred compensation and the deferred compensation in a 401(k) plan (see pages 149–151) is that there is no limit to the amount of salary you can defer, while the 401(k)'s limit for 1995 is $9,240.

If you defer some of your salary, you are not subject to current taxes because you have not received this income. Your corporation is the stakeholder: the deferred compensation is an asset of the corporation and becomes a benefit to the corporation because it can be carried as an asset, as a balance-sheet item.

Deferred-compensation plans offer an advantage to your corporation, too. If the corporation puts $200,000 into your deferred-compensation plan, it has an expense of $200,000. But if the $200,000 grows to $300,000, depending on the terms of the deferred-compensation agreement, your corporation can either pay out the $300,000 and write off an expense of $300,000 or pay out the $200,000, write off $200,000, and keep $100,000 as an asset.

However, there is a disadvantage to deferred-compensation plans: if the corporation goes bankrupt, the assets of the plan can be attached by creditors.

Deferred-compensation plans are not for the average employee because he or she needs current income. Plans could be set up for $50 a month, and many state and city employees and employees of large corporations participate in such plans. But deferred compensation really becomes very advantageous to the higher-paid employee who doesn't need all that current income. Instead of taking $60,000 a year, the employee may take a salary of $40,000 and defer $20,000.

In order to do this, a deferred-compensation agreement must be drawn up by a lawyer, setting up the amount or percentage of salary to be deferred, the number of years the funds will be deferred, and the terms of the payout. The agreement can be drawn flexibly enough so that you agree to defer your bonus, which, in a one-person corporation, you control completely. The cost of drawing up a deferred-compensation agreement varies; if you find a lawyer who's done many of these and is familiar with them, the bill should be for no more than two or three hours of his or her time.

The deferred-compensation agreement must be a valid plan, in writing. It must impose reasonable obligations on the corporation to pay the deferred compensation, and it must anticipate that at the end of the time period the money will be paid to the employee. The deferred-compensation agreement can't be a sham, where at the end of 10 years the corporation throws the money away and can't pay. The corporation must intend to repay the funds.

Now: what happens to the deferred-compensation funds? The corporation carries them as an asset. There is no current write-off to the corporation, but there is no income to the employee, either.

Because deferred-compensation plans are not qualified under Section 401 of the Internal Revenue Code, your corporation can make use of these assets, borrow against them, use them as collateral, etc. Your corporation can fund the plan any way it wants to. It doesn't even have to fund the plan: it can just pay you the agreed-upon sum at the end of the time period. The deferred-compensation plan permits your corporation to accumulate money in a special fund—without regard to the $150,000/$250,000 limitation—because it's for a valid business purpose and therefore not subject to the accumulated earnings tax discussed in Chapter 1, "So You Want to Be a Corporation."

Deferred compensation is not only a way for you to avoid paying taxes on a salary you do not need, it's also a way for your corporation to accumulate funds in excess of $150,000/$250,000 without being subjected to the accumulated earnings tax.

Deferred compensation can also work for smaller amounts of money. It can work for amounts as small as $5,000 or $10,000 a year or for a one-shot lump sum, as in the case of a prizefighter or an author who signs a contract for a large advance. In these cases, a deferred-compensation plan could be drawn up along with the contract.

Deferred compensation isn't for everyone, but if you think it may be for you, consult your lawyer and your accountant.

BUY/SELL AGREEMENTS

You and your older brother each own 50 percent of your corporation. He decides to retire. How will you be able to buy him out?

Enter buy/sell agreements and insurance policies to fund them.

If your brother should become incapacitated or die, "key man" insurance policies will provide the funds to purchase his shares.

THE ESTATE FREEZE

Over the past two years, you may have heard about the estate freeze, an estate-planning strategy that permitted a business owner to transfer the right to future appreciation to family members while retaining such vital rights as control of the company and the right to receive dividend income. This was usually done by recapitalizing the corporation, converting the senior owner's common stock into preferred stock, and giving newly issued common stock to the next generation. Often, the senior and junior owners would agree secretly that the dividends on the preferred stock would not be paid.

Because of this frequent collusion, the estate freeze was eliminated in 1987. Then it was reinstated in late 1990, but with more stringent rules, in order to prevent this playing around with dividends. The new law contains special transfer valuation rules which state that dividends on the preferred stock issued to the senior owner cannot be deducted by the corporation. As such, the dividends become a cash hemorrhage, and many tax professionals now advise that the new estate freeze is not practical for many small corporations.

Still, the new estate freeze is probably worth an hour's consultation with your tax professional. There may be a way for your corporation to benefit.

YOUR S CORPORATION AS AN ESTATE-PLANNING TOOL

There are several estate-planning tools especially suited to an S corporation. For a complete discussion, see pages 110–112.

JUST THE BEGINNING

These tax-deferral and estate-planning strategies are just the beginning. You are probably just starting up your corporation now, and you, your corporation, and the tax laws are certain to change over the years. Keep one eye on the present and one on the future, and you're bound to succeed!

18

IF YOU SHOULD DIE FIRST

If you should die before liquidating your corporation, using the example of XYZ Corporation in Chapter 16, your heirs can use your stock's value on the date of your death as the adjusted cost. Thus, instead of your basis of $20,000, your heirs can use the new stepped-up figure of $50,000. Then, when they have liquidated the corporation at $50,000, they would not have to pay any capital-gains taxes, since under the law there was no gain ($50,000 − $50,000 = $0).

Your heirs will be able to choose the same liquidation options—§331 or the installment method—as you would have had.

If the distribution (either pension or the liquidation of the corporation) is taken as a lump sum by your beneficiaries, it is included in your estate. However, if the distribution is taken as an annuity, it will bypass the estate and not be subject to estate taxes. Therefore, the shortest length of annuity that will satisfy the IRS would seem to be an ideal way to save paying estate taxes.

19

BACK TO
THE FUTURE—
AND THE PRESENT

Since I started writing the first edition of *Inc. Yourself* back in 1976, I have interviewed hundreds of experts and given seminars for thousands of new entrepreneurs in New York, Boston, Washington, San Francisco, Los Angeles, and San Diego. Many of these entrepreneurs are recent immigrants, and their ambition and desire to build a prosperous new life are inspiring. They remind me of my grandparents, who arrived here speaking less than ten words of English and lived to see all six of their grandchildren become successful professionals, two in *Who's Who*. These new entrepreneurs and professionals give me faith that the American Dream still lives.

At the same time, I am horrified by the massive downsizing occurring in corporate America, especially among giant corporations. Virtually not a day goes by without the headline XYZ TO LAY OFF 2,000 MANAGERS. My files are full of these disturbing clippings; each represents thousands of untold personal tragedies. Recently, as I was completing this book, the phone rang. An engineer from Monsanto in St. Louis had tracked me down. He was one of 2,600 engineers whom Monsanto had laid off. He was planning to set up his own corporation, and he wanted advice. He told me he felt he was one of the lucky ones because he was able to make plans for his future. Many of his coworkers were not so lucky, he said. They had given their lives to the corporation and then were thrown out, no longer needed.

An April 1995 study by Challenger, Gray & Christmas, a leading outplacement firm, points out dramatically what happens to managers and executives when their companies institute massive layoffs:

Move to a smaller company	60%
Change industries to find a new job	49
Relocate to another region	17
Start your own business if you're over 40 (emphasis mine)	*71*
Go without work for a long time	3.6 months, median

What's the bottom line on all this? Clearly, more than ever, self-employment is the wave of the future, and incorporation is the way to obtain enormous tax and fringe benefits and to insulate yourself from liability. As it has helped hundreds of thousands of entrepreneurs and professionals, I hope that *Inc. Yourself* will help you in your endeavors.

APPENDIX A

STATE REQUIREMENTS FOR GENERAL BUSINESS AND PROFESSIONAL CORPORATIONS

State	Professions Covered by P.C. Act	Title and No. of P.C. Act
Alabama	All licensed professions	Revised Professional Corp. Act et seq. Section 10-4-380
Alaska	All licensed professions	Alaska Statute 10.45
Arizona	Accountants, dentists, doctors, lawyers, real estate brokers, and salespeople	Arizona Revised Statute 10-901-909
Arkansas	All licensed professions	Act 155 of 1963
California	Accountants, chiropractors, clinical social workers, dentists, doctors, lawyers, marriage and family & child counselors, optometrists, osteopaths, physical therapists, podiatrists, psychologists, shorthand reporters, speech pathologists	Part 4, Division 3, Title 1, California Corps. Code and Business and Professions Code
Colorado	Accountants, architects, chiropractors, dentists, doctors, lawyers, optometrists, veterinarians	Title 12
Connecticut	All licensed professions	Professional Service Corps. Chap. 594a

Min. No. of Shareholders/ Incorporators/ Directors	Title of Form to Be Filed	Address and Telephone No.	Filing Fee
1	Articles of Incorporation	Judge of Probate of county where corporation's registered office will be located	$50 for Secretary of State, $35 (est.) for Probate Judge
1	Duplicate Originals of Articles of Incorporation or write your own	Dept. of Commerce & Economic Development Division of Banking, Securities, & Corporations P.O. Box 110808 Juneau, AK 99811 (907) 465-2530	$250
1	Articles of Incorporation	Arizona Corporation Commission 1300 West Washington St. Phoenix, AZ 85007 (602) 542-3135	$60 + $35 optional 24-hr. expediting fee
1	Duplicate Originals of Articles of Incorporation	Sec'y of State Corporation Division State Capitol Bldg. Room 058 Little Rock, AR 72201-1094 (501) 682-3557	$50
1	Articles of Incorporation*	Sec'y of State—Corporate Filings 1500 11th St., 3d fl. Sacramento, CA 95814 (916) 657-5448	$900, incl. prepaid franchise tax**
1	Articles of Incorporation	Sec'y of State 1560 Broadway Suite 200 Denver, CO 80202 (303) 894-2251	$50
1	Certificate of Incorporation	Sec'y of State P.O. Box 846 30 Trinity St. Hartford, CT 06106 (203) 566-4128	$320

*After incorporation, application is made to the proper licensing board of the profession for a Certificate of Authority, which, when granted, legally permits the corporation to practice the profession.
**At press time, there was talk of a further increase.

State	Professions Covered by P.C. Act	Title and No. of P.C. Act
Delaware	Accountants, architects, chiropodists, chiropractors, dentists, doctors, engineers, lawyers, optometrists, osteopaths, veterinarians	Chapter 6, General Corp. Law
District of Columbia	Accountants, architects, doctors, engineers, lawyers	Title 29, Chap. 6
Florida	Accountants, architects, chiropodists, chiropractors, dentists, doctors, lawyers, life insurance agents, osteopaths, podiatrists, veterinarians	Professional Corp. Act Chap. 621
Georgia	Accountants, architects, chiropractors, dentists, doctors, engineers, land surveyors, lawyers, optometrists, osteopaths, podiatrists, psychologists (applied), veterinarians	Georgia Professional Corp. Act No. 943
Hawaii	Accountants, chiropractors, dentists, doctors, lawyers and district court practitioners, naturopaths, opticians, optometrists, osteopaths, pharmacists, veterinarians	Chap. 415A, Professional Corp. Act
Idaho	All licensed professions	Title 30, Chap. 13
Illinois	All licensed professions	Professional Service Corp. Act
Indiana	All licensed professions	Professional Corp. Act 1983

Min. No. of Shareholders/ Incorporators/ Directors	Title of Form to Be Filed	Address and Telephone No.	Filing Fee
1	Certificate of Incorporation*	Sec'y of State Division of Corporations P.O. Box 898 Dover, DE 19903 (302) 739-3073	$50 min.
1	Articles of Incorporation	Dept. of Consumer & Regulatory Affairs Business Regulation Admin. Corporations Division P.O. Box 37200 Washington, DC 20013-7200 (202) 727-7278	$120 min.
1	Articles of Incorporation	Department of State Division of Corporations P.O. Box 6327 Tallahassee, FL 32314 (904) 487-6052	$122.50
1	Articles of Incorporation BSR Form 227 (Transmittal Form)	Sec'y of State Business Services & Regulations Suite 315, West Tower 2 Martin Luther King Jr. Dr., SE Atlanta, GA 30334 (404) 656-2817	$100
1	Articles of Incorporation and Affidavits of Officers	Dept. of Commerce & Consumer Affairs Business Registration Division P.O. Box 40 Honolulu, HI 96810 (808) 586-2727	$50 min. + optional $40 expediting fee**
1	None	Division of Corporations Boise, ID 83720 (208) 334-2301	$100
1	Articles of Incorporation	Sec'y of State Business Services Dept. 328 Centennial Bldg. Springfield, IL 62756 (217) 782-6961	$75 + applicable franchise tax
1	Articles of Incorporation	Corporations Division 302 West Washington Room E018 Indianapolis, IN 46204 (317) 232-6576	$90

*Corporation must have registered office with registered agent in state.
**Paying this fee guarantees three-day service; without it, incorporators may have to wait two to three months.

State	Professions Covered by P.C. Act	Title and No. of P.C. Act
Iowa	Accountants, architects, chiropractors, dentists, doctors, engineers, land surveyors, lawyers, nurses, optometrists, osteopaths, physical therapists, podiatrists, veterinarians	Professional Corp. Act 496C
Kansas	All licensed professions	Professional Corp. Law of Kansas Chap. 17
Kentucky	All licensed professions	Professional Service Corps., Kentucky Revised Statutes Chap. 274
Louisiana	Accountants, architects, chiropractors, dentists, doctors, engineers, lawyers, nurses, occupational therapists, veterinarians	Louisiana Revised Statutes 12:8, 9, 11, 12, 14–21
Maine	Accountants, architects, chiropodists, chiropractors, dentists, doctors, lawyers, life insurance agents, osteopaths, podiatrists	Professional Service Corp. Act Chap. 22
Maryland	Accountants, doctors, funeral directors, real estate agents, lawyers, veterinarians. Architects and engineers can choose P.C.s or general business corporations.	Title 5, Maryland Code, Revised 1993
Massachusetts	Accountants, dentists, doctors, lawyers, psychologists, veterinarians*	Professional Corps., Chap. 156A
Michigan	All licensed professions	Act 192, P. A. of 1962, as amended

*Unless particular statutes or the regulations of the appropriate regulatory board mandate otherwise, all other professionals can choose to be incorporated either as professional corporations or business corporations. (Incorporating as a business corporation is more flexible and therefore more desirable.)

Min. No. of Shareholders/ Incorporators/ Directors	Title of Form to Be Filed	Address and Telephone No.	Filing Fee
1	Articles of Incorporation	Sec'y of State Corporation Division Hoover Bldg. Des Moines, IA 50319 (515) 281-8370	$50
1	Articles of Incorporation	Sec'y of State Corporation Division State Capitol—2nd floor Topeka, KS 66612–1594 (913) 296-2236	$75
1	Articles of Incorporation—original + 2 conforming copies	Sec'y of State P.O. Box 718 Frankfort, KY 40602–0718 (502) 564-2848	$50 min.
1	Articles of Incorporation. Notarized affidavit of registered agent must accompany filing	Sec'y of State Corporations Division P. O. Box 94125 Baton Rouge, LA 70804–9125 (504) 925-4704	$60
1	Articles of Incorporation	Bureau of Corporations State House Station 101 Augusta, ME 04333 (207) 287-4195	$105 min.
1	Articles of Incorporation Form No. 25 (every year)	State Dept. of Assessments & Taxation 301 W. Preston St. Baltimore, MD 21201 (301) 225-1340	$40 min.
1	Articles of Organization	Sec'y of the Commonwealth Corporation Division One Ashburton Pl. Boston, MA 02108 (617) 727-9640	$200 min.
1	Articles of Incorporation Form C&S 101	Michigan Dept. of Commerce Corporation & Securities Bureau Box 30054 Lansing, MI 48909 (517) 334-6206	$60 min.

State	Professions Covered by P.C. Act	Title and No. of P.C. Act
Minnesota	Accountants, architects, chiropractors, dentists, doctors, engineers, interior designers (certified), landscape architects, lawyers, nurses, optometrists, osteopaths, pharmacists, podiatrists, psychologists, surveyors, veterinarians	Minnesota Professional Corps. Act, Minn. Stat. 319A
Mississippi	All licensed professions	Mississippi Professional Corp. Law
Missouri	Accountants, architects, chiropodists, chiropractors, dentists, doctors, engineers, lawyers, optometrists, osteopaths, podiatrists, veterinarians	Title XXIII, Chap. 356 Revised Statutes of Missouri 1969, as amended
Montana	All licensed professions	Title 35, Chap. 4, Montana Codes Annotated
Nebraska	All registered professions	Nebraska Professional Corp. Act, Chap. 21, Article 22
Nevada	All licensed professions	Chapter 89, Professional Corps. and Associations Act
New Hampshire	All licensed professions	Revised Statutes Annotated—Chaps. 294A, Professional Corps.
New Jersey	All licensed professions	Professional Service Corp. Act NJSA 14A:17-1 et seq.

Min. No. of Shareholders/ Incorporators/ Directors	Title of Form to Be Filed	Address and Telephone No.	Filing Fee
1	Articles of Incorporation	Sec'y of State Business Services Division 180 State Office Bldg. St. Paul, MN 55155 (612) 296-2803	$135
1	Articles of Incorporation	Sec'y of State P.O. Box 136 Jackson, MS 39205 (601) 359-1350	$50 min.
1	Articles of Incorporation Corp. Form #41	Sec'y of State Corporation Division New Corporation Desk Jefferson City, MO 65102 (314) 751-2359	$58 min.
1	Articles of Incorporation— furnished by state	Sec'y of State P.O. Box 202801 Helena, MT 59620-2801 (406) 444-3665	$70 min.
1	Articles of Incorporation	Sec'y of State Corporation Division 1301 State Capitol Bldg. Lincoln, NE 68509 (402) 471-4079	$60 min. + $5 per page recording fee
1	Articles of Incorporation	Sec'y of State Corporation Division Capitol Complex Carson City, NV 89710 (702) 687-5203	$125 min.
1	Articles of Incorporation	Sec'y of State Corporation Division State House Room 204 107 North Main St. Concord, NH 03301 (603) 271-3244	$85
1	Certificate of Incorporation	New Jersey Department of State Commercial Recording Bureau Corporate Filing Section CN-308 Trenton, NJ 08625 (609) 530-6400	$100

State	Professions Covered by P.C. Act	Title and No. of P.C. Act
New Mexico	All licensed professions	Professional Corp. Act Sections 51-22-1 to 51-22-13 NMSA 1953 Compilation
New York	All licensed professions	Business Corp. Law Article 15
North Carolina	Accountants, architects, chiropractors, dentists, doctors, engineers, landscape architects, lawyers, optometrists, osteopaths, podiatrists, psychologists, surveyors, veterinarians	Professional Corp. Act Chap. 55B
North Dakota	All licensed professions	Professional Associations Act Chap. 10–31
Ohio	All licensed professions	Chap. 1701 or 1785, Ohio Revised Code
Oklahoma	Accountants, architects, chiropodists, chiropractors, dentists, doctors, nurses, optometrists, osteopaths, physical therapists, podiatrists, psychologists, veterinarians	Professional Corp. Act Title 18
Oregon	All licensed professions	Oregon Revised Statutes, Chap. 58, Professional Corps.

Min. No. of Shareholders/ Incorporators/ Directors	Title of Form to Be Filed	Address and Telephone No.	Filing Fee
1	Articles of Incorporation	State Corporation Commission Corporation & Franchise Tax Depts. P. O. Drawer 1269 Santa Fe, NM 87504-1269 (505) 827-4511	$100 min.
1	Certificate of Incorporation	New York State Division of Corporations 162 Washington Ave. Albany, NY 12231-0001 (518) 473-2492	$135 min.
1	Articles of Incorporation; Certification of Eligibility to Practice from licensing board	Sec'y of State Corporations Division 300 N. Salisbury St. Raleigh, NC 27603-5909 (919) 733-4201	$100
1	Duplicate Originals of Incorporation	Sec'y of State Division of Corporations Bismarck, ND 58505 (701) 328-4284	$90 min.
1	Articles of Incorporation	Sec'y of State Division of Corporations State Office Tower, 14th Fl. 30 E. Broad St. Columbus, OH 43266-0418 (614) 466-3910	$75 min.
1	Duplicate Originals of Certificates of Incorporation	Sec'y of State Rm. 101 Oklahoma State Capitol Bldg. Oklahoma City, OK 73105 (405) 521-3911	$50 min.
1	Articles of Incorporation 11-P	Secretary of State Corporation Division 255 Capitol St. NE Suite 151 Salem, OR 97310-0210 (503) 986-2200	$50

State	Professions Covered by P.C. Act	Title and No. of P.C. Act
Pennsylvania	Accountants, architects, auctioneers, chiropractors, dentists, doctors, engineers, funeral directors, landscape architects, lawyers, nurses, optometrists, osteopaths, pharmacists, podiatrists, psychologists, veterinarians	Pennsylvania General Associations Act of 1988, as amended by Act 198 of 1990
Rhode Island	Accountants, architects, chiropodists, chiropractors, dentists, doctors, engineers, nurses, optometrists, veterinarians	Title 7, Chap. 5.1 Professional Service Corps.
South Carolina	All licensed professions	South Carolina Professional Association Act
South Dakota	Accountants, chiropractors, dentists, doctors, lawyers, optometrists, veterinarians	SDCL Chapter 47-11 through 47-138-18
Tennessee	All licensed professions	Tennessee Professional Corp. Act 48-3-401
Texas	Accountants, dentists, nurses, optometrists, osteopaths, psychologists, surveyors, veterinarians	Texas Rev. Civ. Stat. Ann. Art. 1528e
	Doctors and podiatrists	Texas Rev. Civ. Stat. Ann. Art. 1528f
Utah	All licensed professions	Title 16, Chap. 11, Professional Corp. Act

Min. No. of Shareholders/ Incorporators/ Directors	Title of Form to Be Filed	Address and Telephone No.	Filing Fee
1	Articles of Incorporation— Domestic Professional Corp.	Commonwealth of Pennsylvania Corporation Bureau 308 North Office Bldg. Harrisburg, PA 17120-0029 (717) 787-1057	$100
1	Duplicate Originals of Articles of Incorporation	Sec'y of State 100 North Main St. Providence, RI 02903-1335 (401) 277-3061	$150 min.
1	Articles of Association	Filed at courthouse in county where professional corporation is located	$110 + $25 annual report
1	Articles of Incorporation	Sec'y of State Corporate Division 500 East Capitol Pierre, SD 57501 (605) 773-4845	$40 min.
1	Corporation Charter	Sec'y of State Corporation Division Suite 1800 James K. Polk Bldg. Nashville, TN 37243–0306 (615) 741-0537	$100
1	Articles of Incorporation	Sec'y of State Corporation Division 1019 Brazos P.O. Box 13697 Austin, TX 78711–3697 (512) 463-5555 (512) 463-5709 (fax)	$300; $310 to expedite in 24 hrs.
1	Application for a Certificate of Authority; Articles of Incorporation	Business Regulation Office Corporation Division 160 East 300 South P. O. Box 45801 Salt Lake City, UT 84145-0801 (801) 530-4849	$75 min.

State	Professions Covered by P.C. Act	Title and No. of P.C. Act
Vermont	All licensed professions	Title 11
Virginia	All licensed professions	Chap. 7, Professional Corps.
Washington	All licensed professions	RCW 18.100
West Virginia	All licensed professions	Under general corporation laws, Chap. 31-3
Wisconsin	All licensed professions	Service Corp. Law, Wisconsin Statute 180.1901–1921
Wyoming	Not specifically covered by statute	Wyoming Statutes 1957 17-3-101–104

Min. No. of Shareholders/ Incorporators/ Directors	Title of Form to Be Filed	Address and Telephone No.	Filing Fee
1	DCI Articles of Association with proof of profession attached	Sec'y of State Corporations Division Montpelier, VT 05602-2710 (802) 828-2386	$75
1	Articles of Incorporation	Clerk of the Commission State Corporation Commissioner Box 1197 Richmond, VA 23209 (804) 371-9733	$75 min.
1	Forms not supplied	Corporations Division Republic Bldg., 2nd Fl. 505 E. Union Olympia, WA 98504-0234 (360) 753-7115	$175
1	Form 101, Articles of Incorporation	Sec'y of State Corporation Division Charleston, WV 25305 (304) 558-8000 (304) 558-0900 (fax)	$30 min.
1	Articles of Incorporation, Form 2	Sec'y of State Corporation Division P.O. Box 7846 Madison, WI 53707 (608) 266-3590	$90 min.
No provision for minimum	No forms are furnished	Sec'y of State Division of Corporations Cheyenne, WY 82002 (307) 777-7311	$90

State	Title and No. of General Business Corp. Act	Min. No. of Shareholders/ Incorporators/ Directors	Title of Form to Be Filed	Address and Telephone No.	Filing Fee
Alabama	Alabama Business Corp. Act, Sec. 10-2A-1; Title 10-2B-1.01 1975 Code of Alabama	1	Articles of Incorporation	Judge of Probate of county where corporation's registered office will be located	$50 for Secretary of State, $35 (est.) for Probate Judge
Alaska	Alaska Statute 10.06	1	Duplicate Originals of Articles of Incorporation or write your own	Dept. of Commerce and Economic Development Division of Banking, Securities & Corporations P.O. Box 110808 Juneau, AK 99811 (907) 465-2530	$250
Arizona	Arizona Revised Statutes 10-002-10-105, 10-125–10-149	1	Articles of Incorporation	Arizona Corporations Commission 1300 West Washington St. Phoenix, AZ 85007 (602) 542-3135	$60 + $35 optional 24-hr. expediting fee
Arkansas	Act 576 of 1965	1	Duplicate Originals of Articles of Incorporation	Sec'y of State Corporation Dept. State Capitol Bldg. Room 058 Little Rock, AR 72201-1094 (501) 632-3557	$50
California	Title 1, Division 1, Calif. Corps. Code	1	Articles of Incorporation	Sec'y of State—Corporate Filings 1500 11th St., 3d fl. Sacramento, CA 95814 (916) 657-5448	$900, incl. prepaid franchise tax*
Colorado	Title 7, Volume 3, Articles 1–10	1	Articles of Incorporation	Sec'y of State 1560 Broadway Suite 200 Denver, CO 80202 (303) 894-2251	$50

*At press time, there was talk of a further increase.

State	Title and No. of General Business Corp. Act	Min. No. of Shareholders/ Incorporators/ Directors	Title of Form to Be Filed	Address and Telephone No.	Filing Fee
Connecticut	Stock Corporation Act Chap. 599	1	Certificate of Incorporation	Sec'y of State P. O. Box 846 30 Trinity St. Hartford, CT 06106 (203) 566-4128	$320
Delaware	Title 8, General Corp. Law	1	Certificate of Incorporation*	Sec'y of State Division of Corporations P. O. Box 898 Dover, DE 19903 (302) 739-3073	$50 min.
District of Columbia	Title 29, Chap. 3	1	Articles of Incorporation	Dept. of Consumer & Regulatory Affairs Business Regulation Admin. Corporations Division P.O. Box 37200 Washington, DC 20013-7200 (202) 727-7278	$120 min.
Florida	Florida Business Corp. Act Chap. 89-607	1	Articles of Incorporation	Department of State Division of Corporations P. O. Box 6327 Tallahassee, FL 32314 (904) 487-6052	$122.50
Georgia	Georgia Title 22—Corporations	1	Articles of Incorporation BSR Form 227 (Transmittal Form)	Sec'y of State Business Services & Regulations Suite 315, West Tower 2 Martin Luther King Jr. Dr., SE Atlanta, GA 30334 (404) 656-2817	$100

*Corporation must have registered office with registered agent in state.

State	Title and No. of General Business Corp. Act	Min. No. of Shareholders/ Incorporators/ Directors	Title of Form to Be Filed	Address and Telephone No.	Filing Fee
Hawaii	Chap. 415, Hawaii Revised Statutes	1	Articles of Incorporation and Affidavits of Officers	Dept. of Commerce & Consumer Affairs Business Registration Division P. O. Box 40 Honolulu, HI 96810 (808) 586-2727	$50 min. + optional $40 expediting fee*
Idaho	Title 30, Chap. 1	1	None	Division of Corporations Boise, ID 83720 (208) 334-2300	$100
Illinois	Business Corp. Act of 1983	1	Articles of Incorporation	Sec'y of State Business Services Dept. 328 Centennial Bldg. Springfield, IL 62756 (217) 782-6961	$75 + applicable franchise tax
Indiana	Indiana Business Corp. Law	1	Articles of Incorporation	Corporations Division 302 West Washington Room E018 Indianapolis, IN 46204 (317) 232-6576	$90
Iowa	490 Iowa Business Corp. Act of 1989	1	Articles of Incorporation	Sec'y of State Corporation Division Hoover Bldg. Des Moines, IA 50319 (515) 281-8370	$50

*Paying this fee guarantees three-day service; without it, incorporators may have to wait two to three months.

State	Title and No. of General Business Corp. Act	Min. No. of Shareholders/ Incorporators/ Directors	Title of Form to Be Filed	Address and Telephone No.	Filing Fee
Kansas	Kansas General Corp. Code Chap. 17	1	Articles of Incorporation	Sec'y of State Corporation Division State Capitol—2nd floor Topeka, KS 66612-1594 (913) 296-2236	$75
Kentucky	Kentucky Business Corp. Act, Kentucky Revised Statutes Chap. 271B	1	Articles of Incorporation— original + 2 conforming copies	Sec'y of State P.O. Box 718 Frankfort, KY 40602-0718 (502) 564-2848	$50 min.
Louisiana	Louisiana Revised Statutes 12:1, 2	1	Articles of Incorporation Notarized affidavit of registered agent must accompany filing	Sec'y of State Corporations Division P.O. Box 94125 Baton Rouge, LA 70804-9125 (504) 925-4704	$60
Maine	Maine Business Corp. Act Title 13-A	1	Articles of Incorporation	Bureau of Corporations State House Station 101 Augusta, ME 04333 (207) 287-4195	$105 min.
Maryland	Corps. and Assns. Article of Annotated Code of Maryland	1	Articles of Incorporation Form No. 1 (every year)	State Dept. of Assessments & Taxation 301 W. Preston St. Baltimore, MD 21201 (301) 225-1340	$40 min.

State	Title and No. of General Business Corp. Act	Min. No. of Shareholders/ Incorporators/ Directors	Title of Form to Be Filed	Address and Telephone No.	Filing Fee
Massachusetts	Business Corps. Chap. 156B	1	Articles of Organization	Sec'y of the Commonwealth Corporation Division One Ashburton Pl. Boston, MA 02108 (617) 727-9640	$200 min.
Michigan	Act 284, P. A. of 1972, as amended	1	Articles of Incorporation Form C&S 101	Michigan Dept. of Commerce Corporation & Securities Bureau Box 30054 Lansing, MI 48909 (517) 334-6206	$60 min.
Minnesota	Minn. Stat. Ch. 302A	1	Articles of Incorporation	Sec'y of State Business Services Division 180 State Office Bldg. St. Paul, MN 55155 (612) 296-2803	$135
Mississippi	Mississippi Business Corp. Law	1	Articles of Incorporation	Sec'y of State P. O. Box 136 Jackson, MS 39205 (601) 359-1350	$50 min.
Missouri	Title XXIII, Chap. 351 Revised Statutes of Missouri 1969, as amended	1	Articles of Incorporation Corp. Form #41	Sec'y of State Corporation Division New Corporation Desk Jefferson City, MO 65101 (314) 751-2359	$58 min.

State	Title and No. of General Business Corp. Act	Min. No. of Shareholders/ Incorporators/ Directors	Title of Form to Be Filed	Address and Telephone No.	Filing Fee
Montana	Title 35, Chap. 1, Montana Codes Annotated	1	Articles of Incorporation— furnished by state	Sec'y of State P.O. Box 202801 Helena, MT 59620-2801 (406) 444-3665	$70 min.
Nebraska	Nebraska Business Corp. Act, Chap. 21, Article 20	1	Articles of Incorporation	Sec'y of State Corporation Division 1301 State Capitol Bldg. Lincoln, NE 68509 (402) 471-4079	$60 min. + $5 per page recording fee
Nevada	Private Corps. Chap. 78	1	Articles of Incorporation	Sec'y of State Corporation Division Capitol Complex Carson City, NV 89710 (702) 687-5203	$125 min.
New Hampshire	Revised Statutes Annotated (1955) Chap. 293-A, Business Corps.	1	Articles of Incorporation	Sec'y of State Corporation Division State House Room 204 107 North Main St. Concord, NH 03301 (603) 271-3244	$85
New Jersey	New Jersey Business Corp. Act NJSA 14:A 1-1 et seq.	1	Certificate of Incorporation	New Jersey Department of State Commercial Recording Bureau Corporate Filing Section CN-308 Trenton, NJ 08625 (609) 530-6400	$100

State	Title and No. of General Business Corp. Act	Min. No. of Shareholders/ Incorporators/ Directors	Title of Form to Be Filed	Address and Telephone No.	Filing Fee
New Mexico	Business Corp. Act Sections 51-24-1–51-31-11, NMSA 1953 Compilation	1	Articles of Incorporation	State Corporation Commission Corporation & Franchise Tax Depts. P.O. Drawer 1269 Santa Fe, NM 87504-1269 (505) 827-4511	$50 min.
New York	Business Corp. Law	1	Certificate of Incorporation	New York State Division of Corporations 162 Washington Ave. Albany, NY 12231-0001 (518) 473-2492	$135 min.
North Carolina	Business Corp. Act Chap. 55	1	Articles of Incorporation	Sec'y of State Corporations Division 300 N. Salisbury St. Raleigh, NC 27603-5909 (919) 733-4201	$100
North Dakota	North Dakota Business Act Chap. 10–19	1	Articles of Incorporation	Sec'y of State Division of Corporations Bismarck, ND 58505 (701) 328-4284	$90 min.

State	Title and No. of General Business Corp. Act	Min. No. of Shareholders/ Incorporators/ Directors	Title of Form to Be Filed	Address and Telephone No.	Filing Fee
Ohio	Chap. 1701, Ohio Revised Code	1	Articles of Incorporation	Sec'y of State Division of Corporations State Office Tower, 14th Fl. 30 E. Broad St. Columbus, OH 43266-0418 (614) 466-3910	$75 min.
Oklahoma	General Business Corp. Act Title 18	1	Duplicate Originals of Certificate of Incorporation	Sec'y of State Rm. 101 Oklahoma State Capitol Bldg. Oklahoma City, OK 73105 (405) 521-3911	$50 min.
Oregon	Oregon Revised Statutes, Chap. 60, Private Corporations	1	Articles of Incorporation 11-B	Secretary of State Corporation Division 255 Capitol St. Suite 151 Salem, OR 97310-0210 (503) 986-2200	$50
Pennsylvania	General Associations Act of 1988, as amended by Act 198 of 1990	1	Articles of Incorporation— Domestic Business Corp.; Docketing Statement (triplicate)	Commonwealth of Pennsylvania Corporation Bureau 308 North Office Bldg. Harrisburg, PA 17120-0029 (717) 787-1057	$100

State	Title and No. of General Business Corp. Act	Min. No. of Shareholders/ Incorporators/ Directors	Title of Form to Be Filed	Address and Telephone No.	Filing Fee
Rhode Island	Title 7, Corporations, Associations, and Partnerships	1	Duplicate Originals of Articles of Incorporation	Sec'y of State 100 North Main St. Providence, RI 02903-1335 (401) 277-3061	$150 min.
South Carolina	Chap. 1 of 1962 Code—Vol. 3	1	Articles of Incorporation	Sec'y of State Box 11350 Columbia, SC 29211 (803) 734-2158	$110 + $25 annual report
South Dakota	SDCL 47-1–47-31	1	Articles of Incorporation	Sec'y of State Corporate Division 500 East Capitol Pierre, SD 57501 (605) 773-4845	$40 min.
Tennessee	Tennessee Business Corp. Act, 48-11-101	1	Corporation Charter	Sec'y of State Corporation Division Suite 1800 James K. Polk Bldg. Nashville, TN 37243-0306 (615) 741-0537	$100
Texas	Texas Rev. Civ. Stat. Ann., Vol. 3A, Texas Business Corp. Act	1	Articles of Incorporation	Sec'y of State Corporation Division 1019 Brazos P.O. Box 13697 Austin, TX 78711-3697 (512) 463-5555 (512) 463-5709 (fax)	$300; $310 to expedite in 24 hrs.

State	Title and No. of General Business Corp. Act	Min. No. of Shareholders/ Incorporators/ Directors	Title of Form to Be Filed	Address and Telephone No.	Filing Fee
Utah	Title 16, Chap. 10	1	Application for Certificate of Authority; Articles of Incorporation	Business Regulation Office Corporation Division 160 East 300 South P. O. Box 45801 Salt Lake City, UT 84145-0801 (801) 530-4849	$75
Vermont	Title 11A	1	DCI—Articles of Association	Sec'y of State Corporations Division Montpelier, VT 05602-2710 (802) 828-2386	$75
Virginia	Virginia Stock Corp. Act	1	Articles of Incorporation	Clerk of the Commission State Corporation Commission Box 1197 Richmond, VA 23209 (804) 371-9733	$75 min.
Washington	RCW 23B	1	Articles of Incorporation— forms supplied	Corporations Division Republic Bldg., 2nd Fl. 505 E. Union Olympia, WA 98504-0234 (360) 753-7115	$175
West Virginia	Chap. 31 Article 1	1	Articles of Incorporation	Sec'y of State Corporation Division Charleston, WV 25305 (304) 348-0262	$30 min.

State	Title and No. of General Business Corp. Act	Min. No. of Shareholders/ Incorporators/ Directors	Title of Form to Be Filed	Address and Telephone No.	Filing Fee
Wisconsin	Wisconsin Business Corp. Law, Chap. 180	1	Articles of Incorporation, Form 2	Sec'y of State Corporation Division P.O. Box 7846 Madison, WI 53707 (608) 266-3590	$90 min.
Wyoming	Wyoming Statutes 1957 17-16-101–1803	No provision for minimum	No forms are furnished	Sec'y of State Division of Corporations Cheyenne, WY 82002 (307) 777-7311	$90

APPENDIX B

SAMPLE MINUTES AND BYLAWS FOR A SMALL CORPORATION

(FOR USE IF THERE IS ONE INCORPORATOR)

MINUTES OF ORGANIZATION MEETING OF (NAME OF YOUR CORPORATION)

The undersigned, being the sole incorporator of this corporation, held an organization meeting at the date and place set forth below, at which meeting the following action was taken:

It was resolved that a copy of the Certificate of Incorporation together with the receipt issued by the Department of State showing payment of the statutory organization tax and the date and payment of the fee for filing the original Certificate of Incorporation be appended to these minutes.

Bylaws regulating the conduct of the business and affairs of the corporation, as prepared by _____ _____ , counsel for the corporation, were adopted and ordered appended hereto.

The persons whose names appear below were named as directors.

The board of directors was authorized to issue all of the unsubscribed shares of the corporation at such time and in such amounts as determined by the board and to accept in payment money or other property, tangible or intangible, actually received or labor or services actually performed for the corporation or for its benefit or in its formation.

The principal office of the corporation was fixed at

Dated at

this   day of   , 19   _____

                                            Sole Incorporator

The undersigned accept their nomination as directors:

Type director's name	Signature

The following are appended to the minutes of this meeting:

Copy of Certificate of Incorporation, filed on ____(date)____
Receipt of Department of State
Bylaws

(FOR USE IF THERE IS MORE THAN ONE INCORPORATOR)

MINUTES OF ORGANIZATION MEETING OF
(NAME OF YOUR CORPORATION)

The organization meeting of the incorporators was held at
on the   day of   , 19 , at   o'clock
M.
The following were present:

being a quorum and all of the incorporators.

One of the incorporators called the meeting to order. Upon motion duly made, seconded, and carried, _____ was duly elected chairman of the meeting and _____ duly elected secretary thereof. They accepted their respective offices and proceeded with the discharge of their duties.

A written Waiver of Notice of this meeting signed by all the incorporators was submitted, read by the secretary, and ordered appended to these minutes.

The secretary then presented and read to the meeting a copy of the Certificate of Incorporation of the corporation and reported that on the   day of   , 19 , the original thereof was duly filed by the Department of State.

Upon motion duly made, seconded, and carried, said report was adopted and the secretary was directed to append to these minutes a copy of the Certificate of Incorporation, together with the original receipt issued by the Department of State, showing payment of the statutory organization tax, the filing fee, and the date of filing of the certificate.

The chairman stated that the election of directors was then in order.

The following were nominated as directors:

Upon motion duly made, seconded, and carried, it was unanimously
RESOLVED, that each of the abovenamed nominees be and hereby is elected a director of the corporation.

Upon motion duly made, seconded, and carried, and by the affirmative vote of all present, it was

RESOLVED, that the board of directors be and it is hereby authorized to issue all of the unsubscribed shares of the corporation at such time and in such amounts as determined by the board, and to accept in payment money or other property, tangible or intangible, actually received or labor or other services actually performed for the corporation or for its benefit or in its formation.

The chairman presented and read, article by article, the proposed bylaws for the conduct and regulation of the business and affairs of the corporation as prepared by _____ _____, counsel for the corporation.

Upon motion duly made, seconded, and carried, they were adopted and in all respects ratified, confirmed, and approved, as and for the bylaws of this corporation.

The secretary was directed to cause them to be inserted in the minute book immediately following the receipt of the Department of State.

Upon motion duly made, seconded, and carried, the principal office of the corporation was fixed at _____, County of _____, State of New York.

Upon motion duly made, seconded, and carried, and by the affirmative vote of all present, it was

RESOLVED, that the signing of these minutes shall constitute full ratification thereof and Waiver of Notice of the Meeting by the signatories.

There being no further business before the meeting, the same was, on motion, duly adjourned.

Dated this   day of   , 19   .

_____
Secretary of meeting

_____
_____
Chairman of meeting

_____

_____

_____

The following are appended to the minutes of this meeting:

    Waiver of Notice of organization meeting
    Copy of Certificate of Incorporation, filed on ___(date)___
    Receipt of Department of State
    Bylaws

WAIVER OF NOTICE OF ORGANIZATION MEETING
OF
(NAME OF YOUR CORPORATION)

We, the undersigned, being all the incorporators named in the Certificate of Incorporation of the above corporation, hereby agree and consent that the organization meeting thereof be held on the date and at the time and place stated below and hereby waive all notice of such meeting and of any adjournment thereof.

Place of meeting:
Date of meeting:
Time of meeting:

_____
Incorporator

_____
Incorporator

_____
Incorporator

Dated:

BYLAWS
OF
(NAME OF YOUR CORPORATION)

Article I   Offices

The principal office of the corporation shall be in the   of   , County of   , State of New York. The corporation may also have offices at such other places within or without the State of New York as the board may from time to time determine or the business of the corporation may require.

Article II   Shareholders

1. *Place of Meetings.* Meetings of shareholders shall be held at the principal office of the corporation or at such place within or without the State of New York as the board shall authorize.

2. *Annual Meeting.* The annual meeting of the shareholders shall be held on the   day of   at   M. in each year if not a legal holiday, and, if a legal holiday, then on the next business day following at the same hour, when the shareholders shall elect a board and transact such other business as may properly come before the meeting.

3. *Special Meetings.* Special meetings of the shareholders may be called by the board or by the president and shall be called by the president or the secretary at the request in writing of a majority of the board or at the request in writing by shareholders owning a majority in amount of the shares issued and outstanding. Such request shall state the purpose or purposes of the proposed meeting. Business transacted at a special meeting shall be confined to the purposes stated in the notice.

4. *Fixing Record Date.* For the purpose of determining the shareholders entitled to notice of or to vote at any meeting of shareholders or any adjournment thereof, or to express consent to or dissent from any proposal without a meeting, or for the purpose of determining shareholders entitled to receive payment of any dividend or the allotment of any rights, or for the purpose of any other action, the board shall fix, in advance, a date as the record date for any such determination of shareholders. Such date shall not be more than fifty nor less than ten days before the date of such meeting, nor more than fifty days prior to any other action. If no record date is fixed, it shall be determined in accordance with the provisions of law.

5. *Notice of Meetings of Shareholders.* Written notice of each meeting of shareholders shall state the purpose or purposes for which the meeting is called, the place, date, and hour of the meeting, and unless it is the annual meeting, shall indicate that it is being issued by or at the direction of the person or persons calling the meeting. Notice shall be given either personally or by mail to each shareholder entitled to vote at such meeting, not less than ten nor more than fifty days before the date of the meeting. If action is proposed to be taken that might entitle shareholders to payment for their shares, the notice shall include a statement of that purpose and to that effect. If mailed, the notice is given when deposited in the United States mail, with postage

thereon prepaid, directed to the shareholder at his or her address as it appears on the record of shareholders, or, if he or she shall have filed with the secretary a written request that notices to him or her be mailed to some other address, then directed to him or her at such other address.

6. *Waivers.* Notice of meeting need not be given to any shareholder who signs a waiver of notice, in person or by proxy, whether before or after the meeting. The attendance of any shareholder at a meeting, in person or by proxy, without protesting prior to the conclusion of the meeting the lack of notice of such meeting, shall constitute a waiver of notice by him.

7. *Quorum of Shareholders.* Unless the Certificate of Incorporation provides otherwise, the holders of (a majority) (your own determination of a quorum, expressed either as a fraction or a percentage) of the shares entitled to vote thereat shall constitute a quorum at a meeting of shareholders for the transaction of any business, provided that when a specified item of business is required to be voted on by a class or classes, the holders of (a majority) (your own determination of a quorum, expressed either as a fraction or a percentage) of the shares of such class or classes shall constitute a quorum for the transaction of such specified item or business.

When a quorum is once present to organize a meeting, it is not broken by the subsequent withdrawal of any shareholders.

The shareholders present may adjourn the meeting despite the absence of a quorum.

8. *Proxies.* Every shareholder entitled to vote at a meeting of shareholders or to express consent or dissent without a meeting may authorize another person or persons to act for him or her by proxy.

Every proxy must be signed by the shareholder or his or her attorney-in-fact. No proxy shall be valid after expiration of eleven months from the date thereof unless otherwise provided in the proxy. Every proxy shall be revocable at the pleasure of the shareholder executing it, except as otherwise provided by law.

9. *Qualification of Voters.* Every shareholder of record shall be entitled at every meeting of shareholders to one vote for every share standing in his or her name on the record of shareholders, unless otherwise provided in the Certificate of Incorporation.

10. *Vote of Shareholders.* Except as otherwise required by statute or by the Certificate of Incorporation:

(Create your own election requirements, or use the following:)

a. Directors shall be elected by a plurality of the votes cast at a meeting of shareholders by the holders of shares entitled to vote in the election.

b. All other corporate action shall be authorized by a majority of the votes cast.

11. *Written Consent of Shareholders.* Any action that may be taken by vote may be taken without a meeting on written consent, setting forth the action so taken, signed by the holders of all the outstanding shares entitled to vote thereon or signed by such lesser number of holders as may be provided for in the Certificate of Incorporation.

Article III   Directors

1. *Board of Directors.* Subject to any provision in the Certificate of Incorporation, the business of the corporation shall be managed by its board of directors, each of whom shall be at least 18 years of age and (choose the number) be shareholders.

2. *Number of Directors.* The number of directors shall be _____. When all of the shares are owned by less than three shareholders, the number of directors may be less than three but not less than the number of shareholders.

3. *Election and Term of Directors.* At each annual meeting of shareholders, the shareholders shall elect directors to hold office until the next annual meeting. Each director shall hold office until the expiration of the term for which he or she is elected and until his or her successor has been elected and qualified, or until his or her prior resignation or removal.

4. *Newly Created Directorships and Vacancies.* Newly created directorships resulting from an increase in the number of directors and vacancies occurring in the board for any reason except the removal of directors without cause may be filled by a vote of a majority of the directors then in office, although less than a quorum exists, unless otherwise provided in the Certificate of Incorporation. Vacancies occurring by reason of the removal of directors without cause shall be filled by vote of the shareholders unless otherwise provided in the Certificate of Incorporation. A director elected to fill a vacancy caused by resignation, death, or removal shall be elected to hold office for the unexpired term of his or her predecessor.

5. *Removal of Directors.* Any or all of the directors may be removed for cause by vote of the shareholders or by action of the board. Directors may be removed without cause only by vote of the shareholders.

6. *Resignation.* A director may resign at any time by giving written notice to the board, the president, or the secretary of the corporation. Unless otherwise specified in the notice, the resignation shall take effect upon receipt thereof by the board or such officer, and the acceptance of the resignation shall not be necessary to make it effective.

7. *Quorum of Directors.* Unless otherwise provided in the Certificate of Incorporation, (a majority) (your own determination of a quorum, expressed either as a fraction or a percentage) of the entire board shall constitute a quorum for the transaction of business or of any specified item of business.

8. *Action of the Board.* Unless otherwise required by law, the vote of (a majority) (your own determination of a quorum, expressed either as a fraction or a percentage) of directors present at the time of the vote, if a quorum is present at such time, shall be the act of the board. Each director present shall have one vote regardless of the number of shares, if any, which he or she may hold.

9. *Place and Time of Board Meetings.* The board may hold its meetings at the office of the corporation or at such other places, either within or without the State of New York, as it may from time to time determine.

10. *Regular Annual Meeting.* A regular annual meeting of the board shall be held immediately following the annual meeting of shareholders at the place of such annual meeting of shareholders.

11. *Notice of Meetings of the Board, Adjournment.*

a. Regular meetings of the board may be held without notice at such time and place as it shall from time to time determine. Special meetings of the board shall be held upon notice to the directors and may be called by the president upon three days' notice to each director either personally or by mail or by wire; special meetings shall be called by the president or by the secretary in a like manner on written request of two directors. Notice of a meeting need not be given to any director who submits a Waiver of Notice whether before or after the meeting or who attends the meeting without protesting prior thereto or at its commencement, the lack of notice to him or her.

b. A majority of the directors present, whether or not a quorum is present, may adjourn any meeting to another time and place. Notice of the adjournment shall be given all directors who were absent at the time of the adjournment and, unless such time and place are announced at the meeting, to the other directors.

12. *Chairman.* The president, or, in his or her absence, a chairman chosen by the board, shall preside at all meetings of the board.

13. *Executive and Other Committees.* By resolution adopted by a majority of the entire board, the board may designate from among its members an executive committee and other committees, each consisting of three or more directors. Each such committee shall serve at the pleasure of the board.

14. *Compensation.* No compensation, as such, shall be paid to directors for their services, but by resolution of the board, a fixed sum and expenses for actual attendance at each regular or special meeting of the board may be authorized. Nothing herein contained shall be construed to preclude any director from serving the corporation in any other capacity and receiving compensation therefor.

Article IV   Officers

1. *Offices, Election, Term.*

a. Unless otherwise provided for in the Certificate of Incorporation, the board may elect or appoint a president, one or more vice-presidents, a secretary, and a treasurer, and such other officers as it may determine, who shall have such duties, powers, and functions as hereinafter provided.

b. All officers shall be elected or appointed to hold office until the meeting of the board following the annual meeting of shareholders.

c. Each officer shall hold office for the term for which he or she is elected or appointed and until his or her successor has been elected or appointed and qualified.

2. *Removal, Resignation, Salary, Etc.*

a. Any officer elected or appointed by the board may be removed by the board with or without cause.

b. In the event of the death, resignation, or removal of an officer, the board in its discretion may elect or appoint a successor to fill the unexpired term.

c. Unless there is only one shareholder, any two or more offices may be held by the same person, except the offices of president and secretary. If there is only one shareholder, all offices may be held by the same person.

d. The salaries of all officers shall be fixed by the board.

e. The directors may require any officer to give security for the faithful performance of his or her duties.

3. *President.* The president shall be the chief executive officer of the corporation; he or she shall preside at all meetings of the shareholders and of the board; he or she shall have the management of the business of the corporation and shall see that all orders and resolutions of the board are effected.

4. *Vice-presidents.* During the absence or disability of the president, the vice-president, or, if there are more than one, the executive vice-president, shall have all the powers and functions of the president. Each vice-president shall perform such other duties as the board shall prescribe.

5. *Secretary.* The secretary shall:

a. attend all meetings of the board and of the shareholders;

b. record all votes and minutes of all proceedings in a book to be kept for that purpose;

c. give or cause to be given notice of all meetings of shareholders and of special meetings of the board;

d. keep in safe custody the seal of the corporation and affix it to any instrument when authorized by the board;

e. when required, prepare or cause to be prepared and available at each meeting of shareholders a certified list in alphabetical order of the names of shareholders entitled to vote thereat, indicating the number of shares of each respective class held by each;

f. keep all the documents and records of the corporation as required by law or otherwise in a proper and safe manner;

g. perform such other duties as may be prescribed by the board.

6. *Assistant Secretaries.* During the absence or disability of the secretary, the assistant secretary, or, if there are more than one, the one so designated by the secretary or by the board, shall have all the powers and functions of the secretary.

7. *Treasurer.* The treasurer shall:

a. have the custody of the corporate funds and securities;

b. keep full and accurate accounts of receipts and disbursements in the corporate books;

c. deposit all money and other valuables in the name and to the credit of the corporation in such depositories as may be designated by the board;

d. disburse the funds of the corporation as may be ordered or authorized by the board and preserve proper vouchers for such disbursements;

e. render to the president and the board at the regular meetings of the board, or whenever they require it, an account of all his or her transactions as treasurer and of the financial condition of the corporation;

f. render a full financial report at the annual meeting of the shareholders if so requested;

g. be furnished by all corporate officers and agents, at his or her request, with such reports and statements as he or she may require as to all financial transactions of the corporation;

h. perform such other duties as are given to him or her by these bylaws or as from time to time are assigned to him or her by the board or the president.

8. *Assistant Treasurer.* During the absence or disability of the treasurer, the assistant treasurer, or, if there are more than one, the one so designated by the secretary or by the board, shall have all the powers and functions of the treasurer.

9. *Sureties and Bonds.* In case the board shall so require, any officer or agent of the corporation shall execute to the corporation a bond in such sum and with such surety or sureties as the board may direct, conditioned upon the faithful performance of his or her duties to the corporation and including responsibility for negligence and for the accounting for all property, funds, or securities of the corporation which may come into his or her hands.

Article V   Certificates for Shares

1. *Certificates.* The shares of the corporation shall be represented by certificates. They shall be numbered and entered in the books of the corporation as they are issued. They shall exhibit the holder's name and the number of shares and shall be signed by the president or a vice-president and the treasurer or the secretary and shall bear the corporate seal.

2. *Lost or Destroyed Certificates.* The board may direct a new certificate or certificates to be issued in place of any certificate or certificates

theretofore issued by the corporation, alleged to have been lost or destroyed, upon the making of an affidavit of that fact by the person claiming the certificate to be lost or destroyed. When authorizing such issue of a new certificate or certificates, the board may, in its discretion and as a condition precedent to the issuance thereof, require the owner of such lost or destroyed certificate or certificates, or his or her legal representative, to advertise the same in such manner as it shall require and/or to give the corporation a bond in such sum and with such surety or sureties as it may direct as indemnity against any claim that may be made against the corporation with respect to the certificate alleged to have been lost or destroyed.

3. *Transfers of Shares.*

a. Upon surrender to the corporation or the transfer agent of the corporation of a certificate for shares duly endorsed or accompanied by proper evidence of succession, assignment, or authority to transfer, it shall be the duty of the corporation to issue a new certificate to the person entitled thereto and to cancel the old certificate; every such transfer shall be entered in the transfer book of the corporation, which shall be kept at its principal office. No transfer shall be made within ten days next preceding the annual meeting of shareholders.

b. The corporation shall be entitled to treat the holder of record of any share as the holder in fact thereof and, accordingly, shall not be bound to recognize any equitable or other claim to or interest in such share on the part of any other person whether or not it shall have express or other notice thereof, except as expressly provided by the laws of the State of New York.

4. *Closing Transfer Books.* The board shall have the power to close the share transfer books of the corporation for a period of not more than ten days during the thirty-day period immediately preceding (1) any shareholders' meeting, or (2) any date upon which shareholders shall be called upon to or have a right to take action without a meeting, or (3) any date fixed for the payment of a dividend or any other form of distribution, and only those shareholders of record at the time the transfer books are closed, shall be recognized as such for the purpose of (1) receiving notice of or voting at such meeting, or (2) allowing them to take appropriate action, or (3) entitling them to receive any dividend or other form of distribution.

Article VI   Dividends

Subject to the provisions of the Certificate of Incorporation and to applicable law, dividends on the outstanding shares of the corporation may be declared in such amounts and at such time or times as the board may determine. Before payment of any dividend, there may be set aside out of the net profits of the corporation available for dividends such sum or sums as the board from time to time in its absolute discretion deems proper as a reserve fund to meet contingencies, or for equalizing dividends, or for repairing or maintaining any property of the corporation, or for such other purpose as the board shall think conducive to the interests of the corporation, and the board may modify or abolish any such reserve.

Article VII   Corporate Seal

The seal of the corporation shall be circular in form and bear the name of the corporation, the year of its organization, and the words "Corporate Seal, New York." The seal may be used by causing it to be impressed directly on the instrument or writing to be sealed, or upon adhesive substance affixed thereto. The seal on the certificates for shares or on any corporate obligation for the payment of money may be a facsimile, engraved, or printed.

Article VIII   Execution of Instruments

All corporate instruments and documents shall be signed or countersigned, executed, verified, or acknowledged by such officer or officers or other person or persons as the board may from time to time designate.

Article IX   Fiscal Year

This fiscal year shall begin the first day of (month) in each year.

Article X   References to Certificate of Incorporation

References to the Certificate of Incorporation in these bylaws shall include all amendments thereto or changes thereof unless specifically excepted.

Article XI   Bylaw Changes

Amendment, Repeal, Adoption, Election of Directors

a. Except as otherwise provided in the Certificate of Incorporation, the bylaws may be amended, repealed, or adopted by vote of the holders of the shares at the time entitled to vote in the election of any directors. Bylaws may also be amended, repealed, or adopted by the board, but any bylaws adopted by the board may be amended by the shareholders entitled to vote thereon as hereinabove provided.

b. If any bylaw regulating an impending election of directors is adopted, amended, or repealed by the board, there shall be set forth in the notice of the next meeting of shareholders for the election of directors the bylaw so adopted, amended, or repealed, together with a concise statement of the changes made.

MINUTES OF FIRST MEETING OF BOARD OF
DIRECTORS
OF
(NAME OF YOUR CORPORATION)

The first meeting of the board was held at   on the
day of   , 19 , at   o'clock   M.
The following were present:

being a quorum and all of the directors of the corporation.

_____ was nominated and elected temporary chairman and acted as such until relieved by the president.

_____ was nominated and elected temporary secretary, and acted as such until relieved by the permanent secretary.

The secretary then presented and read to the meeting a Waiver of Notice of Meeting, subscribed by all the directors of the corporation, and it was ordered that it be appended to the minutes of this meeting.

The following were duly nominated and, a vote having been taken, were unanimously elected officers of the corporation to serve for one year and until their successors are elected and qualified:

President:

Vice-President:

Secretary:

Treasurer:

The president and secretary thereupon assumed their respective offices in place and stead of the temporary chairman and the temporary secretary.

Upon motion duly made, seconded, and carried, it was

RESOLVED, that the seal now presented at this meeting, an impression of which is directed to be made in the margin of the minute book, be and the same is hereby adopted as the seal of this corporation, and further

RESOLVED, that the president and treasurer be and they hereby are authorized to issue certificates for shares in the form as submitted to this meeting, and further

RESOLVED, that the share and transfer book now presented at this meeting be and the same hereby is adopted as the share and transfer book of the corporation. Upon motion duly made, seconded, and carried, it was

RESOLVED, that the treasurer be and hereby is authorized to open a bank account in behalf of the corporation with (name of bank) located at (address) and a resolution for that purpose on the printed form of said bank was adopted and was ordered appended to the minutes of this meeting. Upon motion duly made, seconded, and carried, it was

RESOLVED, that the corporation proceed to carry on the business for which it was incorporated.

(The following is the appropriate form to be included here if a proposal or offer for the sale, transfer, or exchange of property has been made to the corporation:)

The secretary then presented to the meeting a written proposal from _____ _____ to the corporation.

Upon motion duly made, seconded, and carried, the said proposal was ordered filed with the secretary, and he or she was requested to spread the same at length upon the minutes, said proposal being as follows:

(Insert proposal here.)

The proposal was taken up for consideration, and, on motion, the following resolution was unanimously adopted:

WHEREAS, a written proposal has been made to this corporation in the form as set forth above in these minutes, and

WHEREAS, in the judgment of this board the assets proposed to be transferred to the corporation are reasonably worth the amount of the consideration demanded therefor, and that it is in the best interests of this corporation to accept the said offer as set forth in said proposal,

NOW, THEREFORE, IT IS RESOLVED, that said offer, as set forth in said proposal, be and the same hereby is approved and accepted, and that in accordance with the terms thereof, this corporation shall, as full payment for said property, issue to said offeror(s) or nominee(s) (number of shares) fully paid and nonassessable shares of this corporation, and it is

FURTHER RESOLVED, that upon the delivery to this corporation of said assets and the execution and delivery of such proper instruments as may be necessary to transfer and convey the same to this corporation, the officers of this corporation are authorized and directed to execute and deliver the certificate or certificates for such shares as are required to be issued and delivered on acceptance of said offer in accordance with the foregoing.

The chairman presented to the meeting a form of certificate required under Tax Law Section 275A to be filed in the office of the tax commission.

Upon motion duly made, seconded, and carried, it was

RESOLVED, that the proper officers of this corporation are hereby authorized and directed to execute and file such certificate forthwith. On motion duly made, seconded, and carried, it was

RESOLVED, that all of the acts taken and decisions made at the organization meeting be and they hereby are ratified, and it was

FURTHER RESOLVED, that the signing of these minutes shall

constitute full ratification thereof and Waiver of Notice of the Meeting by the signatories.

There being no further business before the meeting, on motion duly made, seconded, and carried, the meeting was adjourned. Dated this   day of   , 19 .

_____   _____

                                                        Secretary

_____   _____

                                                        Chairman

_____

_____

   A true copy of each of the following documents referred to in the foregoing minutes is appended hereto.
Waiver of Notice of Meeting
Specimen certificate for shares
Resolution designating depository of funds

WAIVER OF NOTICE OF FIRST MEETING OF BOARD
OF
(NAME OF YOUR CORPORATION)

We, the undersigned, being all the directors of the above corporation, hereby agree and consent that the first meeting of the board be held on the date and at the time and place stated below for the purpose of electing officers and the transaction thereat of all such other business as may lawfully come before said meeting and hereby waive all notice of the meeting and of any adjournment thereof.

Place of meeting:
Date of meeting:
Time of meeting:

_____
Director

_____
Director

_____
Director

Dated:

MINUTES OF FIRST MEETING OF SHAREHOLDERS
OF
(NAME OF YOUR CORPORATION)

The first meeting of the shareholders was held at   on the   day of   , 19   , at   o'clock   M.

The meeting was duly called to order by the president, who stated the object of the meeting.

The secretary then read the roll of the shareholders as they appear in the share record book of the corporation and reported that a quorum of the shareholders was present.

The secretary then read a Waiver of Notice of Meeting signed by all the shareholders and on motion duly made, seconded, and carried, it was ordered that the said waiver be appended to the minutes of this meeting.

The president then asked the secretary to read the minutes of the organization meeting and the minutes of the first meeting of the board.

On motion duly made, seconded, and unanimously carried, the following resolution was adopted:

WHEREAS, the minutes of the organization meeting and the minutes of the first meeting of the board have been read to this meeting, and

WHEREAS, at the organization meeting the bylaws of the corporation were adopted, it is

RESOLVED, that this meeting hereby approves, ratifies, and adopts the said bylaws as the bylaws of the corporation, and it is

FURTHER RESOLVED, that all of the acts taken and the decisions made at the organization meeting and at the first meeting of the board hereby are approved and ratified, and it is

FURTHER RESOLVED, that the signing of these minutes shall constitute full ratification thereof and Waiver of Notice of the Meeting by the signatories.

There being no further business, the meeting was adjourned. Dated this   day of   , 19   .

_____

                                    Secretary

_____

_____

_____

The following is appended hereto:
Waiver of Notice of Meeting

WAIVER OF NOTICE OF FIRST MEETING OF
SHAREHOLDERS
OF
(NAME OF YOUR CORPORATION)

We, the undersigned, being all of the shareholders of the above corporation, hereby agree and consent that the first meeting of the shareholders be held on the date and at the time and place stated below for the purpose of electing officers and the transaction thereat of all such other business as may lawfully come before said meeting and hereby waive all notice of the meeting and of any adjournment thereof.

Place of meeting:
Date of meeting:
Time of meeting:

_____

_____

_____

Dated:

MINUTES OF A SPECIAL MEETING OF
SHAREHOLDERS
OF
(NAME OF YOUR CORPORATION)

MINUTES of a special meeting of shareholders held at   , in the State of   , on the   day of   , 19   , at   o'-clock   M.

The meeting was duly called to order by the president, who stated the object of the meeting.

On motion duly made, seconded, and unanimously carried, the following resolution was adopted:

WHEREAS, the corporation's clients are delaying payments for work performed earlier and are now paying in the month of January, rather than in December, it is

RESOLVED, that a feasibility study be made as to shifting from a calendar year to a January fiscal year so that income more appropriately matches the work done, and it is

˙ FURTHER RESOLVED, that if such a study indicates that a January fiscal-year election is appropriate, that such an election be made.

There being no further business, the meeting was adjourned. Dated the   day of   , 19   .

_____

Secretary

_____

President

APPENDIX C
ADOPTION AGREEMENT

1. Information about the Employer

Name _____

Business Address _____

_____

Nature of Business _____

Tax Identification # _____

Employer's Fiscal Year _____
S Corporation ☐ Yes ☐ No

Date of Incorporation _____

2. The Trustee

The Employer appoints the following Trustee(s) in accordance with the Trust Agreement, effective on the date that the Employer and Trustee execute said Agreement.

Name(s) _____

_____

Business Address _____

_____

3. Plan Manager

The Employer appoints the following Plan Manager to perform the duties provided in the Plan and Trust Agreement.

Name(s) _____

_____

265

Business Address _____

_____

4. Plan Year

The Effective Date of the Plan shall be _____ .

Plan Year shall mean the Employer's fiscal year unless a different Plan Year is selected as follows: _____ to _____ .

Anniversary date shall be the last day of the Plan Year unless a different date is selected as follows: _____ .

5. Plan Compensation

Plan Compensation shall mean all income paid the Participant.
- ☐ A. In the Plan Year
- ☐ B. In the Fiscal Year ending within the Plan Year

Unless the following item(s) would be excluded:
- ☐ C. Bonus
- ☐ D. Overtime
- ☐ E. Commission payments
- ☐ F. Other remuneration _____

      If integrated formula is selected (under option 15(c)), there shall be no exclusions.

No more than $100,000 of the earnings of a more than 5% shareholder in an S corporation may be considered.

6. Application of Forfeitures

In accordance with Section 4 of Article VIII, forfeitures under the Plan shall be applied in the following manner:
- ☐ A. Be reallocated in the same proportion that the current year's contribution is allocated among Participants.
- ☐ B. Be used to reduce subsequent contributions by the Employer.
- ☐ C. Be reallocated among all Participants except for those who have a greater than 5% stock interest in the corporation, in the proportion that the current year's contribution for such Participant bears to the total contribution for all such Participants.

7. Years of Service

In accordance with Section 5 of Article III, years of service shall include previous service with _____

_____

8. Normal Retirement Age

Normal Retirement Age under the Plan shall be the _____ birthday (no less than 60 nor more than 70). The Normal Retirement Age shall be 65 unless otherwise specified. If an integrated formula is selected, the Normal Retirement Age shall not be less than 65.

9. Early Retirement

☐ A. There shall be no early retirement under the Plan.
☐ B. A Participant who has attained age _____ (no less than 50) with _____ years of participation shall be fully vested and shall be entitled to take an early retirement if he or she so desires.

10. Eligibility Requirements

A. Employee Classification
☐ i. All Employees
☐ ii. Salaried Employees Only
☐ iii. Hourly Employees Only
☐ iv. All Employees except for those who are subject to a Collective Bargaining Agreement unless such agreement provides for their inclusion hereunder
☐ v. All Employees except for commission salesmen
☐ vi. All Employees at _____
      (specific site, department, or division)
B. An Employee is one who after commencing employment works 1,000 hours during the following 12 months.
C. Years of Service
   Immediate Vesting Requirement
   All present Employees who have completed three years of service.
   Employees hired after the effective date when they have completed three years of service.

Otherwise, all present and future Employees after completing one year of service and reaching the minimum age.

D. Minimum Age

☐ i. Present Employees: _____ years of age (maximum of 21)

☐ ii. Future Employees: _____ years of age (maximum of 21)

All officers, shareholders, supervisors, and highly compensated employees must be able to meet the eligibility requirements for future employees on the Plan's effective date under options C and D above.

11. Mandatory Contributions

In accordance with Article IV of the Plan, a Participant must make contributions in accordance with the following formula:

☐ A. No Mandatory Contributions shall be required under the Plan.

☐ B. For an otherwise eligible Participant hereunder, he or she must contribute _____% of his compensation (percentage selected by Employer cannot exceed 6%).

☐ C. For an otherwise eligible Participant to participate hereunder, he must contribute _____% (not to exceed 6%) of his compensation in excess of his or her Social Security Wage Base (unless option A above is indicated, this formula must be used if the Plan is to be integrated with Social Security on an excess basis only).

12. Voluntary Contributions by Employees

☐ A. An Employee is permitted to contribute an amount not to exceed 10% of his or her Plan Compensation each year.

☐ B. _____% is to be read in place of 10% above.

☐ C. Participants shall not be permitted to make Voluntary Contributions hereunder.

13. Vesting

The Employee's interest in Employer contributions shall become nonforfeitable in accordance with the following schedule:

☐ A. 100% immediately upon becoming a Participant

☐ B. Six-Year Rule

Years of Service	Nonforfeitable Percentage
2	20
3	40
4	60
5	80
6	100

☐ C. Other _____

_____

_____

14. Contributions by the Employer

In accordance with Article VI of the Plan, the Employer shall annually make contributions out of its Net Profits in accordance with the following:

☐ A. The Employer shall contribute such amount as annually determined by its Board of Directors.

☐ B. The Employer shall contribute such amount as annually determined by its Board of Directors; however, in the event that the Board of Directors does not act within its fiscal year, the company shall make a contribution in accordance with the following:

    ☐ i. The company shall contribute _____% of the compensation of the Participants.

    ☐ ii. The company shall contribute _____% of its Net Profits for such year.

☐ C. The Employer shall contribute _____% of the compensation of the Participants.

☐ D. The Employer shall make contributions in accordance with the level of its Net Profits as follows:

If the Annual Net Profit is:			*The Employer's Contribution as a Percentage of the Participant's Compensation Shall Be:*
1. Less than $_____			_____%
2. $_____	or more, but less than	$_____	_____%
3. $_____	or more, but less than	$_____	_____%
4. $_____	or more, but less than	$_____	_____%
5. $_____	or more		_____%

☐ E. The Employer shall make a contribution of _____% (not more than 7.51%) of compensation in excess of the Social Security Wage Base (as defined hereunder). This option may be chosen by itself or in conjunction with any other contribution formula hereunder.

15. Allocation of the Employer's Contribution

☐ A. In the proportion that each Participant's individual compensation bears to the total compensation of all Participants.

☐ B. In the proportion that each Participant's points bear to the total points of all Participants where each Participant is credited with _____ point(s) (no more than 2) for each full year of continuous service and _____ point(s) (no more than 2) for each full $100 of compensation.

☐ C. Allocated on the basis of _____% (not more than 7%) of the Participant's compensation in excess of Social Security Wage Base, the balance, if any, to be allocated in the proportion that each Participant's individual compensation bears to the total compensation of all Participants.

If contribution option 14E is chosen in conjunction with this allocation formula or if another contribution formula is chosen and contributions are made in a manner so that there are no participants other than those participating on an excess basis, then any forfeitures will be used to reduce the amount of Employer contributions for such year. Any balance remaining shall be allocated in the proportion that each Participant's compensation bears to the total compensation of all Participants. For purposes of allocating such remaining balance, a Participant shall include Employees who are otherwise eligible except for the fact that their compensation is below the maximum amount of wages subject to Social Security taxes.

If this option is chosen and there are Participants for whom an allocation is made other than on an excess basis only, then forfeiture will be allocated as follows:

☐ i. To reduce Employer contributions.

☐ ii. In proportion that each Participant's compensation bears to that total compensation of all Participants.

16. Social Security Wage Base

For purposes of this Plan, Social Security Wage Base shall mean:

☐ A. The Social Security Wage Base in effect for the year in which the Plan Year begins.

☐ B. A stated dollar amount of $ _____ (may not be more than the Social Security Wage Base as in effect when the Plan is adopted or amended).

The Employer (a) acknowledges receipt of the current Prospectus of the named fund or security, and represents that each Participant has received such Prospectus, (b) represents that each new Participant will receive the then-current Prospectus, (c) on behalf of himself and each Participant consents to the Plan and Trust Agreement, (d) represents that he will file such information with the Internal Revenue Service as the Service may require, and any other filings required by the State or Federal laws for any taxable year, (e) agrees to vote or instruct the voting of shares as requested by Participants concerning their Mandatory and Voluntary Contributions, (f) realizes that neither the Sponsor nor Broker-Dealer can furnish legal advice, and (g) acknowledges and agrees to the Fee Schedule listed under the investment instructions for the maintenance of Participant accounts, if applicable.

DATE: _____

EMPLOYER: _____

By: _____

(Authorized Signature)

The named Trustee(s) acknowledges receipt of a copy of the Plan and Trust Agreement and hereby accepts its appointment as of this _____ day of _____, 19_____.

TRUSTEE(S):

_____

_____

_____

INDEX

Accident insurance. *See* Disability insurance

Accountant, use of, *xvii,* 33, 44, 46, 59, 112, 128, 133, 211

Accounting, as "perilous profession," *xv,* 11*n*, 32, 45, 76

Accumulated earnings, accumulated earnings tax, 11–12, 14, 16, 78, 108, 109, 211

Actuarial science, as "perilous profession," *xv,* 11*n*, 32, 45, 76

Affirmative action projects, 118–19

Agent, as profession, 55, 77, 116

Alabama
 S corporation treatment, 100
 state corporation requirements, 218–19, 232

Alaska
 S corporation treatment, 100
 state corporation requirements, 218–19, 232

Ameritech
 layoffs by, 11

Alter, Murray, 99

Annuities, 208, 214

Architects, disability insurance rating of, 131

Architecture, as "perilous profession," *xv,* 11*n*, 32, 45, 76

Arizona
 S corporation treatment, 100
 state corporation requirements, 218–19, 232

Arkansas
 S corporation treatment, 100
 state corporation requirements, 218–19, 232

Art and antiques, 170–71, 203
 in pension fund, 153

Artists, 77, 116

Assets, corporate, 33–34, 81, 108*n*, 203–4, 209

AT&T
 layoffs by, 11

Auxier, George, 63

Azar, Brian, 3–4, 62–63

Bank accounts
 checking, 34*n*, 39, 40–41, 43–44, 50, 53, 54
 savings, 39, 50

Banks, relationship with, 114, 115, 117, 119–20, 147, 163–64

Basis of stock, 81, 98, 203, 204, 214

BatorLink, 122

Beal, Bernard B., 114

Blue Cross/Blue Shield, 136

Boeing
 layoffs by, 11

Bonds, 153, 154, 159, 164, 170, 171
 municipal, 21, 116

Bonuses, 131, 157. *See also* Salaries for owner-employees

Bookkeeping, 7, 13, 16, 24, 26, 27, 43–44, 47–52
 worksheets, 48–49

Borchers, Melody, 118, 119

Brokerage accounts, 34*n*, 147, 159–60, 162–63

Buckaroo Bagels, 121

Business incubators, 119–22

Business plan(s), 61–71
 financial summary in, 67–71
 independent studies in, 66
 market potential assessment in, 62, 65–66, 68

Business plan(s) *(cont'd)*
  marketing strategy in, 62, 65–66, 68
  packaging of, 63–64, 65
Buy/sell agreements, 211–12
Bylaws, 16, 34, 46, 247–57

Calendar year, 27, 32–33
California
  S corporation treatment, 100–101
  state corporation requirements, 218–19, 232
Capital-gains tax, 161*n*, 170, 202, 204, 206
"Cash or deferred arrangement" plans. *See* 401(k) plans
Certificate of incorporation, 26–27, 28–31, 33, 34
  state requirements for, 217–41
Challenger, Gray & Christmas, 216
Clay, Carrie L., 117–18
Clients, number of, 20
CODA plans. *See* 401(k) plans
Collins, Peter R., 119, 120, 121
Colorado
  S corporation treatment 101
  state corporation requirements, 218–19, 232
Commercial rent tax
  avoidance of, 57
Commissioner v. *Soliman,* 53–54
Common stocks, 115–16, 153, 159, 161, 164, 166, 170, 171. *See also* Dividends
Computers, computer programs, 47, 110. *See also* Office equipment
Connecticut
  S corporation treatment, 101
  state corporation requirements, 218–19, 233
Construction industry, 5
Consultants, 17
Consulting, as "perilous profession," *xv,* 11*n*, 32, 45, 76

Consumer Price Index 132
Coopers & Lybrand, 63–65, 99, 117, 119, 123
  Choosing a Business Entity in the 1990's, 73–74
  Public Financing Sources, 123
Corestates Financial
  layoffs by, *xiii*
Corporate accounts and discounts, 6, 17
Corporate layoffs, *xiii,* 11, 17, 203–4, 215–16
Corporate-loss carryforwards, 78
Corporate name, 22–23
"Corporate pocketbook," 14, 115
Corporate records, 34, 39, 47–49, 157
Corporate seal, 34, 34*n,* 39, 256, 258
Corporate surplus, 11–i2, 14, 45, 57, 109, 161–71
Corporation(s):
  advantages of, *xv, xvii, xviii,* 5–6, 8–9, 11–12, 17, 20, 47, 57, 114, 161, 162, 216
  age of incorporators, 10
  assets of, 33, 81, 98, 108*n,* 203–4
  bank accounts for, 34*n,* 39, 40–41, 44, 50, 54
  basis of stock in, 81, 98, 203, 204, 214
  bookkeeping requirements for, 7, 13, 16, 24, 26, 27, 43–44, 47, 50
  bylaws of, 16, 34, 46, 235–45, 247–57
  calendar for, 50–52
  deferred-compensation plans of, 149, 209–11
  definition of, *xvii,* 5, 13, 50
  dividend exclusion for, 6, 16, 20*n,* 21, 108, 109, 116, 164–68, 170, 172, 173–74, 203–4
  dividends paid by, 7, 11–12, 14, 43, 56, 78, 111–12, 169, 203, 212

Corporation(s) *(cont'd)*
  fiscal year of, 27, 32–33, 35–58,
    263–64
  fringe benefits of, 6, 99, 108–9,
    216
  income limitations for, 11–13
  income-splitting feature of, 7–9,
    13, 14–15 45, 77, 99, 107, 172
  investing surplus of, 109, 161–68,
    170–71
  limited liability of, 5, 17, 216
  liquidation of, 76, 78, 108, 202–3,
    204–6, 214
  loans from, 99–100, 108
  loans to, 42–43, 98–99, 117
  losses of, 78, 81, 98–99
  minority-owned, 113, 114, 117–19,
    120, 123
  minutes of, 34, 46, 56–57, 139,
    169, 243–47, 257–64
  no-par-value stock of, 33–34
  office expenses of, 42, 44
  par-value stock of, 33–34
  personal-holding, 20–21, 115–16,
    168, 204
  personal-service, *xv*, 11*n*, 32, 34,
    45, 77, 81, 203
  powers of, 5, 22
  professional, *xv, xvii–xviii*, 5, 20,
    32, 43, 45, 107, 109, 204,
    217–42
  records and resolutions of, 34,
    136
  retained earnings of, 11–12, 14,
    16, 45, 57, 109, 161–71
  sample tax returns, 82–85, 92–93,
    175–76, 184–85, 193–94
  seal of, 34, 34*n*, 39, 256, 258
  §1244 stock for, 44, 46
  seed money for, 42–44
  for spouse, 16
  state requirements for, 217–41
  stock, basis of, 81, 98, 203, 204,
    214
  stock of, 33–34, 111
  transfer of assets to, 39, 42, 203–4
  validity of, 17
  women-owned, 113–19, 120, 123
  See also Employees;
    Owner-employees; Pension and
    profit-sharing plans; S
    corporations; Tax(es)
Crain's business magazines, 122–23
Credit, establishment of, 114–15
Credit cards, 50, 115
CT Corporation System, 23

Death benefits, 108. *See also* Life
    insurance
Deferred-compensation plans, 149,
    209–11
Deficit Reduction Act of 1984, *xiv*
Delaware
  S corporation treatment, 101
  state corporation requirements,
    220–21, 233
Delta Airlines
  layoffs by, 11
Dental benefits, 108, 109. *See also*
    Medical benefits
Dentist
  transfer of assets to corporation
    by, 39, 42
Dentistry, as "perilous profession,"
    xv, 11*n*, 32, 45, 76
Digital Equipment Corporation
  layoffs by, 11
Disability, disability insurance, 6, 18,
    108, 109, 129, 130–33, 134
  inflation feature of, 132
District of Columbia
  S corporation treatment, 101–2
  state corporation requirements,
    220–21, 233
Dividends
  paid by corporation, 7, 11–12, 14,
    43, 56, 78, 112, 168–69, 203,
    212
  received by corporation, 6, 16,
    20–21, 20*n*, 108, 109, 116,
    164–68, 169, 172, 173–74,
    203–4

Doctors
    disability insurance rating of, 131
    See also Health professions
Dow Jones Industrial Average, 161
Dun & Bradstreet Information
    Services, 113

Eastman Kodak
    layoffs by, 11
Economic Recovery Tax Act of
    1981, *xiv*, 12
Einstein, Albert, 63
Employees, 6, 17, 124–27, 133,
    136
    independent contractors, 17–20,
        124
    part-time, 124–25
    See also Owner-employees
Employees' Retirement Income
    Security Act (ERISA), 142, 155,
    156. *See also* Pension
    and profit-sharing plans
Employees' Stock Ownership Plan
    (ESOP), 148–49
Employer Identification Number,
    24, 25, 39, 43, 156
Engineering, as "perilous
    profession," *xv*, 11*n*, 32, 45,
    76
Entrepreneurs, 61, 63, 65, 117, 216
    quiz to predict success of, 3–4
Equity capital, 43
ERISA. *See* Employees' Retirement
    Income Security Act
Errors & Omissions insurance, 133
ESOP. *See* Employees' Stock
    Ownership Plan
Estate planning, 111–12, 209, 212
    estate freeze in, 212
Estate taxes, 111, 214

Fiscal year, 27, 32–33, 35–38
Florida 263–64
    S corporation treatment, 102
    state corporation requirements,
        220–21, 233

Fortune 500 companies
    affirmative action programs, 114
    layoffs by, 17.
    See also indiv. companies
401(k) plans, 149–51, 209
Fringe benefits, 6, 99, 108–9, 216.
    See also specific benefits

Georgia
    S corporation treatment, 102
    state corporation requirements,
        220–21, 233
GTE
    layoffs by, 11
Guardian Insurance Co., 130*n*

Hawaii
    S corporation treatment, 102
    state corporation requirements,
        220–21, 234
Health professions, as "perilous
    professions," *xv*, 11*n*, 32, 45, 76
"Hidden employee" trap, 17–20
Home office, 53–60
    zoning regulations for, 54–55

Idaho
    S corporation treatment, 102
    state corporation requirements,
        220–21, 234
Illinois
    S corporation treatment, 102–3
    state corporation requirements,
        220–21, 234
IBM Corporation
    layoffs of, 11
    stock performance of, 165
Imputed income, 129–30
Income splitting, 7–9, 13, 14–15, 45,
    77, 99, 107, 172
Income taxes
    corporate, 6–9, 11–12, 14–16, 44, 47,
        75, 77–78, 81, 107, 108, 216
    individual, 6*n*, 6–9, 11–12, 14–16,
        47, 56, 75, 77–78, 81, 98–99,
        108, 209

Income taxes *(cont'd)*
    sample returns, 82–97, 175–201
    See also Taxes
Incorporation statistics, *xiv*
Incubators, 119–22
Independent contractors, 124
    IRS test for, 17–20
Indiana
    S corporation treatment, 103
    state corporation requirements,
        220–21, 234
Individual proprietors. *See* Sole
    proprietors
Insurance, 17, 129–34
    comparison shopping for, 134
    disability, 6, 18, 108, 109, 129,
        130–33, 134
    errors and omissions, 133
    "key man," 212
    life, 6, 108, 109, 129–30
    office general liability, 133–34
    overhead expense, 133
    workers' compensation, 6, 17, 18,
        129
    See also Medical benefits
Internal Revenue Code §401, 211
Internal Revenue Code §448, *xv*
Internal Revenue Service, 24, 26, 42,
        98, 142
    on accumulated earnings, 11–12,
        11*n*
    on annuity payments, 208, 214
    on asset-liability balance, 42
    on asset valuation, 98
    on constructive use of funds, 158,
        160
    on corporate loans, 43
    on "corporate pocketbook," 13,
        115
    dealing with, 24, 26
    on deferred-compensation plans,
        211
    on dividends, 14
    on fiscal-year election, 27, 32–33
    on fringe benefits, 129–30, 135–36
    on "hidden employees," 17–20

    on independent contractors,
        17–20, 124
    on insurance, 129
    on liquidation of corporation,
        202–3, 214
    on loans to corporations, 43
    on lump-sum pension payments,
        208
    on medical-reimbursement plans,
        135–36
    on pension and profit-sharing
        plans, 126, 142, 144, 147,
        152, 154, 157
    on "perilous professions," *xv*, 76
    on personal holding corporations,
        20–21, 116, 168
    private-letter rulings of, 110
    on recordkeeping, 47
    on rent, 57, 59
    on S corporation election, 24, 76
    on S corporation reelection, 110
    on salaries for owner-employees,
        14–15
    on seed money, 42–44
    on sham corporations, 17
    on telephone expenses, 55
    tests for disqualifying
        corporations, 13, 17–20
    on transfer of assets to
        corporation, 39
    See also specific taxes
Inventories, 12
Investments, 20–21, 147, 153–54,
        161–71
    art and antiques, 153, 170–71, 203
    banks as managers of, 163–64
    bonds, 153, 154, 159, 164, 170,
        171
    capital-gains treatment of, 170,
        202, 204, 206
    common stocks, 115–16, 153, 159,
        161, 164, 166, 170, 171
    individual research on, 163
    liquidation of, on retirement,
        202–3
    municipal bonds, 21, 116

Investments *(cont'd)*
  mutual funds, 147, 148, 153,
      157–58, 162, 170
  pooled trusts, 163
  preferred stocks, 115–16, 153, 159,
      161, 164–66, 170
  professional management of,
      162–63
  real estate, 78*n*, 153, 159, 170
  variables governing, 161–62
  yield on, 164, 166–67.
  See also Dividends; Pension and
      profit-sharing plans
Investor's Business Daily, xiii
Iowa
  S corporation treatment, 103
  state corporation requirements,
      222–23, 234

Job Creation and Wage
      Enhancement Act of 1995, 53

Kansas
  S corporation treatment, 103
  state corporation requirements,
      222–23, 235
Kelso, Louis, 148
Kentucky
  S corporation treatment, 103
  state corporation requirements,
      222–23, 235
Keogh plans, 145, 6, 24, 124
  transfer of, to corporate pension
      and profit-sharing plans,
      156–60
"Key man" insurance, 212

Law professions, as "perilous
      professions," *xv,* 11*n*, 32, 45,
      76
Lawyer(s), 27
  disability insurance ratings of, 131
  errors and omissions insurance
      for, 133
  use of, *xvii,* 33, 34, 39, 44, 46,
      112, 128, 147, 211

Life insurance, 6, 108, 109, 129–30
Limited liability, 5, 17, 204
Limited liability companies (LLCs),
      xv, 45, 72–74
Lines of credit, 114–15
Liquidation of corporation, 76, 78,
      108, 202–6
  by heirs, 214
  installment method, 204, 205–6
  lump-sum method, 204–5
Loans
  from corporation, 99–100, 108
  to corporation, 42–43, 98–99, 117
  interest free, 43
  See also Seed money
Louisiana
  S corporation treatment, 103
  state corporation requirements,
      222–23, 235

Maine
  S corporation treatment, 103
  state corporation requirements,
      222–23, 235
Maryland
  S corporation treatment, 103
  state corporation requirements,
      222–23, 235
Massachusetts
  S corporation treatment, 103–4
  state corporation requirements,
      222–23, 236
McDonnell Douglas
  layoffs by, 11
Medical benefits, 6, 6*n*, 17, 108, 109,
      135–41, 172
  exclusions from, 136
  minutes for adoption of, 139
  sample corporate plan, 137–38
Medical professions. *See* Health
      professions
Medicare taxes, 135*n*
Michigan
  S corporation treatment, 104
  state corporation requirements,
      222–23, 236

Minnesota
 S corporation treatment, 104
 state corporation requirements,
  224–25, 236
Minorities, as business owners, 113,
  114, 117–19, 120, 123
Minutes, 34, 46, 56–57, 139, 169,
  243–47, 257–64
Mississippi
 S corporation treatment, 104
 state corporation requirements,
  224–25, 236
Missouri
 S corporation treatment,
  104
 state corporation requirements,
  224–25, 236
Monsanto Corporation
 layoffs by, 215–16
Montana
 S corporation treatment, 104
 state corporation requirements,
  224–25, 237
Mutual funds, 147, 148, 153,
  157–58, 162, 170

National Business Incubation
  Association, 121–22
National Foundation of Women
  Business Owners,
  113–14
NCR
 layoffs by, 11
Nebraska
 S corporation treatment, 104
 state corporation requirements,
  224–25, 237
Nevada
 S corporation treatment, 104
 state corporation requirements,
  224–25, 237
New Hampshire
 S corporation treatment,
  105
 state corporation requirements,
  224–25, 237

New Jersey
 S corporation treatment, 105
 state corporation requirements,
  224–25, 237
New Mexico
 S corporation treatment, 101
 state corporation requirements,
  226–27, 238
New York City
 commercial rent tax, avoidance
  of, 57
 S corporation treatment, 105
 zoning regulations, 54–55
New York Court of Appeals, 55
New York State
 S corporation treatment, 105
 state corporation requirements,
  226–27, 238
No-par-value stock, 33–34
North Carolina
 S corporation treatment, 105
 state corporation requirements,
  226–27, 238
North Dakota
 S corporation treatment, 105
 state corporation requirements,
  226–27, 238
NYNEX
 layoffs by, 11

OBRA. *See* Omnibus Budget
  Reconciliation Act of 1989
Office, 53–60
 lease for, 58
 zoning regulations, 54–55
Office equipment, 39, 81, 109,
  120
Office general liability insurance,
  133–34
Ohio
 S corporation treatment, 105
 state corporation requirements,
  226–27, 239
Ohio Department of Development,
  118, 119
 Mini Loan program, 118

Oklahoma
  S corporation treatment, 105
  state corporation requirements,
    226–27, 239
Olin Corporation, 121
Omnibus Budget Reconciliation Act
  of 1987. *See* Revenue Act of
  1987
Omnibus Budget Reconciliation Act
  of 1989 (OBRA), *xiv*
Omnibus Budget Reconciliation Act
  of 1993, *xv*
Oregon
  S corporation treatment, 106
  state corporation requirements,
    226–27, 239
Overhead expense insurance, 133
Owner-employees, 34, 99
  insurance for, 6, 129
  salaries for, 5, 8–9, 12–16, 27, 32,
    50, 57, 77
  sample tax returns, 86–91, 94–97,
    177–78, 186–87, 195–96

Pacific Bell
  layoffs by, 11
Partnerships, 3, 32, 37
  incorporation of, 42
Par-value stock, 33–34
Passive income, 78
Passive losses, 78
Pennsylvania
  S corporation treatment, 106
  state corporation requirements,
    228–29, 239
Pension and profit-sharing plans,
    142–55
  adoption agreement, 265–72
  borrowing from, 108, 109
  changes in, 155
  contributions to, 10, 15, 108, 109,
    112, 125–26, 169
  cost-of-living adjustments in,
    152n
  coverage of employees, 125–26,
    127–28

defined-benefit plans, 142, 143,
    151–52, 154–55, 156, 156n,
    157
  defined-contribution plans,
    142–51, 152, 154, 156, 156n
  documents for, 144, 147–48, 152,
    154, 159, 265–72
  integrated plans, 126, 128, 148
  investments for, 147, 153–54
  Keogh plan transfer to, 156–60
  liquidation of, 206–8, 214
  lump-sum payments of, 206–8
  minimum distribution allowance
    in, 207
  money-purchase plans, 142, 143,
    144–45
  for one-person corporations, 143,
    149, 153
  payments from, 15, 206–8, 214
  profit-sharing plans, 142, 143–48
  profits and losses in, 154–55
  prototype plan, 147, 156, 159
  target-benefit plans, 127–28
  "top-heavy," 125–26
  vesting in, 125–26, 143, 148, 149,
    268–69
  voluntary contributions in, 142,
    207, 268
  See also Employees' Stock
    Ownership Plans; 401(k)
    plans
Perdreau, Michel, 111
Performing arts, as "perilous
    professions," *xv,* 11n, 32, 45,
    76
Personal holding corporations,
    20–21, 168, 204
  women as, 115–16
Personal service corporations, *xv,*
    11n, 32, 34, 45, 77, 81, 203.
    See also Professional
    corporations
Philip Morris
  layoffs by, 11
Preferred stocks, 116, 200, 153, 159,
    161, 164–66, 170, 171, 212

Procter & Gamble
  layoffs by, 11
Professional corporations, *xv,
    xvii–xviii*, 5, 20, 32, 43, 107,
    109, 204
  state requirements for, 217–42
  See also Personal service
    corporations
Profit-sharing plans
  adoption agreement, 144, 147–48,
    265–72
  model trust agreement, 144, 147,
    154
Prototype plan, 147, 156, 159
"Prudent man" investments, 153,
    159, 170

Raytheon
  layoffs by, *xiii*
Real estate investments, 78*n*, 170
  in pension fund, 153, 159
Recordkeeping. *See* Bookkeeping
Rent paid by corporation, 53–60
Retained earnings, 11–12, 14, 16, 45,
    57, 109
  investment of, 161–71
Revenue Act of 1987 (Omnibus
    Budget Reconciliation Act of
    1987), *xiv, xv,* 20*n*, 33, 45, 76
Revenue Reconciliation Act of 1990,
    xiv
Rhode Island
  S corporation treatment, 106
  state corporation requirements,
    228–29, 240
Ridlon, Dean, 10

S Corporation Reform Act, *xv,*
    76*n*
S corporations, 24, 45–46, 75–112
  advantages of, *xv,* 45, 75, 76–78,
    81, 107–10
  disadvantages of, 32, 99–100,
    107–8, 135, 135*n*
  as financial-planning tool,
    110–12

fringe-benefit limitations of,
    99–100, 107–8, 135, 135*n*
  ownership of, 76
  pension-plan limitations of,
    99–100, 107–8
  profits and losses in, 98–99, 108,
    109–10
  reelection of, 110, 110*n*
  sample tax returns, 82–91
  states' recognition of, 100–107
  tax on, 45, 75, 77–78, 81, 108
Salaries for owner-employees, 5,
    8–9, 13–16, 27, 32, 50, 57,
    77
Science Park, 121
Scott Paper
  layoffs by, 11
Sears, Roebuck
  layoffs by, 11
§79 insurance, 129–30
§331 liquidation, 204–5, 208, 214
§453 liquidation, 205
§1244 stock, 44, 46
Seed money, 42–44
Small Business Administration, 63,
    117–18, 122
  7A Direct Guarantee Program,
    117–18
Social Security taxes, 15, 18, 57,
    124, 126, 135*n*, 150
Sole proprietors, 5, 6, 6*n*, 7–8, 13,
    32, 33, 47, 50, 129, 139–40,
    157, 206, 209
  sample tax returns, 179–83,
    188–92, 197–201
South Carolina
  S corporation treatment, 106
  state corporation requirements,
    228–29, 240
South Dakota
  S corporation treatment, 106
  state corporation requirements,
    228–29, 240
Spokane Business Incubator, 121
Standard & Poor's Corporation,
    166

State requirements for corporations,
217–42
and S corporation recognition,
100–107
Stern, Leonard, 130n, 131–32
Stock, basis of, 81, 98, 203, 204, 214
Stocks, 116, 153, 154, 159, 161, 164,
166, 170, 171. *See also*
Dividends, Preferred stock.
Subchapter S Revision Act of 1982,
xiv, 99, 102

Tax(es)
accumulated earnings, 11–12, 14,
16, 78, 108, 109, 211
capital gains, 161n, 170, 202, 204,
207
corporate income, *xiv–xv*, 6–9,
11–12, 14, 15–16, 45, 75–76,
77–78, 107–10, 166–70, 172–74
on dividends, 6, 15, 16, 20–21,
20n, 109, 161, 161n, 162, 164,
165, 166–69, 170, 172–74,
203–4
enhanced estimated payment
system, 33
estate, 111, 214
individual income, 6n, 6–9, 13,
14–16, 47, 56, 75, 77–78, 81,
98–99, 108
on pension fund distributions,
206–8
on pension fund underpayments,
155
on personal-holding corporations,
20–21
on personal service corporations,
xv, 45, 107
on professional corporations, 20,
45, 107
on S corporations, 45, 75–76,
77–78, 107–8
on sale of home used by
corporation, 59
on transfer of assets to
corporation, 42, 204

Tax Equity and Fiscal
Responsibility Act of 1982
(TEFRA), *xiv*, 6, 152, 153,
205
Tax Fairness and Deficit Reduction
Act of 1995, *xv*
Tax Reduction Act of 1975, 12
Tax Reform Act of 1976, 135
Tax Reform Act of 1986, *xiv*, 20n,
32, 45, 75, 202
Technical and Miscellaneous
Revisions Act of 1988
(TAMRA), *xiv*
TEFRA. *See* Tax Equity and Fiscal
Responsibility Act of 1982
Telephone expenses, 55
Tennessee
S corporation treatment, 106
state corporation requirements,
228–29, 240
Texas
S corporation treatment, 106
state corporation requirements,
228–29, 240

Unincorporated business taxes, 7
U.S. Department of Labor, 142
U.S. Federal Laboratory
Consortium, 122
U.S. Supreme Court, 53–54
United Technologies
layoffs by, 11
Utah
S corporation treatment, 107
state corporation requirements,
228–29, 241

Value Line convertible bond service,
166
Vermont
S corporation treatment, 107
state corporation requirements,
230–31, 241
Vesting. *See* Pension and
profit-sharing plans: vesting
in

Virginia
  S corporation treatment, 107
  state corporation requirements,
    230–31, 241

Washington
  S corporation treatment, 107
  state corporation requirements,
    230–31, 241
West Virginia
  S corporation treatment, 107
  state corporation requirements,
    230–31, 241
Wisconsin
  S corporation treatment, 107
  state corporation requirements,
    230–31, 241

Women, as corporate owners,
    113–19, 120, 123
*Women-Owned Businesses: Breaking
    the Boundaries,* 113
Woolworth
  layoffs by, 11
Workers' compensation, 6, 17, 18,
    129
Writers, 77, 116
Wyoming
  S corporation treatment,
    107
  state corporation requirements,
    230–31, 241

Yale University, 121